MODERN JEWISH HISTORY

Songs of Sonderling

Commissioning Jewish Émigré Composers in Los Angeles, 1938–1945

Jonathan L. Friedmann
and John F. Guest

TEXAS TECH UNIVERSITY PRESS

This book is typeset in EB Garamond. The paper used in this book meets the
minimum requirements of ANSI/NISO Z39.48-1992 (R1997). ∞

Designed by Hannah Gaskamp

Cover photo courtesy of the Westen States Jewish History Association

Library of Congress Control Number: 2020947799

ISBN 978-1-68283-079-6 (cloth)
ISBN 978-1-68283-080-2 (eBook)
ISBN 978-1-68283-244-8 (paperback)

First paperback edition 2025

Texas Tech University Press
Box 41037
Lubbock, Texas 79409-1037 USA
800.832.4042
ttup@ttu.edu
www.ttupress.org

CONTENTS

ILLUSTRATIONS

*Images courtesy of Western States Jewish History Association
Archives*

FOREWORD

A PERSONAL APPRECIATION OF RABBI JACOB SONDERLING AND HIS COMMISSIONING PROJECT

A couple of years before his untimely death, George Korngold came by my office to chat. A highly regarded classical record producer, as well as the son of Erich Wolfgang Korngold, George wanted to explore some possible recording projects with the Nuremberg Symphony Orchestra, an ensemble with which I had begun working only a short time before. Toward the end of the conversation—which was focused on nineteenth-century Czech orchestral works—he mentioned a choral composition, *A Passover Psalm*, by his father, and asked if I would consider programming it in Los Angeles. He described the premiere, enthusiastically recounting that when the performance ended, a member of the congregation (Edward G. Robinson, no less!) stood, declared that it was the most beautiful thing he'd ever heard, and suggested, because of its brevity, that perhaps it could be repeated. And it was. A couple of days later, George brought me a tape cassette recording of the premiere, apologizing that he had been unable to find the sheet music. We listened to the cassette together, and I promised to look for an opportunity to perform it, fully understanding why Edward G. Robinson wanted to hear it twice. But George Korngold died in 1987, before we could record in Nuremberg or present his father's composition in Los Angeles. And he never said anything to me about the commissioning of *A Passover Psalm*.

Sometime before George Korngold died, I was contacted by Malcolm Cole, a distinguished musicologist at UCLA and a close friend. Malcolm wanted me to consider performing choral music by a composer totally unknown to me: Eric Zeisl. He introduced me to Zeisl's daughter, Barbara Schoenberg, who in turn introduced me to her husband, Ronald Schoenberg, son of Arnold Schoenberg. Together, Malcolm and Barbara gently nudged me into including Zeisl's *Harlemer Nachtlied* in a February 1988 concert. Soon after this concert, the Schoenbergs introduced me to Hugo Schally, diplomat in charge of cultural affairs at the Austrian Consulate in Los Angeles, who had a very interesting idea for two concerts during the upcoming Mozart Year (1991) that would include music by Korngold, Zeisl, and Schoenberg as well as Mozart. I conducted these concerts with the Choral Society of Southern California. A few days after the first concert (which concluded with Zeisl's *Requiem Ebraico*) I received, in close succession, phone calls from Barbara Schoenberg and Neal Brostoff, each inviting me to conduct the Choral Society in Zeisl's *Requiem Ebraico* and the premiere of the organ version of Schoenberg's *Kol Nidre* in an upcoming concert that Neal was organizing. This concert took place on May 28, 1992. And this is when I first learned about Rabbi Jacob Sonderling and his commissioning of music.

Jacob Sonderling was obviously successful as a rabbi and civic leader in Los Angeles. However, his commissioning project may overshadow all else. When he arrived, Jewish composers in Southern California were aligned in two distinct camps: those who worked exclusively in the synagogue or the secular Yiddish-speaking world of the Workmen's Circle (*Der Arbeiter Ring*, which had been established in Los Angeles in 1900), and those who worked either in Hollywood's sprawling entertainment industry or in the realm of classical concert music (or both). Rabbi Sonderling saw an opportunity for émigré composers from the latter group to produce music that would not only connect with his own congregation but also, potentially, connect with a much broader audience. He apparently imposed no stylistic restraints, and the works were to be composed in a genre most familiar to the composers: that is to say, with orchestral accompaniment.

These commissions provided the composers with a unique opportunity to embrace their cultural and religious heritage: Erich Wolfgang Korngold reconnected to the Jewish community at a profound level; Ernst Toch produced a major work on a topic that, because of the family-oriented nature of the Passover liturgy, had been largely ignored by Jewish composers; Eric Zeisl honored the memory of his parents and all other Holocaust victims in a way that illuminated Sabbath ritual; and Arnold Schoenberg, the Christian convert who had returned to his ancestral religion, came to grips with a liturgical, theological, and moral issue that had apparently bothered him all his life.

Moreover, Sonderling's commissions—while not the first such projects in the United States—were certainly influential beyond the boundaries of Los Angeles, providing, for example, an impetus for Park Avenue Synagogue in New York City, following the earlier example of Salomon Sulzer in Vienna, to begin its very successful project of commissioning composers (Jewish and Gentile) to compose small liturgical works expressly for worship. Further, Sonderling's spirit may be discerned in the current efforts of a number of prominent and enterprising conductors—Joshua Jacobson, Coreen Duffy, Iris Levine, and Noreen Green, for example—who have worked tirelessly to introduce Jewish music to a broad non-Jewish audience.

In my case, I might never have become involved in Jewish music had it not been for the efforts of Rabbi Sonderling. His commissions opened the door to a brave new world of music that I have been exploring with great delight now for many years. At the time of George Korngold's death, I had just begun studying Holocaust-related music. But I knew nothing of Jewish music in general. With the notable exceptions of Ernest Bloch's *Avodath Hakodesh*, Leonard Bernstein's *Chichester Psalms* and *Kaddish*, and Louis Lewandowski's *Hallelujah* (which I learned in a church youth choir), the first Jewish works I encountered were Korngold's *A Passover Psalm*, Schoenberg's *Kol Nidre*, and Zeisl's *Requiem Ebraico*, all commissioned by Rabbi Sonderling. In the intervening years, I have performed a great many Jewish works, including all of Sonderling's commissions. Particularly, the compositions of Eric Zeisl and Arnold Schoenberg now occupy foundational positions in my repertoire: I have conducted virtually all of their choral compositions, including the premieres of several large cantatas by Zeisl that had been otherwise unjustly neglected.

Now, thanks to Jonathan L. Friedmann and John F. Guest, we have this book, which not only presents a biography of Rabbi Sonderling and lucid analyses of the music he commissioned but also places the discussion within the important contexts of other commissioning projects and Jewish musical life in Los Angeles and other important American cities during Sonderling's day. It is meticulously researched and quite objective. Still, the authors' admiration of his accomplishment reminds me of an occurrence in Berlin in 2012. I conducted the last two sections of *Requiem Ebraico* in the Berliner Dom as part of an interfaith concert organized by the Dom and the Cantors Assembly. It was attended by many dignitaries. At the concert's conclusion, I was approached by Joachim Gauck, then president of Germany. As he shook my hand he said, in English, "Thank you! Thank you for this gift! You really have given us a very great gift!" I suspect that Cantor Friedmann and Cantor Guest would like to say this to Rabbi Sonderling but, obviously, they cannot. However, because of their book, Rabbi Jacob Sonderling is no longer a footnote in the history of Jewish music in America.

NICK STRIMPLE

Rabbi Jacob Sonderling in his study, 1951.

PREFACE

R abbi Jacob Sonderling (1878–1964) was many things: a descendant of Chassidic rebbes; a rationalist; a Reform rabbi; a Zionist; an army chaplain; a celebrated orator; an artistic soul. From his early career at the Hamburg Temple and German Army service in World War I to his wandering years in the eastern United States and founding of the Society for Jewish Culture–Fairfax Temple in Los Angeles, Sonderling cultivated a unique aesthetic vision of Judaism—a "five-sense appeal"—that would yield liturgical commissions from exiled Viennese Jewish composers who arrived in Los Angeles in the 1930s and '40s. Through these commissions, activities at the Fairfax Temple, and involvement with the Los Angeles campus of the Hebrew Union College-Jewish Institute of Religion, Sonderling made an indelible mark on the city's Jewish community and the wider musical world, both Jewish and non-Jewish.

This is the first book-length study to examine the life and contributions of Rabbi Jacob Sonderling and his synagogue commissions from Ernst Toch, Arnold Schoenberg, Erich Wolfgang

Korngold, and Eric Zeisl. It joins a number of valuable books documenting the migration and impact of German-speaking artists, musicians, writers, and scholars who settled in the Los Angeles area during the 1930s and '40s. These include *Driven into Paradise: The Musical Migration from Nazi Germany to the United States*, edited by Reinhold Brinkmann and Christopher Wolff,[1] David Wallace's *Exiles in Hollywood*,[2] Ehrhard Bahr's *Weimar on the Pacific: German Exile Culture in Los Angeles and the Crisis of Modernism*,[3] and Dorothy Lamb Crawford's *A Windfall of Musicians: Hitler's Émigrés and Exiles in Southern California*.[4] Among online resources covering the subject, Michael Haas' excellent blog *Forbidden Music* (forbiddenmusic.org) deserves special mention.[5]

Although Toch, Schoenberg, Korngold, and Zeisl are profiled in some of these sources, their contributions to Sonderling's project are treated only cursorily. The present volume fleshes out the narrative with a biography of Rabbi Sonderling, an assessment of his place among commissioners of synagogue song, an examination of Jewish aspects of the composers' lives and works, an exploration of how the commissions came about, and an analysis of the resulting compositions. What emerges is a rich and colorful story at the intersection of American Jewish history, musicology, and Holocaust studies.

Research for this book was aided by a number of archives and institutions, especially: The Jacob Rader Marcus Center of the American Jewish Archives at Hebrew Union College-Jewish Institute of Religion (HUC-JIR) in Cincinnati; HUC-JIR Archives in Los Angeles; Jewish Museum Berlin (Jüdisches Museum Berlin); Milken Archive of Jewish Music; Online Archive of California; Los Angeles Museum of the Holocaust; The OREL Foundation; Western States Jewish History Archive at the Charles E. Young Research Library, University of California, Los Angeles; and the Western States Jewish History Association Archives.

PREFACE

Thank you to Diane Sonderling Gray and Steven D. Sonderling, who graciously agreed to be interviewed about their grandfather, and to Neal Brostoff, an independent Jewish music scholar, who generously commented on an earlier draft of the book. Gratitude is owed to Travis Snyder, acquisitions editor at Texas Tech University Press, for enthusiastically embracing this project, and to Christie Perlmutter for her expert proofreading. The authors are eternally indebted to their wives, Debbie Guest and Elvia Friedmann, whose patience, support, and advice were vital to every stage of this book's maturation.

INTRODUCTION

T he history of Los Angeles in the nineteenth and early twentieth centuries is one of transformation from a dusty outpost
to a major metropolitan center. The discovery of gold at Sutter's
Mill in Coloma, north central California, turned "the little village
of Los Angeles," home to just 1,600 inhabitants in 1850, into
a major supplier for northern miners.[1] A census taken that year
listed just eight recognizably Jewish names. The eight men lived in
their stores on the ground level of a two-story commercial building on the southwest corner of Aliso and Los Angeles Streets. Six
were German born, one was Polish, and another migrated from
Portland, Oregon. All were unmarried, seven were merchants, and
one was a tailor.[2]

As Gold Rush prosperity flowed down from the northern part
of the state, Jews migrated to the nascent "southern metropolis"
from San Francisco, the East Coast, and directly from Europe,
many of them setting up shops, wagons, and pushcarts. A small
group of traditionalists convened the first Jewish worship services
in Los Angeles in 1851. In 1854, the Hebrew Benevolent Society

(now Jewish Family Service of Los Angeles) was established as the city's first social welfare organization and served as a burial society, social / fraternal club, Jewish philanthropic agency, general charity, and "as needed" congregation for the High Holidays.[3] The city's first synagogue, Congregation B'nai B'rith (now Wilshire Boulevard Temple) received its charter from the State of California in 1862 and formally joined the Reform movement in 1903.[4] Meanwhile, Jewish merchants helped found the Chamber of Commerce, Masonic order, Library Association, Odd Fellows order, and Turnverein (German American athletics club).[5] By 1870, Los Angeles was home to 5,728 residents, among them 330 Jews.[6] Transcontinental rail service helped grow the city's population from 11,183 in 1880 to 50,395 in 1890.[7] Rapid expansion continued into the new century. Between 1900 and 1930, the population increased more than tenfold, from 102,479 to 1,238,048.[8] During this period, the astonishing rate of growth was dwarfed by that of the city's Jewish population, which grew from 2,500 to over 70,000.[9]

Musical advancement lagged behind the rapid population growth. The region was dismissed nationally as a "cultural desert," referring to its paucity of support for, and interest in, the European arts. According to Zubin Mehta, Los Angeles still had this reputation when he became assistant director of the Los Angeles Philharmonic in 1961.[10] The impression was only partially deserved. By 1906, Los Angeles was home to eight vaudeville houses.[11] The Los Angeles Philharmonic was formed in 1919 with English Jewish conductor Walter Henry Rothwell at the helm, replacing the semi-professional Los Angeles Symphony and Woman's Symphony Orchestra as the city's major musical institution.[12] *Los Angeles Times* critic Edwin Schallert praised the Philharmonic's 1919 debut:

> Convincingly proving his ability to weld into shape a new organization and his capacity for realizing both the musical and

artistic content of his programme, Walter Henry Rothwell, as conductor of the Philharmonic Orchestra, yesterday startled Los Angeles out of her symphonic slumbers and introduced what might be termed a new epoch in local musical history.[13]

The Los Angeles reporter for the San Francisco-based *Pacific Coast Musical Review*, Bruno David Ussher, who had previously dubbed Los Angeles a "city haphazard,"[14] wrote enthusiastically: "New symphony orchestra arouses musical public of southern metropolis to highest pitch of enthusiasm."[15] The Los Angeles Opera Association recruited touring opera companies to give local concerts between 1924 and 1934. Theatrical and other performances were mounted at the John Anson Ford Amphitheatre beginning in 1920 and at the Hollywood Bowl beginning in 1922.

Notwithstanding these achievements, the city had no resident professional dance, vocal, or chamber music organizations, and the only public art museum was housed in a small portion of the Los Angeles County Museum of History, Science, and Art in Exposition Park (now the Natural History Museum of Los Angeles County).[16] In his book *Musical Metropolis: Los Angeles and the Creation of a Music Culture, 1880–1940*, Kenneth H. Marcus details how the ethnic diversity and decentralization of the region's music culture contributed both to its "haphazard" character and to its eventual emergence as a hotbed of creative energy. Geographic dispersion prevented Los Angeles, the central city, from exerting a musical hegemony, such that "what was playing downtown was not necessarily what was playing in Pomona."[17] The unevenness of local amateur and semi-professional Southland orchestras, choral groups, and pageant associations further contributed to the perception of Los Angeles as culturally inferior. Yet, the city also attracted nearly five hundred music teachers by the turn of the twentieth century, making it the music teaching center of the American West.[18]

To be sure, distinctions between "high culture" and "low culture" should be understood in light of the prevailing Eurocentrism of the time, which valued classical art forms such as opera, ballet, and concert music as superior to popular entertainment and folk arts. Despite its carefully manicured image as an Anglo "white spot," sold through a variety of local interests—including the chamber of commerce, merchants association, citrus industry, Hollywood, Santa Fe and Southern Pacific railroads, *Los Angeles Times*, and sheet music publishers—Los Angeles was home to diverse ethnic communities, both native and foreign-born, with thriving cultures of their own.[19] That the music of Native Americans, Mexican Americans, African Americans, and others did not qualify as "culture" tells us more about the critics than it does about the sonic reality.

Still, the region's "lowbrow" reputation played to the advantage of the fledgling film industry and the many Jews who helped create it. Following historical patterns that saw enterprising Jews enter fields considered undesirable and financially risky, only to turn them into major industries—such as banking, garment manufacturing, department stores, and popular music—motion pictures began as an unrestricted fringe industry in an underdeveloped locale. Without the dominating presence of non-Jews, motion pictures offered opportunities at all levels, from production to acting to screenwriting to composing. And, similar to the mercantile businesses, once a profitable niche was found, Jews brought their friends and relatives with them. Neal Gabler, in his influential book *An Empire of Their Own: How the Jews Invented Hollywood*, sums up the attraction:

> The movie industry held out a number of blandishments to these Jews, not the least of which was that it admitted them. There were no social barriers in a business as new and faintly disreputable as the movies were in the early years of [last]

century. There were none of the impediments imposed by loftier professions and more firmly entrenched businesses to keep Jews and other undesirables out.[20]

Jewish émigré film composers, most of whom were high artists in the European mold, occupied a gray area in the high art / low art dichotomy. They had benefited from Europe's enthrallment with concert music before being pushed out of that rich environment and into a strange new land where, by and large, they struggled to find audiences for their non-film work. The composers themselves generally considered movie music a lesser art form, even as they used the same tools, styles, and techniques found in their concert pieces. Further complicating the situation, many Jewish émigrés, composers included, depended on studio jobs to obtain visas and circumvented strict immigration quotas through the assistance of other Hollywood immigrants. Among them were German actor and director William Dieterle and his wife, German actress and writer Charlotte Hagenbruch Dieterle, Austrian actress and screenwriter Salka Viertel, Czech talent agent Paul Kohner, and German head of Universal Pictures Carl Laemmle Sr., who helped with affidavits and money and arranged employment opportunities at movie studios, colleges, and universities.[21]

The state of synagogue music in Los Angeles before the 1930s is lightly documented. For the most part, the musical aesthetic paralleled the "church style" promoted by the Reform movement's *Union Hymnal*, published in three editions between 1897 and 1932, and showcased at Congregation B'nai B'rith, the city's influential "cathedral synagogue."[22] At Sinai Temple, the city's first Conservative synagogue, services followed a similar, if more traditionalist-leaning, organ-choir aesthetic. In a 1919 essay, San Francisco-based lawyer and theater director Jerome Bayer criticized the widely held preference for a "Protestant" sound: "To substitute Christian church melodies for traditional Jewish melodies is absurd; to substitute them for those chants which contain the very essence of the Jewish spirit, is unpardonable folly."[23] While customary synagogue modes were still being chanted by prayer leaders in the smaller, more traditional synagogues, the picture painted by Bayer is one of a Judaically barren musical landscape.[24]

Bayer proposed specific recommendations for a Jewish musical revival, including a "mighty symphony" propelled by a "particularly Jewish religious fervor," a tone poem capturing the spirit of the "Giving of the Law," and a "turbulent Jewish rhapsody" brimming with the tragedy of Jewish life, but hopeful of future redemption.[25] Beginning a little over a decade later, Jewish music in California would receive a significant boost from European composers. At San Francisco's prestigious Congregation Emanu-El, Cantor Reuben Rinder commissioned Swiss-born composer Ernest Bloch to write *Avodath Hakodesh* (Sacred Service, 1933), French-born composer Darius Milhaud to write *Service sacré pour le samedi matin* (Sacred Service for Sabbath Morning, 1947), and other renowned Jewish composers to write shorter synagogue works.

The 1930s brought a similar revival to Los Angeles. During that decade, the city's Jewish population grew by forty-four percent to 103,634.[26] Roughly 10,500 of the new Jewish residents were German speakers who had fled the Nazis, including a remarkable array of cultural elites: theater and film director Otto Preminger, conductors Otto Klemperer, Bruno Walter, and Hugo Strelitzer, cellist Emanuel Feuermann, novelist and playwright Lion Feuchtwanger, among many others. A number of prominent Jewish composers arrived in this wave. Most had little, if any, history of composing on Jewish themes and were not naturally inclined to pursue that path. However, Nazi horrors forced some to confront their dormant or semi-dormant Jewish identities, making them a potential resource for new Jewish music.

The West Coast was a particularly ripe environment for synagogue musical innovation. Geographically distant from Jewish spheres of influence, the Jews of Los Angeles were not beholden to established norms or expectations in the same way as East Coast Jews. Rabbi Leonard Beerman, who arrived in Los Angeles in the 1950s and was founding rabbi of the politically progressive Leo Baeck Temple, spoke for many who came before and after him: "This was a place not known for following everybody else. A place where somebody like me could come along, stir things up, and not get kicked out."[27]

Several factors contributed to the atmosphere of freedom in the American West, and Los Angeles in particular. Western Jews, especially during the pioneer period (1840s–early 1900s), tended to be less religious—or at least less meticulous about adhering to ancient folkways—than Jews who stayed in large Eastern cities. Whereas pious Jews needed access to kosher food, a *mikveh* (ritual bath), and a synagogue within walking distance, Jews who came west had to forgo these customary necessities. Without an authoritative model or structure to emulate, Jewish communal life in Los Angeles developed organically. For example, services at Congregation B'nai B'rith originally followed Orthodox customs under its Polish-born founding rabbi, Abraham Wolf Edelman, but by the twentieth century had, through the experiments of successive rabbis, gradually evolved into a Classical Reform synagogue. This experimental approach to change would play out in other Los Angeles area synagogues.

Antisemitism was also rare in the western states during the nineteenth and early twentieth centuries. Jews largely evaded prejudices that followed them elsewhere, as well as suspicions and bigotry directed at non-Anglo natives and immigrants. Their skin tone allowed them to "pass" as just another Anglo group, free to climb the social and economic ladder of the ostensibly wide-open region. Jewish Angelinos were elected to public office at nearly every level and filled the ranks of civic groups, private clubs, and business leaders. Among the many successful Jews of early Los Angeles were German-born dry goods proprietor Isaias W. Hellman (1842–1920), who helped found the University of Southern California and formed Wells Fargo Bank; Prussian-born marksman Emil Harris (1839–1921), who became the city's chief of police in 1878; and Prussian-born hides and wool businessman Kaspare Cohn (1839–1916), who helped initiate what are today the City of Hope National Medical Center, Vista Del Mar Child and Family Services, and Cedars-Sinai Medical Center. Numerous other Central European Jewish immigrants and migrants achieved similarly remarkable accomplishments.[28]

This tolerance was undermined somewhat in later decades, as nativism and xenophobia accompanied the Immigration Act of 1924, Great Depression, rise of Nazism, and the Red Scare following World War II. During the first third of the twentieth century, most of the city's Jewish arrivals were "re-immigrants" or "re-migrants" of Eastern European origin, who came from the East Coast and Midwest. Their numbers turned Los Angeles into a demographically significant "Jewish city." In 1933, the city's *B'nai B'rith Messenger* became the first American newspaper to call for a boycott of German goods.[29] In 1935, a mass meeting took place at the Philharmonic Auditorium to protest the treatment of Jews in Germany.[30] The Jewish Community Committee hired private investigators to shadow local Nazi groups.[31] By the end of the decade, members of the German American Bund were organizing pro-Nazi rallies at Hindenburg Park, named for former German president Paul von Hindenburg, in nearby La Crescenta. Yet, through these comparatively turbulent decades, Los Angeles Jews as a whole remained upwardly mobile, owing to the city's rapid industrialization, access to public higher education, the growth of Hollywood, and New Deal initiatives. Economic advances enabled the westward movement of eastside Jews, notably from Boyle Heights, who formed Jewish enclaves in areas such as West Hollywood and the Fairfax District, where Rabbi Jacob Sonderling set up his synagogue.

Perhaps most important is a generalization made by Rabbi Mordecai Kaplan, father of the Reconstructionist movement and spiritual founder of Los Angeles' University of Judaism (now American Jewish University, est. 1947). During a talk at Wilshire Boulevard Temple in the late 1950s, Kaplan was asked to identify the primary difference between Jews in Los Angeles and those on the East Coast. He responded that Jews came West to start a new life, not to repeat the patterns of the past.[32] Sonderling gave a similar assessment in a 1946 Yom Kippur sermon: "We find in this soil, in this climate, a future life."[33] In the absence of an entrenched Jewish establishment or ritual blueprints copied from the Old Country, services across denominations evolved through a process of trial and error. Synagogues were more likely to adapt to changing tastes of congregants than to impose expectations upon them. Musically, this meant an open door to composers to introduce new musical languages into Jewish ritual—so long as the right candidate was met with the right encouragement.

Southern California's spirit of reinvention, individualism, and self-determination resonated with many refugees from Nazi Europe. Unlike the state-sanctioned, violent, racial antisemitism that had infected that continent, preventing even the least observant Jew from attaining complete assimilation, Los Angeles permitted one to be a "non-Jewish Jew," a "Jew in name only," adopt a new name entirely, or simply define for themselves the extent to which Jewishness factored into their lives. While the dominance of Jews in the movies attracted antisemitic vitriol, from fiery early twentieth-century sermons to propaganda from the

German American Bund and red-baiters in the 1930s–1950s, it was generally not as dire and certainly not as life-threating as the European "Jewish Question."[34] Without downplaying the tragic consequences of these attacks on the lives and careers of some Hollywood Jews, especially during the McCarthy era, most who endeavored to "punch into the American mainstream" succeeded in doing so, even if it meant creating their own country clubs or forging their own social networks.[35]

Contrast this with Vienna before the Anschluss of 1938, where the four composers commissioned by Sonderling resided. Jews mainly lived in the district of Leopoldstadt, which garnered the nickname *Mazzesinsel* (Isle of Matzos). Assimilated families in the district were able to accumulate wealth and contribute to Vienna's cultural glory, yet they were never fully accepted or secure. Rather than a pathway to integration, assimilation proved to be another means by which Jews were otherized. Discarded folkways, such as dietary laws, customary dress, and Sabbath observance, were replaced by exaggerated tendencies toward liberalism, socialism, humanism, and modernism. Jewish satirist and social critic Karl Kraus, himself the product of a wealthy Austrian family, remarked that, despite the Jews' near indistinguishability from their Christian neighbors, they could always be identified by the stress they placed on that fact.[36]

Jewish émigré composers in Los Angeles were mostly active in the lucrative film industry. Hitler's rise to power and the concomitant banning of Jewish musicians coincided with the emergence of sound technology in Hollywood films, which matured rapidly following the release of *The Jazz Singer* in 1927.[37] The medium was starved for skilled technicians who could work under harsh deadlines and mold the "Hollywood sound." Some, like Arnold Schoenberg and Ernst Krenek, failed to adapt their modernist styles to the industry's predilection for accessible scores. Others, like Franz Waxman, Erich Wolfgang Korngold, Hanns Eisler, Ernst Toch, and Eric Zeisl, found varying levels of success writing music for films, despite frequent complaints of meddling producers, unreasonable working conditions, and the damage it caused to their reputations in concert music circles. Importantly, the seven composers listed above were all born and/or raised in Vienna, where they made names for themselves as composers of serious music. Exiled from their culturally rich homeland, they were frustrated by the comparatively "primitive" audiences of Los Angeles, who were generally unreceptive to their concert works.[38] For the most part, they were resigned to write "lower music" for films and/or teach at colleges and universities in the Los Angeles area.

A catalyst appeared in this landscape in the form of Rabbi Dr. Jacob Sonderling. A German immigrant himself, and a longtime proponent of fusing the arts and Jewish worship, Rabbi Sonderling arrived in Los Angeles in 1934, founded the Society for Jewish Culture–Fairfax Temple, and made the acquaintance of a number of exiled composers who had landed in the region. Described by a contemporary as "a very unusual personality, very magnetic and equally popular with young and old,"[39] Sonderling had the character, credentials, and charisma to initiate a renewal of synagogue song in Los Angeles. Four émigré composers wrote new liturgical works for religious events organized by Rabbi Sonderling between 1938 and 1945: *Cantata of the Bitter Herbs* (1938) by Ernst Toch; *Kol Nidre* (1938) by Arnold Schoenberg; *A Passover Psalm* (1941) and *Prayer* (1941) by Erich Wolfgang Korngold; and *Requiem Ebraico* (1945) by Eric Zeisl.

These were among the first American synagogue works written by composers who were well known in the classical music world. They stand in company with, and chronologically between, Ernest Bloch's *Avodath Hakodesh* and Darius Milhaud's *Service sacré*. Sonderling's commissions provided a much-needed outlet for personal musical expression, as well as a platform to explore complex emotions surrounding exile, loss, and Jewish identity. The works can be heard as real-time reflections on the horrors of the Holocaust, although in highly personalized and sometimes indirect ways.

Sonderling was uniquely positioned to inspire and guide these compositions to fruition. Beyond the financial incentive to accept the commissions, Sonderling was a product of the same German-speaking world that had celebrated these composers, and his congregation, comprising Central European refugees, was equally receptive to their music. Fairfax Temple was, in a sense, a variation of the *landsmanshaft shuls* of earlier decades, which preserved the homeland customs of immigrant communities and provided a place from which to navigate the new environment.[40] In the case of Sonderling's synagogue, the homeland retained was essentially that of pre-war Weimar Germany, which was fertile ground for intellectuals, artists, and musicians, especially of a modernist or innovative bent. Los Angeles' German-speaking émigré community remained close-knit through the war years.

The composers also resonated with the rabbi's idiosyncratic brand of "Neo-Chassidism," which emphasized the experiential stimulation of all five senses, rather than placing textual study or ritual observance at Judaism's core. Sonderling elsewhere described this as "aesthetic Judaism." Music on a grand emotional scale, for which the composers were known, was key to achieving the holistic engagement Sonderling sought, and he apparently had little difficulty selling the concept to his commissionees.

At the same time, Sonderling was grounded in a universalism derived from the Haskalah (Enlightenment) and Reform movement—usually seen as incompatible with Chassidic mysticism. As both a descendant of Chassidic rabbis and a student of modern Judaism, Sonderling blended the emotionality of the former and the universalism of the latter, with the arts as the "universal language" tying them together. In this way, he agreed with Mordecai Kaplan, who believed that aesthetic engagement of the five senses could simultaneously revitalize collective values, reinvigorate connections to heritage, and renew Judaism for modern times. Kaplan's words in this regard could have come from Sonderling himself:

> [T]he long overdue flowering of creativity in the domain of new Jewish cultural values, where the arts reign supreme. This is the area in which it should be possible to render Jewish life visibly, audibly and tangibly beautiful and fascinating. For the development of that area we need the best that the most gifted of our sons and daughters can contribute.[41]

Sonderling had meaningful interactions with Kaplan before coming to Los Angeles and seems to have modeled his Society for Jewish Culture–Fairfax Temple partly on Kaplan's Society for the Advancement of Judaism, which promoted Judaism as an all-embracing "civilization" inclusive of literature, languages, food, customs, civil and criminal law, visual arts, and music—elements often considered "secular." This reframing of Jewish life appealed to the four composers commissioned by Sonderling, each of whom was non-observant: Toch had a universalist view of religion; Schoenberg expressed a political Jewish identity; Korngold never viewed himself as particularly Jewish; and Zeisl was a cultural Jew.[42]

The commissions also gave the composers a creative platform at a time when such opportunities were lacking. Aside from Schoenberg, the composers primarily worked in film, where they used their talents to accompany, convey, and shape someone else's vision—a functional process that, while invariably drawing from their backgrounds and life experiences, differs from laboring to transmit "the inner workings of the soul."[43] It is a tribute to

Sonderling's artistic sensitivity that he allowed the composers to infuse their Jewish works with intimate meanings and individual styles, rather than have them adjust their voices to the functionalist constraints of synagogue song. The resulting pieces fuse the liturgical with the universal and the communal with the personal.

Like the synagogue works of Bloch, Milhaud, and other contributors to "the modern renaissance of Jewish music,"[44] the five pieces examined in this book are best understood as concert works for Jewish liturgy. In terms of style, form, and performance demands, their natural setting was the concert hall more than the sanctuary. This was a welcome development for those who had grown tired of the *Gebrauchsmusik* (utility music) of the American synagogue, both folk melodies and hymns, which favored accessibility over higher artistic ideals. With these commissions, distinctions between "high culture" and "low culture" had entered the synagogue, much to the delight of Jewish cultural critics and music organizations.[45]

Of course, different considerations apply when music is created for listening and aesthetic pleasure versus the historically participatory religious service. For a variety of reasons that will be explored, the liturgical works of Toch, Schoenberg, Korngold, and Zeisl are almost never performed during Jewish rituals and are only occasionally heard in concert and classical radio programs. Still, the existence of the pieces was well known and helped to inspire more practical liturgical commissions, as well as settings from cantors, synagogue organists, and music directors who were likewise dedicated to raising the artistic level of Jewish ritual, albeit in a more pragmatic manner.

The remarkable burst of new Jewish liturgical music, which Sonderling fostered, blazed a trail for the next wave of synagogue music that would soon emerge from talented Los Angeles-based composers, such as Sinai Temple organist Max Helfman, Leo

Baeck Temple cantor William Sharlin, and Valley Beth Shalom music director Aminadav Aloni, as well as from cantors, composers, and synagogue musicians in New York City, Chicago, and other American cities. Rabbi Sonderling thus deserves recognition as a driving force of the twentieth-century renaissance of American synagogue music.

Chapter 1 presents a biography of Rabbi Sonderling drawn from his own writings, letters, programs, newspaper articles, synagogue records, and a variety of archival materials. Because of the wandering nature of Sonderling's early career and the loss of documents from his time in Los Angeles, the resulting biography, although detailed, has some gaps. Missing information and aspects of Sonderling's writings that cannot be corroborated are noted in the text. Chapter 2 positions Sonderling within the broader history of synagogue music commissions, both in Europe and the United States. Chapters 3 through 6 profile Toch, Schoenberg, Korngold, and Zeisl individually, focusing on expressions of "Jewishness" in their lives and works, their relationships with Sonderling, and the liturgical compositions that grew from those relationships. The authors hope not only to shed light on this dimly studied episode in Jewish music history but also to bring together larger themes of the Holocaust, Jewish identity, and the refugee experience.

Songs of
Sonderling

CHAPTER I
A BIOGRAPHY OF RABBI SONDERLING

J acob Sonderling, the eldest son of Wilhelm and Johanna (née Lebowitsch) Sonderling, was born in Lipine, Upper Silesia, Germany, on October 19, 1878.[1] Although the hour of his birth is lost to history, some would later claim that the future rabbi was born on Simchat Torah, which began at sundown on October 19, 1878, thus foretelling his lifelong love of Torah.[2]

Jacob's father, Wilhelm (c. 1855–1935), is said to have been "ordained" (*semikhah l'rabbanut*) by the Sanzer Rebbe in Galicia, presumably either Rabbi Chaim Halberstam (1793–1876) or his son, Rabbi Aaron Halberstam (1826–1903), although Wilhelm never functioned as a rabbi.[3] However, family lore holds that he did serve as a *hazzan* (cantor).[4] If true, Jacob may have inherited his interest in Jewish liturgical music from his father.

Jacob's mother, Johanna (c. 1855–1918), was descended from the family of Rabbi Moshe Teitelbaum (Yismach Moshe, 1759–1841), who is considered the founder of Hungarian Chassidism.[5] Johanna's mother, Katerina Lebowitch, was a successful corset-maker who set each of her four daughters up in corset shops of their own.[6] A few years after Johanna gave birth to Jacob in 1878, his younger brother Georg in 1880, and a third son, Sigmund, in 1881, she and Wilhelm opened a corset shop in Brünn, the capital of Moravia, now Brno in the Czech Republic.[7]

Referring to his family's connection to two Chassidic sects, one from Galicia and the other from Hungary, Jacob Sonderling later wrote, "I have been all my life closely attached to those two different viewpoints in Jewish life."[8] In all likelihood, Sonderling did not mean that the Galician and Hungarian approaches to Chassidism were dramatically different from one another—they share a strong sense of community, strict adherence to *halakha* (Jewish ritual law), and an emphasis on religious study—but that both differed from the approach to Judaism with which his American readers would have been familiar in the 1950s, when he wrote those words.

Another strong influence on young Jacob was the spiritual and political leader of the Jewish community in Brünn, Rabbi Dr. Baruch Jacob Placzek (1835–1922).[9] Placzek assumed the position as "Landesrabbiner" or chief rabbi of Moravia in 1884, a post previously held by his father, Rabbi Avraham Placzek, who had succeeded Rabbi Samson Raphael Hirsch, founder of the *Torah im Derekh Eretz* (Torah with the Way of the Land) school of contemporary Orthodox Judaism.[10] In addition to being a rabbi, Placzek was a novelist and a botanist. Through his botany research, he became a close friend of Gregor Mendel and a correspondent with Charles Darwin. He saw no contradiction between Darwin's theory of evolution and rabbinic thought. He was also a strong proponent of secular education, insisting that only those candidates with both a secular academic education and theological training could be appointed as rabbis in Moravia.

According to Sonderling's autobiographical sketch, Chief Rabbi Placzek became interested in him while young Jacob was a student in a Jewish preparatory school in Brünn. Placzek "decided that [Sonderling] had to become a rabbi also" and "sent [him] to a gymnasium in Nikolsburg" at the age of fifteen (c. 1893).[11] Run by a Catholic priest, the Nikolsburg *gymnasium* was one of the few places in that small city where Christians and Jews interacted. For five hours a day, Sonderling studied secular subjects, including Greek and Latin. In the afternoons, he studied Talmud with Rabbi David Feuchtwang (1864–1936), a noted scholar of Assyriology and philology, outspoken critic of antisemitism, and ultimately chief rabbi of Vienna from 1933 to 1936.[12]

HIGHER EDUCATION

After completing his studies at the *gymnasium* in Nikolsburg, Sonderling attended university in Vienna, followed by seminaries in Vienna, Breslau, and Berlin.[13] He may have also studied at the University of Breslau.[14] At university, he studied art history and philosophy, including aesthetics, earning a PhD in philosophy from the University of Tübingen with a dissertation on Kantian logic, "The Relationships of the Kant-Jaschian Logic to Georg Friedrich Meier's 'Excerpts from the Doctrine of Reason'" ("Die Beziehungen der Kant-Jäscheschen Logik zu George Friedrich Meiers 'Auszug aus der Vernunftlehre'").[15] Although the historical record is unclear, it appears that his seminary studies took him from the Israelitische-Theologische Lehranstalt in Vienna to Das Jüdisch-Theologische Seminar in Breslau, and then to the Hochschule für die Wissenschaft des Judentums in Berlin. If so, the young Sonderling would have been exposed to a variety of approaches to the modernization of Judaism in Central Europe.

Vienna's Israelitische-Theologische Lehranstalt was founded in 1893, so Sonderling would have been among its first rabbinic students. The seminary reflected Viennese Jewry at the time, wherein a spirit of compromise prevailed.[16] While some Vienna synagogues modified their services to minimize mention of the sacrifices in the ancient Jerusalem Temple and the return to Zion, they were not officially aligned with the emerging Reform movement. Rather, they adhered to the Vienna Rite (Wiener Ritus), which originated with preacher Isaak Noah Mannheimer (1793–1865) and Cantor Salomon Sulzer (1804–1890) of Vienna's influential Stadttempel.[17] Departing from the radical Reform ideology, the moderate Vienna Rite retained traditional elements, such as Hebrew text and customary chant patterns (stripped of "foreign" accretions and undignified coloraturas), but incorporated modern tastes for decorum, German sermons, choral singing, and art music. Communal unity through moderate change was of greater value than ideology and was enshrined in the *Unity Prayerbook* (*Einheitsgebetbuch*) of 1840, edited by Mannheimer.[18]

The rector of the Vienna seminary, Dr. Adolf Schwartz, a graduate of the Breslau seminary, had studied with Adolf Jellinek (1823–1893), one of Vienna's leading Jewish preachers and scholars. What was said of Jellinek could also be said of Schwartz and of the ideal graduate of the seminary: "a religious leader who did not create ideological division, an accomplished preacher who provided his listeners with memorable artistic experiences, and a man who expressed [his listeners'] own feelings, reconfirming both Jewish loyalties and universal convictions."[19]

Das Jüdisch-Theologische Seminar in Breslau, the oldest of the three seminaries, opened in 1854. Its first director was Zacharias Frankel (1801–1875), considered the ideological founder of present-day Conservative Judaism. Frankel set the philosophical direction for the seminary, championing a moderate and gradual religious reform that combined scholarship with faith. His "positive-historical" approach was open to the scholarly, scientific study of Judaism as a culture that had evolved over time ("historical"), but also insisted that Judaism possessed an unchanging, faith-based core ("positive") that transcended history. Ultimate truth was defined by this faith, which imposed limits on the influence of scientific truth. For Frankel and the Breslau seminary, the inherited tradition, even if it were the product of human invention over time, was not to be cast aside lightly.

The Hochschule für die Wissenschaft des Judentums, opened in 1872, was in many respects a response of more liberal reformers to the moderation of Breslau. Abraham Geiger (1810–1874), largely responsible for the development of the Reform ideology, was the most prominent member of its initial faculty. The driving principle of the institution was the free scientific study of Jewish matters without religious sensitivities or other restrictions. Science, not faith, was to be the ultimate arbiter of truth. Among its illustrious graduates were Rabbis Leo Baeck, Emil Fackenheim, Abraham Joshua Heschel, and Solomon Schechter.

Later explaining the wandering nature of his studies, Rabbi Sonderling wrote that he "wanted to get the various views and answers to the never-ending problem of the Jew."[20] He characterized those views and answers as follows: "Vienna was romance" and "typically Austrian: to take matters with a smile, softening the sharpness and avoiding conflicts,"[21] Breslau was "influenced by German correctness," and Berlin was "the Mecca of the people who wanted to disappear and to be nothing but German citizens of Jewish persuasion."[22]

Sonderling became an ardent Zionist by 1897, the year of the First Zionist Congress organized by Theodor Herzl.[23] His Zionist awakening was likely influenced by the ongoing Dreyfus affair in France (which also had an impact on Herzl), and/or the election of Karl Lueger, leader of the antisemitic Christian Social Party, as mayor of Vienna. The Dreyfus affair led to the conviction of Alfred Dreyfus, a French Jewish military officer, who was falsely accused of espionage. It was a watershed event in the history of European antisemitism and caused a political and media scandal that divided the Third French Republic from 1894 until its resolution in 1906. In 1899, Herzl wrote in an American publication that the Dreyfus affair had made him a Zionist. However, scholars question the extent to which this statement is true in light of Herzl's biography.[24]

Karl Lueger had been elected mayor four times prior to 1897, but Emperor Franz Josef repeatedly refused to confirm him, in part because of Lueger's excessive antisemitism. Franz Josef finally relented in 1897 after Pope Leo XIII interceded on Lueger's behalf. The Christian Social Party was not alone is exploiting antisemitism for political gain. From the 1870s to 1938, virtually every political party in Austria was overtly antisemitic or used antisemitic propaganda.[25] Whatever the motivation, Sonderling recounted that he "became imbued with the dream of a Jewish state while still a student, and was one of the first to belong to a youth organization which had as its ideal working for a national homeland in Israel."[26]

Sonderling is remembered as one of Herzl's "first co-workers,"[27] and resembled the father of political Zionism in appearance: "well built, quite good looking, impressive features, longish and well-trimmed beard, neatly dressed in frock suit."[28] He fondly recalled being "knighted" by Herzl as his "fighting rabbi."[29] Yet, Sonderling's relationship with Zionist organizations was not always smooth. He was excluded for seven years from the Zionist Organization in Germany because of his belief in the Jewish people's mission to be a light unto the nations.[30] That mission was associated with the Reform movement, which asserted that diaspora Jews have an obligation to better the world and should thus abandon Zionist aspirations. Zionist organizations would have been suspicious of Sonderling's fusion of Zionism with this ostensibly opposing view.

Reform opposition on the Zionist dream was at least as old as the Hamburg Temple, where Sonderling would later serve. With the Constitution of the Hamburg Temple, approved in 1817, the New Israelite Temple Association of Hamburg initiated the first systematic Reform worship service. Its dedication as a "temple" the following year appropriated a term traditionally reserved for the fallen Jerusalem Temple, thus marking Hamburg—and subsequent city temples—as a replacement for Jerusalem and Zion.[31] At the 1909 World Zionist Congress, held in Hamburg, co-founder Max Nordau publicly criticized the Reform movement: "What have they done, the reformers? They made temples out of synagogues, churches without a cross."[32]

EARLY CAREER

While studying at the Breslau seminary, Sonderling was hired by Josef Kleeman, a wealthy manufacturer, to instruct his children in Hebrew. Sonderling fell in love with Kleeman's eldest daughter, Emma, and the two were married on March 15, 1904.[33] That same year, Sonderling earned a PhD in philosophy from the University of Tübingen and was ordained by the chief rabbi of Moravia, Rabbi Dr. Baruch Jacob Placzek.

Immediately following his ordination, Sonderling and his wife lived in Berlin, where the newly minted rabbi found work as the editor of the official German-Jewish weekly, published by B'nai B'rith. Emma bore Jacob his first son, Egmont, on February 27, 1906.[34] Later that year, Sonderling accepted a position as the rabbi of a congregation in the university town of Göttingen. The position required that Sonderling become a German citizen, a status he did not hold despite being born in Germany. To obtain full citizenship, he served in the military for one year, probably as a reservist. He later wrote proudly of having been "a soldier in the regiment in Göttingen."[35] The citizenship hurdle, which both impeded Sonderling's employment prospects and reinforced his sense of otherness as a German Jew, no doubt furthered his involvement with Zionism and the autonomy it promised.

During the second year of his tenure at Göttingen, Sonderling learned that the Hamburg Temple was looking for a junior preacher to serve alongside Rabbi David Leimdorfer (1851–1922), who had served the congregation since 1883. Having been at Göttingen such a short time, Sonderling struggled with the propriety of applying for the Hamburg position, but he ultimately applied and was selected.[36] His tenure at Hamburg began in September 1908.[37]

The Hamburg Temple was the first permanent synagogue devoted to a "reform" approach to Judaism. Other German congregations had earlier carried out reforms, for example at Seesen (1810–1813) and Berlin (1815–1823), but they collapsed for various reasons in relatively short order.[38] Hamburg, however, endured.

When the Hamburg Temple was dedicated in October 1818, men sat on the ground floor while women sat in a balcony, but there was no *mechitza* (partition) in front of the women's seats. A separate balcony accommodated the organ and choir, which was initially a boys' chorus but became a mixed choir by 1879. The service was shortened by reading the Torah on a triennial cycle (one-third of the weekly portion was read publicly) and eliminating the *haftarah* reading (selections from prophetic books). A sermon delivered in German received a prominent place in the service.

Perhaps most important, the Temple adopted its own prayer book containing the first comprehensive Reform liturgy. Prayers recited aloud, some in Hebrew and some in German, were printed on the top half of the page, while German translations of the

Hebrew prayers appeared on the bottom half. Most of the liturgical references to the sacrificial ritual were omitted. However, the book retained some "irrational" imagery, such as angelic hosts and the resurrection of the dead. The *Aleinu* prayer, which characterizes Jews as a distinctive people, was removed from the Shabbat liturgy. One phrase in that prayer, which implies that Christianity and Islam are "vanity and emptiness," had incurred Church-sponsored attacks for centuries. Another phrase, praising God for not making Jews like the other peoples of the world, was seen by reformers as contrary to their goal of fully integrating Jews into the surrounding society.[39]

The Hamburg prayer book was predictably berated by traditionalists but was also criticized by reformers for its lack of consistency. Some complained that it went too far; others argued it did not go far enough. Nonetheless, the congregation continued using the prayer book, and the Hamburg Temple became an inspiration, if not a model, for would-be reformers in other communities.

By the time Sonderling arrived at Hamburg in 1908, the clergy and congregation were still Reform, but hardly revolutionary. They were comfortably set in their ways. Sonderling shared some of their reticence to adopt radical changes. His relatively conservative sensibilities at times clashed with those of potential patrons, as he recalled in an autobiographical sketch:

> When the Hamburg Temple set out to raise funds for a new building, Mr. Henry Budge, a very rich New York banker who had returned to Europe and lived in Hamburg, had been my first target for a contribution. My president had sent me to him, and I had told him about our plan to build a new temple in Hamburg. Budge had asked me how much it was going to cost. We had figured one million marks. I expected him to give us 5,000 or 10,000 marks. "You can have the million," he said, "under one condition. I would like to have a service like Temple Emanu-El in New York—men and women sitting together,

men without hats and without *talesim* (prayer shawls)." "I have
to refuse your generous offer, Herr Budge—we are building a
Temple for Hamburg Jewry, not for you."[40]

Assuming he would be scolded for refusing such a generous gift,
Sonderling offered his resignation to the Temple's board of trustees. But the board agreed with him, and "in the Hamburg Temple,
the cradle of Reform, men and women remained separated up to
the last moment."[41]

Sonderling did, however, challenge some of the norms of the
Hamburg Temple. For instance, the congregation had eliminated
the title "rabbi" in favor of "preacher"—the same title the senior
clergyman, David Leimdorfer, had held since assuming his post
in 1883. Upon reading a contract identifying him as "preacher,"
Sonderling insisted that he had worked for, and rightly deserved,
the title of "rabbi." Leimdorfer and the Temple administration
opposed the traditional title, which they felt was too strongly
connected to the past. Ultimately, a compromise was struck in
which Sonderling and Leimdorfer were both called "rabbi and
preacher."[42]

Sonderling later reported that Hamburg was his first experience with a "modern service," although it is unclear which aspects
of the service were new to him.[43] He had no adverse reaction to
the organ or female singers, both of which had been part of his
experience in Brünn, Vienna, and Göttingen. But he was irritated
by the Temple's use of German lieder melodies, which Sonderling
associated with the non-Jewish folk songs of Southern Germany.
Those melodies, he wrote, "sounded foreign" to him.[44]

The cantor of the Hamburg Temple during Sonderling's tenure was Moritz Henle (1850–1925), who had been raised in the
southern German town of Laupheim and employed customs of
that region in his own compositions. Henle was also influenced by
the works of Felix Mendelssohn, his wife's cousin, so he was hardly

out of step with the musical trends of the time, Jewish or otherwise.[45] Being a junior clergyman, Sonderling grudgingly acquiesced to the established musical customs of the Hamburg Temple but continued to have strong feelings about the music of Jewish liturgy.

Sonderling's tenure in Hamburg was bumpy at times. He frequently found himself at odds with Leimdorfer. In 1909, Sonderling gave a sermon in which he stated, "I differ with all my colleagues in the Reich. Of course we are a People." He recalled, "the Trustees present almost fainted [in response] and, after services, they approached [Leimdorfer] who reassured them [that] 'we are not a People. We are German citizens of Jewish persuasion.'" Sonderling replied: "You are right. All Hungarians who come to Germany say the very same thing,"[46] by which Sonderling meant that, while Jews can cross national boundaries and change their national identity (from Hungarian to German), they will always be Jews—their Jewish peoplehood is constant and irrevocable. Sonderling later wrote of his tenure in Hamburg: "We lived at the time through the storm and stress of [the question:] what are we, a People or a religion . . . and official Judaism insisted that we are not a People, only a religion."[47]

According to historian Leora Batnitzky, who has charted the uneasy transformation of Judaism from an all-encompassing lifeway to a Protestant-defined "religion," German Judaism at the time had "produced a highly intellectualized tradition of thought that mirrored its German cultural and philosophical surroundings."[48] The idea of Judaism as a religion was "a cultural and political reaction to the gap between the ideal of full Jewish integration into the German state and a far more incomplete and vexed political and cultural reality."[49] The notion was grounded in personal autonomy rather than communitarianism, and was therefore at odds with the Jews' historical practices and identification.[50] Because citizenship in the German state was understood to exclude "the possibility of other types of collective belonging," those Jews who valued complete integration pressed for the reframing of Judaism as a private religion.[51] Sonderling never fully embraced that idea.

WORLD WAR I

During his first years in Hamburg, Sonderling and his family customarily vacationed in Switzerland. They were there in August 1914 when Germany declared war on Russia and entered World War I. Sonderling returned to Hamburg and offered his services as a Jewish chaplain to the German Army. He was commissioned on October 9, 1914, and was ordered to the Eastern Front, attached to the General Staff of Field Marshal Paul von Hindenburg.[52]

By that time, Germany had already repelled Russia's initial invasion of East Prussia at the battles of Tannenberg and Masurian Lakes in August and September 1914. The Germans then launched a successful eastward offensive from East Prussia during the winter of 1914–1915, and another in May to the south, capturing Warsaw in August 1915 and the regions that are now Latvia and Lithuania by the end of September.[53] Thus, a huge segment of Eastern European Jewry came under German control by 1916.

For four years, Sonderling served the army as a chaplain in Poland and what is now Lithuania.[54] He later wrote of the profound impact of his exposure to Eastern European Jewry:

> Here, for the first time, I met people who did not try to give a definition of what they are. They were Jews who did not need sermons to be reminded of their Jewishness. Here I found spirit knowledge, not restricted to professionals, dignity, and inner-independence. In Germany, we were labeled all the time, orthodox, conservative, reformed. Here, I was accepted as a Jew without attributes. Here surrounded by those people, I got answers to my questions. It is more than a jest, and up to this very day, if I am ever reborn I would like to be a Litvac.[55]

Originalaufnahme vom Kriegsschauplatz 1915

Jüdischer Feldgeistlicher
(Dr. Sonderling aus Hamburg)

Rabbi Jacob Sonderling in his chaplaincy uniform, German Army, 1915.

Sonderling recalled finding himself in a *shtetl* one night during the war. Seeing a light inside a small synagogue, he entered and spotted a man cowering in a dimly lit corner. Sonderling asked the man, "What are you doing here, it is very dangerous?" The man replied, "I am the *shames* [caretaker] of the shul and the guardian for the scroll that is left in the ark." Sonderling told him, "I am a rabbi and will become guardian of the scroll in your stead." The *shames* handed him the scroll, containing books of the prophets (*haftarot*), which now resides in the synagogue on the Los Angeles campus of the Hebrew Union College-Jewish Institute of Religion (HUC-JIR).

Another anecdote involves Sonderling's encounter with a Chassidic rebbe, who described Chassidism as "nothing more than finding a place where people do not pass each other in cold indifference, but where they take a sympathetic interest in one another."[56] Sonderling felt this genuine human concern lacking in the hyper-rationality of German Reform Judaism.

Sonderling produced a four-page summary of life-changing incidents that occurred during his chaplaincy.[57] Perhaps the most compelling was an unannounced Friday evening visit to the home of two impoverished Jewish women, "one old, the other young." He recited *Kiddush* (the blessing for wine) and left them money to be used after Shabbat. As he was leaving, the old woman said to her companion, "Do you know who that was? The angel of Shabbes!" The rationalist within Sonderling argued that the woman's utterance was merely superstitious, but a deeper self-identity prevailed. He came to view her words as "truer than fiction," remarking: "That night made me a Chassid."[58]

After the war, Sonderling returned to the Hamburg Temple a changed man. For various reasons, he was no longer content in Hamburg. He found German Jewry to be spiritually "dead," writing: "Those four years in Russia made me a Jew, and coming home, after Germany was defeated, I could not preach anymore."[59] Although he had been a disciple of Hermann Cohen, the leading German-Jewish intellectual in the decades preceding World War I, he came to view Cohen's neo-Kantian philosophy as cold and irrelevant to the lived Jewish experience—a significant shift considering Sonderling's dissertation topic.[60] Having been exposed to the broader Ashkenazi world, Sonderling felt "his sphere of influence in Hamburg was too limited," and he "was dissatisfied with the placid attitude of German Jewry."[61] He may have also had something of a midlife crisis resulting from his mother's death on December 3, 1918, when he was forty years old. Psychological studies suggest that a mother's death can send an adult son into a depressive state characterized by diminished satisfaction with life and an urge to escape responsibilities.[62] Although Sonderling had stable employment, the economic chaos descending on postwar Germany may have further spurred his decision to leave Hamburg in early 1923 and, carrying a letter of recommendation from the Hamburg Temple, travel to the United States.[63]

EASTERN UNITED STATES

Sonderling initially came to the United States without his family. He left Antwerp for New York aboard the *SS Manchuria* in early 1923, along with what he called a "nondescript crowd—chatting, promenading, playing."[64] The only passenger he recognized by reputation was conductor Bruno Walter, who was traveling to his American debut with the New York Symphony Orchestra at Carnegie Hall. The two men bonded over their shared affection for fine cigars. In November 1939, Walter would make his permanent home in Beverly Hills, where his expatriate neighbors included Thomas Mann.

Sonderling was smitten by New York City: "It had attracted me from the very beginning. The fantastic figure of two million Jews in one city never failed to impress me. I loved to exaggerate:

New York is a Jewish city where we permit a few *goyim* (non-Jews) to exist—try not to be Jewish in Brooklyn or the Bronx!"[65] He quickly secured work as a traveling lecturer to German-speaking audiences for the Zionist Organization of America. He may have had some assurance of getting such work before leaving Hamburg. About four weeks into his circuit, he delivered a lecture in Chicago, after which he was asked to become the rabbi of Agudath Achim, an Orthodox Hungarian congregation in that city.[66] He accepted the offer on the condition that the congregation pay to bring his family to the United States from Hamburg.[67]

Sonderling reminisced about his initial encounter with representatives of Agudath Achim:

> One of the first communities I visited was Chicago. Everything was new to me. I was what you call a "greenhorn." Reporters came—I had never met one before, and I took their questions seriously. One of them asked me: "What do you think about American culture?" In all innocence I said, "America is a young country, and culture doesn't travel by express." The papers carried a story about it. So I became nervous. Two days later, five men came to see me. "I don't want to see reporters." "We are not reporters," they answered. "We are officers of a Congregation and, listening to you last night, we decided you have to become our Rabbi." "But I cannot speak English." "You will learn." "What kind of a Congregation are you?" "We are Orthodox." "I'm not Orthodox." "We are semi-Orthodox." I didn't know what it meant. They didn't argue—just took out a contract and asked me to sign it. With the help of a dictionary, I found out that they offered me a decent salary and obligated themselves to bring my family over from Europe and to furnish me with an apartment. I signed. They left, and here I was sitting in my hotel room, believing I had dreamed it. So, four weeks after my arrival in a new continent, I had a Congregation. Another four weeks passed by, and they asked me whether I would agree that they amalgamate with another Congregation. That was new to me. "How do you do that?" "Oh, we sell our

Synagogue." "Whom do you sell it to?" "In our neighborhood is a Negro Congregation—they want to buy the building." I was bedeviled and bewildered. The next Saturday I went to my pulpit and said: "I found a new interpretation for a Bible text: First came the Irish, who built the Church; they left and sold the Sanctuary to Italians; then came the Jews and now the Jews sold it to the Negroes—now I understand what the Bible says 'My House shall be a House of Prayer for all People.'"[68]

Sonderling's tenure in Chicago was relatively brief.[69] In March 1923, shortly after he became rabbi of Agudath Achim, the Hungarian synagogue merged with another congregation of mostly Lithuanian immigrants.[70] The two congregations mustered the resources to build a new sanctuary, but Sonderling was unhappy with the tensions between the Hungarians and the Lithuanians, concluding that "goulash, herring and sour kraut [sic] don't mix."[71] He also observed unethical conduct by some of the board members. For example, he was urged to certify the need for large amounts of sacramental wine so that the congregation could resell it at a profit during Prohibition.[72]

Sonderling presided over the dedication of the new sanctuary on February 25, 1925, joined by renowned cantor Yossele Rosenblatt. But he was anxious to leave.[73] During a conversation with Mordecai Kaplan on July 2, 1925, Sonderling purportedly complained, "ethical considerations play no part whatever in [the congregants'] Judaism, which is strictly orthodox as far as their avowals are concerned while in practice they vary from strict observance to the most indifferent liberty. They give little thought to the Jewish upbringing of their children."[74] There is no record of Kaplan assisting Sonderling in finding another job, but Kaplan and Sonderling were both speakers for the Zionist Organization of America, and Kaplan wrote, "[Sonderling's] approach to Judaism is very similar to mine."[75] Sonderling's next position was in New York City, where Kaplan was already a figure of some prominence.

Although no evidence has come to light regarding how Sonderling landed his first New York pulpit, it can be assumed that Kaplan played a role. This is especially likely given the similarity between Kaplan's framing of Judaism as an evolving "civilization," rather than a set of beliefs or rituals, and his concomitant emphasis on the arts, and Sonderling's interest in the engagement of the senses through a revival of Jewish creative expression. This compatibility extended to their respective engagements in Zionism, which they viewed as a social, cultural, and political movement that, if realized, would enable Jewish culture to survive, evolve, and flourish. For both Sonderling and Kaplan, Zionism, like the Jewish religion, was less concerned with ideology than with the renewal of Jewish life and creativity.

In late 1925, Sonderling became the rabbi of a congregation in the Manhattan Beach neighborhood of Brooklyn.[76] This was most likely Temple Beth El, which had been established in that neighborhood in 1919, and which still exists as a Conservative synagogue.[77] The match may not have been a happy one, as Sonderling never mentioned the congregation's name in his later writings and there is no reference to Sonderling in the temple's public records. Whether the position was at Temple Beth El or at another congregation, his reasons for leaving are veiled from us.

By May 1927, Sonderling had moved on to Temple Israel in the Washington Heights area of Manhattan.[78] That congregation had just dedicated a new building a month earlier, and an impressive new organ was installed during Sonderling's tenure.[79] Sonderling left in 1929, later claiming that he felt disrespected when, unbeknownst to him, the mayor of New York was asked to address the congregation from the pulpit.[80] Financial considerations may have also played a part: the stock market crashed in 1929, Temple Israel dissolved in 1931, and the building was sold to another congregation.[81]

In 1929, Sonderling took a position with Temple Beth-Israel in Providence, Rhode Island. He was proud of the salary he negotiated for the job—$10,000 per year, or about $145,000 in today's money—claiming that the amount, which he requested, factored in his need to start saving for the future.[82] His salary may have caused the temple financial hardship, as he retained the post for just two years.[83] Even so, it was reported:

> Rabbi Sonderling during his short stay at Temple Beth-Israel left a musical legacy. He was greatly interested in the role of music in the service. He was responsible for bringing Igor Greenberg (he later changed his name to Gorin) as Cantor for the High Holy Days of 1930. An interesting story is told about Gorin: "Rabbi Sonderling traveled to Europe every summer. On one occasion he brought back a baritone hazzan (cantor). A reception for him was held at the Temple. One of the women members asked him if he knew a certain person in his home town. He said she was his mother. She said she was her sister, and that was how an aunt and her nephew came to meet. The pandemonium that broke out in the vestry that night was unimaginable." Igor Gorin went on to become a noted concert and motion picture singer. Rabbi Sonderling was also responsible for the installation of an organ—the first in a Conservative Temple.[84]

Sonderling left Temple Beth-Israel in 1931. He later claimed that he resigned because the congregants were not internalizing the message of his sermons. However, correspondence from the congregation's president indicate that his contract was discontinued due to financial difficulties.[85]

At that point, Sonderling was fifty-three years old. He had occupied five different pulpits over the prior decade, and the United States was in the midst of a deep economic depression. It is thus not surprising that he decided to take a sabbatical. He was still a compelling speaker, and congregants in Rhode Island described him as "handsome and dramatic, like an actor, and one woman even likened him to her impression of what God must look like."[86] But his experiences left him brooding: "What is Jewishness? A theology? A number of abstract definitions? A psychological analysis? An ethical guide? . . . I felt I had no purpose."[87] He needed time "to look upon Judaism from the viewpoint of the pew, from a different perspective."[88]

During his sabbatical year (1931–1932), Sonderling attended Orthodox, Conservative, and Reform services "with a non-partisan spirit" in order to understand the experience of religion, "a kind of human experience about which I, only a rabbi, know nothing."[89] It occurred to him that religion, like love, was a coordination of all the senses, and that institutional Judaism's focus on hearing to the detriment of the other four senses was problematic. "If one could only investigate the four other senses, one of them might open and point out a channel leading to the experience of religion."[90]

This attitude was not altogether new for Sonderling, who had described his approach to Judaism as "aesthetic" as early as 1924. An anonymous editorial in the *Jewish Daily Courier* on January 6, 1924, perhaps ghosted by Sonderling himself, describes his approach in some detail:

> The majority of our people look upon Judaism from a purely religious point of view, a cultured minority looks upon it from an ethical point of view, and only a very few select minds, who embody the spirit of artistry, view it from the aesthetic angle. Among this select few is Dr. Jacob Sonderling. . . . To him, Judaism presents itself not only as a religious and ethical, but also as an aesthetic proposition. . . . To him, Judaism is [a] creative religious and aesthetic atmosphere of rhythm and meter, something symphonic, full of harmony, of color and tone. . . . It is obvious that it is much easier to attract a mass by the beautiful than by the good, by the harmonious than by logical truth, because the

reaction of the mass to the beautiful is much stronger than to the good and logical. The mass may not have any reaction to the ethical and religious at all, but it always has some sort of a relationship to the beautiful because it sets the soul of the masses in motion. . . . As far as Jewish theology is concerned, Dr. Sonderling is animated by a certain desire to bring about reconciliation between the rationalistic and somewhat legalistic Jewish conception of the Gaon of [Vilna] and that of the founder of Hasidism. In short, to him ideal Judaism means a synthesis between the straight lines of rationalistic Misnagdism and the mystical aestheticism of the Hasid.[91]

These thoughts on "aesthetic Judaism" may have been reinforced by Sonderling's time in the pews. However, he longed for some ancient authority to bolster his intuition. By happenstance, he found a sentence from Rabbi Moses Isserles' *Torat Ha-Olah* that satisfied his need for support: "The Temple in Jerusalem was surrounded by a wall, and that wall had five gates, according to the five senses." An appeal to the five senses would become Sonderling's touchstone in the years to come.[92]

After his sabbatical, Sonderling considered founding a synagogue in New York based on the engagement of the senses. He prevailed upon Manhattan's Temple Emanu-El to give him a platform from which to introduce the approach. An article dated August 30, 1932, reports:

New York is about to witness an entirely new form of Jewish religious observance combining interpretation of the Scriptures with a colorful ritual described as resembling that of the Ancient Temple. An important part of the ritual provides that members of the congregation attend the services attired as for a social function. Rabbi Jacob Sonderling, exponent of Neo-Chassidism, as this form of Jewish worship is categorized, is reported to have had great success in Germany with the unique ritual of his conception. . . . He gave New York Jewry its first taste of this type of religious expression at a private

demonstration held recently at the Community House of
Temple Emanu-El.[93]

Presumably, this "private demonstration" was the "dramatized Friday (Sabbath) Eve service in the great Temple Emanu-El
in New York," which is referenced in an unsigned biographical
summary held in the HUC-JIR archives. Jacob Rader Marcus,
founder of the American Jewish Archives,[94] received a letter from
the president of the brotherhood at Temple Emanu-El, stating
that Sonderling's service "was considered the greatest demonstration of Sabbath."[95]

A printed program for the evening sheds some light on
Sonderling's vision.[96] The service was held on March 18, 1932.
The "dramatic interpretation and direction" were provided by
Murray Phillips, a fixture of New York theater, with musical
direction by Joseph Yasser, a noted musicologist and organist of
the city's Temple Rodeph Sholom.[97] The program was divided
into two parts. Part One was a modified *ma'ariv* (evening) service,
beginning with organ prelude and Louis Lewandowski's *Lekha
Dodi* as a "processional hymn," moving directly to "*Maariv*,"[98]
"*Ahavah*" (presumably *Ahavat Olam*), *Shema* (by Max Spicker),
and *Hashkiveinu*, then leaping to an "Adoration" (the American
Reform version of *Aleinu*), for which the "audience" was asked
to stand, a "*Kidush Hashem*" (presumably some version of
Kedushat Hashem), a "Traditional" *Kiddush*, the "partaking of
the Sabbath Bread," a benediction, and a recessional hymn (labe-
led "traditional").

Part One ended with a *seudah* (meal), although nothing in the
program indicates how lavish or long the meal might have been. It
may well have been akin to a Passover *seder*, although the service was
held about a month before Passover. Whatever the nature of the
meal, it accomplished Sonderling's goal of appealing to touch, smell,
and taste, while the liturgical service appealed to sight and hearing.

Part Two of the program began with *Veshamru* (by Baruch Schorr). There followed a "Tableau Vivant" entitled "The Sabbath of Yesterday." No details are given, but this was likely a dramatization under the direction of Murray Phillips. On the program, the tableau is followed by a passage from "*Echa*," translated as "How hath the Lord covered the daughter of Zion with a cloud . . . and cast down from heaven unto the earth the beauty of Israel" (Lam. 2:1). The text suggests the initial tableau may have been somewhat grim. A second tableau vivant was then offered, together with Lewandowski's *Tov L'hodos*. A third tableau was either paired with or followed by the celebratory *Ein Keloheinu*. Part Two then ended with an "Address," probably a sermon by Rabbi Sonderling.

A newspaper article from August 30, 1932, described the dramatized Shabbat evening service as a foretaste of another service to be presented by Sonderling:

> On Selichoth, September 24th, Rabbi Sonderling will invite the general public to attend a Neo-Chassidic midnight service at the Level Club. He has also engaged the auditorium of the Level Club with a seating capacity of 2,300 for [Rosh Hashanah and Yom Kippur Services] after which Rabbi Sonderling plans to form a permanent congregation in New York for the followers of Neo-Chassidism.[99]

The article quotes Rabbi Sonderling at length:

> Neo-Chassidism tries to penetrate the channels of the five senses to the soul of man. It is "sense-appeal" and it is in accordance with old Jewish thought. Rabbi Moses Isserles, one of the great authorities of the Middle Ages, stated that the Sanctuary of Old was surrounded by a wall. That wall had five doors leading to the Temple corresponding to the five senses. . . . The synagogue and public services as now conducted do not appeal to the younger generation. The Jewish home is vanishing rapidly. What can be done in order to revive Jewish religiosity? Modern Jewry apparently is not discouraged by the lack of response

of the Jewish masses. It has continued to build magnificent temples and has invested untold millions in structures which remain empty. I suggest that we build, instead of huge synagogues, the Jewish home for the congregation at large. In order to avoid misunderstanding, I insist most emphatically that the Jewish centers as built in recent years are not the things I have in mind. . . . We can't become Jewish by means of a swimming pool . . . neither will bridge parties or similar enterprises help the religious cause. What I plan is a beautiful hall in which the congregation gathers, where people replace the leader, and the service becomes a social gathering.[100]

Another newspaper article from the same year provides a few more details on Sonderling's vision:

[Rabbi Sonderling] proposes departments of painting and sculpture, the crafts, music and drama, and his ideas range from a consideration of incense to the suggestion that evening dress be worn at certain religious festivals. "Steadily," said Rabbi Sonderling in an interview, "the conviction has grown in me that ethics, urged through the spoken word, have been pushed to the exclusion of other values and other modes of worship and that the synagogue has been the loser. Thus I have become an advocate of New-Chassidism, as this form of Jewish worship is categoried [*sic*].[101]

The same article reports:

It is Rabbi Sonderling's impression that there are many to whom sermons do not appeal, although they are drawn by the fusion of religion and art and especially by music. He has been visiting various houses of worship, Christian as well as Jewish, to get ideas. For one thing, the processional in the Riverside Church so impressed him that he hopes to have a synagogue processional. . . . Rabbi Sonderling has been known to borrow a few dozen Oriental rugs in order to create a certain atmosphere of interest and devotion. . . . As the fragrance of a Christmas tree is associated with a [particular] day and as the idea of turkey accords with the American Thanksgiving, so do special fragrances and tastes have a religious meaning, traditionally, for the Jew, declares Rabbi Sonderling.[102]

Sonderling was not the first to use the term "Neo-Chassidism," but the meaning he attached to it was idiosyncratic. The Neo-Chassidic label had initially been used in Poland at the turn of the twentieth century to describe literary works, such as those by Y. L. Peretz, which drew from Chassidic folktales. The term had an aesthetic dimension in that context, although it did not involve the stimulation of all five senses. Neo-Chassidism would later describe attempts to revive interest in some of the values and devotional aspects of Chassidism by such figures as Martin Buber and, later, Abraham Joshua Heschel. In more recent years, the term has been applied to the mystical-experiential teachings and practices of Shlomo Carlebach, Zalman Schachter-Shalomi, Arthur Green, and others.[103] The "mystical aestheticism" of Chassidic practices likely influenced Sonderling's integration of the arts into Jewish ritual, singing and dancing being the most prominent examples. But it is uncertain if he meant to associate himself with the theological attitudes of Chassidism or the philosophical views of figures such as Buber. Although Sonderling, like Buber, used Chassidic stories to highlight theological and human concerns,[104] modern readers should be wary regarding Sonderling as a precursor to the Neo-Chassidism of Carlebach or Schachter-Shalomi.[105] His conception of Neo-Chassidism appears to have been his own.

Although Sonderling later reported that his 1932 Selichot services at Temple Emanu-El "drew a crowd of almost 1700 people,"[106] the showing did not translate into tangible or lasting support for his ideas. He was unable to secure the necessary funds to launch a permanent congregation. The following year, he again announced special services, this time to be held at Town Hall for the High Holidays: "the evening service to inaugurate the Jewish

New Year will be devoted to a German-Jewish service in which the contributions of German Jews to their native German culture will be exemplified by the rendering of music composed by eminent German Jews."[107] This is an intriguing comment in light of Sonderling's later commissions of liturgical works from German-speaking émigré composers in Los Angeles. Unfortunately, as of this writing, the particular composers and works performed at the 1933 service in New York are unknown. Moreover, there is no evidence that the service went forward as advertised, let alone any record of its reception.

While Rabbi Sonderling continued to harbor the hope that his services might lead to a permanent congregation, he narrowed his vision somewhat as 1933 progressed. The Jewish Telegraphic Agency reported in September of that year: "The selection of Town Hall for the High Holiday services by Rabbi Sonderling was motivated by the possibility of founding a permanent synagogue there to be known as the Mid-Town Synagogue, which will serve Jews in the theatrical profession who make their homes in the Times Square district."[108] This plan, too, failed to materialize.

During his years without a pulpit, Sonderling returned to paid speaking engagements on behalf of Zionist causes and for the United Jewish Appeal. One such trip brought him to Los Angeles for two days in July 1934, where he spoke at a fundraising dinner held at the Ambassador Hotel. The audience included top entertainers and film industry bigwigs, such as Eddie Cantor, Irving Thalberg, Harry Warner, and Louis B. Mayer.[109] Sonderling wrote that he "was urged to stay" in Los Angeles.[110] Some of the city's German-Jewish émigrés were presumably impressed by his German sensibilities, oratorical skills, and/or his new approach to Judaism.

Perhaps believing that Los Angeles would be more fertile soil than New York for his Neo-Chassidic approach, Sonderling agreed to settle there. One source suggests that "he decided to settle in

Los Angeles where a preponderance of Jewish artists were living who might become interested in [his 'sense-appeal' approach]."[111] Another account states, "In 1934, Rabbi Sonderling came in search of his artists. He decided there [was] one logical area [in which] to develop his ideas: He settled in Hollywood."[112] Whatever his reasoning, he moved to Los Angeles by September 1934, starting yet another chapter in his wandering career.

LOS ANGELES

The Los Angeles Jewish community to which Sonderling arrived was, if no longer in its infancy, still far from mature. At the turn of the last century, Jewish Angelinos were mostly centered around downtown, although there were no distinctly Jewish neighborhoods. During the 1920s, significant numbers of Eastern European Jews migrated from the Northeast and Midwest to the multiethnic Boyle Heights neighborhood, dubbed "Los Angeles' Lower East Side,"[113] as well as nearby City Terrace in East Los Angeles. By the 1930s, the Jewish population had begun moving west to centers along the Wilshire Boulevard corridor, taking advantage of the upward mobility afforded by New Deal programs, educational opportunities, growth of the Hollywood film industry, and the city's rapid industrialization. This westward shift was solidified with the relocation of Congregation B'nai B'rith to Wilshire Boulevard in 1929, and its subsequent renaming as Wilshire Boulevard Temple. While roughly one-third of Los Angeles Jewry still resided in the Boyle Heights area, making it the largest Jewish community west of Chicago,[114] another third now lived in the Central Wilshire area west of downtown, with Sinai Temple on the eastern end and Wilshire Boulevard Temple on the western end. The balance of the Jewish population was split between the Hollywood area and the West Pico section of Central Los Angeles, around Fairfax Avenue.

Canter's Deli, a fixture of the Fairfax District, Los Angeles, 1948.

Some individual Jews had already moved to the Fairfax District during the 1920s. However, it was not until the 1930s and '40s that the Jewish population was dense enough to require religious institutions. In 1935, Fairfax had four synagogues, including Sonderling's congregation, which began taking shape in 1934. By 1945, that number had increased to twelve.[115]

A shift toward modern practices accompanied this westward migration. The earlier center in Boyle Heights was dominated by two large Orthodox congregations, Beth Israel on Olive Street (Olive Street Shul) and Congregation Talmud Torah on Breed Street (Breed Street Shul), along with several smaller congregations and *shtiebels* (prayer rooms). The eastern edge of the Central Wilshire community was anchored by the Conservative Sinai Temple. Beth Jacob Congregation, a modern Orthodox synagogue a few miles south of Sinai Temple (in the West Adams neighborhood), represented a middle ground between traditional orthodoxy and the American liberal movements. Further west, Wilshire Boulevard Temple stood as the flagship of the city's Reform temples, which came to include Temple Israel of Hollywood (founded in 1926) and the "nearly Reform" Hollywood Temple Beth El (founded in 1922).

Established synagogues were only part of Los Angeles' Jewish religious makeup. Max Vorspan and Lloyd P. Gartner, authors of *History of the Jews of Los Angeles*, wrote that the city was spotted with "unaffiliated little houses of worship," and that ordained rabbis fended off competition from "numerous ill-qualified rabbinic pretenders."[116] These pretenders ran congregations at their private properties, adapting services to the demands of their congregational "customers."[117] According to Vorspan and Gartner: "The large number of irregular and proprietary synagogues tends to show that many Jews participated in worship only on the High Holidays and on the few holidays when the customary 'yizkor' prayer memorialized near relatives. Such behavior was typical in American Jewry."[118] During the Great Depression, laxity in formal Jewish ritual was joined by a weakening of Jewish study at all levels, as congregations decreased their support of Jewish schools. And while there were strong proponents of Yiddish culture, such as the Workmen's Circle, Zionist activities were minimal.[119]

Into this somewhat exhausted Jewish landscape, Rabbi Sonderling brought new energy and ideas. Shortly after relocating to Los Angeles in 1934, he helped to found a congregation that conducted Shabbat evening services in a private home on Manhattan Avenue and rented a larger hall for High Holiday services.[120] By 1938, if not earlier, the congregation had secured space at 525 South Fairfax Avenue and became known as the Society for Jewish Culture–Fairfax Temple.[121] There, Sonderling formed a community through which to pursue the ideas he had introduced in New York in 1932 and 1933. As the Fairfax District's first non-Orthodox synagogue, the denominationally unaffiliated congregation featured Friday evening services in German and English, which catered to the area's German-speaking refugees, as well as a religious school for children, adult education courses, and holiday observances.

The unusual name of Sonderling's new congregation was a first declaration of his goal. He "adopted a name that reflected a purpose broader than the traditional, religious appellations."[122] It was likely an allusion to the short-lived nineteenth-century Verein für Kultur und Wissenschaft der Juden (Society for Jewish Culture and Science), with the reference to science pointedly omitted, and/or a variation on Rabbi Mordecai Kaplan's Society for the Advancement of Judaism in New York. The Verein für Kultur was founded in 1819 by Eduard Gans, Heinrich Heine, Leopold Zunz, and others as an attempt to promote peoplehood based on the entirety of Jewish culture, as opposed to viewing Judaism as simply a religion.[123] Kaplan's Society for the Advancement of Judaism, founded in 1922, espoused a vision of Judaism as a sociocultural phenomenon, wherein Jewish peoplehood was paramount.[124] Given Sonderling's repeated—and, at least in Hamburg, controversial—assertions of Jewish peoplehood, along with the natural link between "culture" and the "sense-appeal" theory, his goals for the new congregation resonated with those of Kaplan and the Verein für Kultur.

Early in his Los Angeles tenure, Sonderling conducted "a dramatized Selichoth service," which was presumably similar to his 1932 Selichot service at New York's Temple Emanu-El.[125] Held in a space at the Carthay Circle Theatre,[126] the service used the talents of choreographer Benjamin Zemach[127] and actor Egon Brecher.[128] Unfortunately, no details have survived.

Indeed, very few records of Sonderling's activities at Fairfax Temple exist. The temple's records were lost when the facility was sold shortly after Sonderling's death in 1964.[129] Rabbi Sonderling's papers, housed at the American Jewish Archives, are unfortunately of little help in this regard. He reportedly "infused drama into his sermons, services, and all synagogue activities,"[130] but the precise form of that "drama" is not clear, even from sermons found in the archives.[131] Rabbi Max Nussbaum, one of Sonderling's contemporaries, commented that Sonderling "initiated the Seder in drama and music, and the dramatization of the Bible at Friday evening services. Basically, Sonderling himself was a fusion of religion and art."[132] According to Nussbaum, Sonderling's ability to innovate owed much to his personal charisma: "He was the most colorful rabbi I have ever known. The long, black, and later white beard—famous on two continents—gave him the appearance of an ancient Patriarch. He called attention to himself by his mere presence."[133]

The Fairfax Temple facility was small, making the weekly services fairly intimate. High Holiday services were conducted in rented spaces that could accommodate larger crowds. Venues included the Ambassador Hotel on Wilshire Boulevard (1944) and the Embassy Auditorium on Grand Avenue (1946).[134] A contemporaneous source relates that the temple's "services are conducted in a modern Conservative style," but with "the wearing of a head-covering as optional."[135] Another describes the temple as a haven where refugees from German-speaking lands "gathered

. . . to socialize and join their relatives in their familiar form of observance."[136]

The communal aspect seems to have been the most important attraction, as many of the refugees—including the commissioned composers—were not necessarily religiously oriented but sought an ethnic community of shared culture, language, and heritage. Sonderling's positioning of the congregation as a social group first and a temple second, enshrined in the name Society for Jewish Culture–Fairfax Temple, was a welcome prioritization for secular Jews who were not ritually inclined but were nonetheless enthusiastic about artistic possibilities at the temple. That Sonderling succeeded in actualizing his vision owes both to the arrival of German-speaking émigrés, who gravitated to the rabbi's "familiar" style, and to the aesthetic values they shared with the rabbi.

During his first decade or so in Los Angeles, Sonderling attracted the services of excellent Jewish émigré musicians. Among them was Joseph Leonard (né Josef Levi), a native of Mannheim, Germany, who, in 1936, joined the faculty of the Pacific Institute of Music and Fine Arts in the Hancock Park neighborhood of Los Angeles at the invitation of the institute's founder, Manuel Compinsky, a conductor, film composer, and celebrated violinist. A blind pianist and organist, Leonard had an extensive performing career in Germany prior to immigrating to the United States.[137] Sonderling hired him to conduct the Fairfax Temple Choir. In that capacity, Leonard served alongside Cantor William Zeisl (brother of Eric) in concerts and worship services. Leonard left Fairfax Temple in the early 1950s to become the organist and choir director at Temple Beth Am, a large Conservative synagogue in Los Angeles.

A notable public performance took place at the Hollywood Inter-Faith Forum on April 7, 1946, hosted by the First Methodist Church of Hollywood. The event, titled "The Communion of

Oriental and Occidental Beliefs, Expressed through the Arts," featured lectures by Rabbi Sonderling, Dr. Ernest Caldecott of the First Unitarian Church, and Swami Prabhavananda, a Hindu monk and founder of the Vedanta Society of California. Occurring just seven months after the end of World War II, the speakers addressed "the all-important current question: 'Has Religion Failed in These Trying Times and Religions' Answer in Defense.'" Leonard, Cantor Zeisl, and the "augmented choir of Fairfax Temple" joined the First Methodist Church Choir and Choral Trio of the Hindu Church in "a dramatized and musical presentation" to supplement the talks.[138]

It is worth noting that Joseph Leonard arrived in Los Angeles with his brother, Alfred, an entrepreneurial classical music enthusiast. Alfred Leonard was the director of symphonic programs on Los Angeles' KFAC, founder of the Los Angeles Music Guild (est. 1944), director of the guild's concert series (1945–1952), owner of a music store, Gateway to Music (1939–1958), and a writer of essays and monographs. Alfred's close circle of friends included Ernst and Lilly (née Zwack) Toch, with whom he exchanged letters, gifts, poetry, and musical manuscripts. Ernst Toch, whom Sonderling would commission, shared the same birthday as Alfred's daughter, Barbara. For several years, Toch sent Barbara a theme and variations based on her name in celebration of their joint birthday.[139]

Sonderling persuaded four preeminent émigré composers to write Jewish liturgical works for use in Fairfax Temple services. As previously noted, the composers were drawn not only to Sonderling's Germanic background but also to his experiential approach to Judaism (dubbed "Neo-Chassidism"), which valued aesthetic involvement as a vitalizing force, as well as the humanistic-universalistic ideals rooted in his rationalist education. Sonderling also encouraged them to express their inner selves through the Jewish texts rather than adhering to preexisting musico-ritual conventions, and offered them a built-in audience at a time when the public at large was uninterested in new music of a classical nature.

The first commissionee was Ernst Toch, who composed *Cantata of the Bitter Herbs* to text adapted by Rabbi Sonderling for a Passover *seder* in 1938. That same year, Sonderling convinced Arnold Schoenberg to compose a new setting of a modified *Kol Nidre* text for Yom Kippur. In 1941, Sonderling commissioned Erich Wolfgang Korngold to write *A Passover Psalm* and *Prayer*. In 1944, Sonderling invited Eric Zeisl to compose something for an interfaith concert, which became *Requiem Ebraico*. These commissions are discussed in detail in the chapters ahead.

Sonderling never stopped trying to actualize his theory of "sense-appeal." He began writing his autobiography late in life, producing only a few short vignettes dealing with his years in Europe and early experiences in America. He intended to write more, as he described in a June 4, 1961 letter to Jacob Rader Marcus:

> [T]he next part will show how I tried, and still try to put into reality the theory of my "sense-appeal." I shall describe two services I gave: One at Temple Emanuel in New York [and a] second one, a midnight service—Selichoth Service—dramatized. . . . Finally, I hope to be able to show that[,] and how[,] I succeeded in getting the cooperation of great musical minds—such as Ernest [*sic*] Toch, Erich Wolfgang Korngold and last, but not least, Arnold Schoenberg.[140]

Sadly, there are no drafts or notes for this unfinished section.

Regardless of how Sonderling attempted to realize the "sense-appeal" theory after 1945, he was doing it for a shrinking congregation. The German-speaking community began to unwind after the war. Some of the leading figures, notably Thomas Mann, returned to Europe permanently. Although Mann was not Jewish, his return to Europe in 1952 impacted the entire émigré community. Others went back to Europe for lengthy stays but ultimately found the continent to be inhospitable. Korngold, for instance, lived in Europe from 1949 to 1952, but resettled in Hollywood when audiences for his music failed to materialize. Illness and age took other community members. Schoenberg died in 1951, Korngold in 1957, and Zeisl in 1959. Toch died in 1964, the same year as Sonderling.

Still, Sonderling continued to attract prominent European refugees to his congregation. Most significant in the postwar period was Alfred Sendrey, a Hungarian-born composer, conductor, organist, and musicologist, who served as music director at Fairfax Temple from 1952 to 1956. Before settling in Los Angeles in the mid-1940s, Sendrey was briefly the director of Central German Radio in Berlin (1933), fleeing soon thereafter to Paris, where he directed Radiodiffusion Nationale (1933–1940). He then immigrated to New York, where he taught music at the 92nd Street YMHA (Young Men's Hebrew Association), before arriving in Los Angeles. After working at Fairfax Temple, Sendrey was hired as musical director of Sinai Temple of Los Angeles (1956–1964), and served as a professor of Jewish music at the University of Judaism (now American Jewish University).[141]

Notwithstanding such collaborations, the offspring of émigrés were more interested in assimilating into American society than asserting their separateness through a Jewish congregation, no matter how modern or cultured. Fairfax Temple, which had always been small, became even smaller in the postwar years. To supplement his income, Sonderling began teaching at the Los Angeles campus of HUC-JIR and at the Brandeis Camp Institute in Simi Valley.[142]

Sonderling taught one or two courses per term at HUC-JIR from fall 1957 through spring 1963.[143] Among his subjects were

homiletics, theology, and the history of Reform Judaism. Rabbi
Alfred Gottschalk, who served as dean of the Los Angeles campus
from 1959 to 1971 and president of the HUC-JIR system from
1971 to 1996, said of Sonderling:

> On the extraordinary faculty in that group of *rishonim*-originals
> was a rabbi who stood out because of his great intellectual and
> spiritual qualities. His name was Jacob Sonderling. . . . He was
> the rabbi of Fairfax Temple, a small congregation of German
> refugees in the Fairfax District of Los Angeles. He used to say
> that while he had the smallest congregation, he enjoyed the
> largest following.[144]

In addition to his professorship, Sonderling remained active in
Zionist causes, especially through the Los Angeles district of the
Zionist Organization of America, for which he served as president
(c. 1939). He also "made the Brandeis Camp Institute his second
home" and "loved to speak at the camp [and] he also served on the
Board of Brandeis."[145] It is unknown precisely when Sonderling
began teaching at the camp, which was inaugurated in 1947, but a
1960 advertisement shows him sitting on the ground and teaching
a circle of eager young students.[146] One of the last photographs of
Sonderling shows him planting a tree at the camp on May 3, 1964.

Sonderling would have been acquainted with Max Helfman,
a charismatic Polish-born composer who led musical activities
for all Brandeis campers from 1947 to 1958 and led five consecu-
tive summers of the Brandeis Arts Institute (1948–1952), which
attracted young Jewish artists and musicians from around the
country. Much like Sonderling's effort to commission specifically
Jewish works from composers of Jewish heritage, Helfman stimulated promising young composers, aged eighteen to twenty-five, to
apply their talents to Jewish thematic works. The institute's teaching staff included three of Sonderling's collaborators: Ernst Toch
and Eric Zeisl, who taught composition, and Alfred Sendrey, who

Rabbi Jacob Sonderling (right) planting a tree at Brandeis Camp Institute, May 3, 1964.

taught conducting.[147] Brandeis also had programs in dance, drama, and visual arts. Several from the musical cohort went on to have notable careers in Jewish and general music, including Charles Feldman, Leon Levitch, Elliot Greenberg, Jack Gottlieb, Gershon Kingsley, Raymond Smolover, Yehudi Wyner, and Sheldon Merel.

Sonderling died of a heart attack on September 30, 1964, at the age of eighty-five.[148] Emma, his wife of sixty years, died three days later. In 1965, the Fairfax Temple property was sold to another congregation. The proceeds of that sale were donated to HUC-JIR to help build a new Los Angeles campus adjacent to the University of Southern California. Max Nussbaum, the first vice president of HUC-JIR Los Angeles, paid tribute to Sonderling in 1965, calling him "a teacher of teachers and a Rabbi of Rabbis; a man who brought drama to religion, Chassidism to Reform, Zionism to American Jewry, and kindness to his fellowman. He represented the totality of our Jewish heritage at its very best."[149]

To this day, a bust of Rabbi Jacob Sonderling occupies a corner of the library at HUC-JIR's Los Angeles campus, creating a small amount of "sense-appeal" for those who happen upon it.

CHAPTER 2

COMMISSIONING JEWISH LITURGICAL MUSIC

R abbi Jacob Sonderling was a pioneer in commissioning new music for the synagogue in the twentieth century. There had been a few such commissions in Europe during the nineteenth century, and Sonderling was likely familiar with some of them. Most famously, the renowned Viennese cantor-composer Salomon Sulzer commissioned Franz Schubert to compose a setting of Psalm 92, *Tov L'hodos*. Schubert delivered a piece that became a regular part of the liturgy of Sulzer's Stadttempel, the main synagogue in Vienna, and was published in the first volume of Sulzer's *Schir Zion* (Songs of Zion) around 1840.[1]

Volume one of *Schir Zion* contains 159 cantorial solos and choral pieces for Sabbath, the Three Pilgrimage Festivals, High Holidays, Purim, Tisha B'Av, weddings, bar mitzvahs, and other occasions. These include thirty-six old melodies, eighty-six Sulzer originals, and thirty-seven original works by other composers. Schubert was one of the guest composers, along with Joseph Drechsler, Ignaz Ritter von Seyfried, Wenzel Wilhelm Würfel, and Franz Volkert. Two Jewish composers also supplied settings: Joseph Fischhof, known mainly for his collection of Beethoven manuscripts, and Sulzer's eldest surviving son, Julius.[2] Viennese Jews were justifiably proud of these Hebrew settings, which symbolized their cultural integration into Western society, a reality made possible by the nineteenth-century Emancipation of European Jewry and the Haskalah (Enlightenment) among Jewish intellectuals. However, Sulzer did not credit any of the commissioned composers in the original edition of *Schir Zion*, presumably to avoid objections from less cosmopolitan Jewish communities where the volume was sold. Sulzer's youngest son Joseph corrected these omissions in his heavily edited 1905 reissue.[3]

Schubert originally composed *Tov L'hodos* (Psalm 92) for baritone cantor and mixed choir for the Stadttempel in July 1828. Because Schubert and the other non-Jewish composers were not familiar with Hebrew declamation, they received guidance from Sulzer (or another member of the Jewish community), worked from marked-up transliterated texts, or had their works edited by Sulzer after submission.[4] As a result, the Hebrew accentuation and syllabic distribution of *Tov L'hodos* are consistent with Sulzer's works. However, the cantor had little influence on the music itself, which is characteristically Schubertian and, from the outset, was deemed "not sufficiently liturgical in spirit" (i.e., not "Jewish" enough) to earn a significant place in synagogue repertoires outside of the Stadttempel.[5] This combination of liturgical guidance and musical freedom would also be a hallmark of Sonderling's synagogue commissions.

Given Sonderling's early years in and around Vienna, it seems likely that he was aware of Sulzer's commissioning activity.

Moreover, Sulzer was an internationally renowned figure.[6] During his career in Vienna, cantors from Central Europe and, later, Eastern Europe trekked to study with him, and notable musicians and critics heard his services at the Stadttempel and penned flattering accounts.[7] Sulzer was purportedly honored with the Russian Golden Medal, the Grand Duke of Baden Golden Medal, knighthood in the Order of Franz Joseph, and Morenu diplomas from the Jewish communities of Lviv, Szegedin (Szeged), and Vienna, and other awards.[8] Jews and non-Jews attended his ceremonious burial in 1890, and newspapers around the world printed laudatory obituaries and appreciations.

Perhaps less likely to be known to Sonderling were the commissions issued to and by Samuel Naumbourg (1817–1880), the Bavarian-born chief cantor of Paris. Through his involvement with the Paris branch of the Consistoire Israélite,[9] established by Napoleon I to administer Jewish worship and congregations in France, and the endorsement of esteemed Parisian Jewish opera composer Fromental Halévy, Naumbourg implemented the improvement of French synagogue music. Much like Sulzer, who initiated the modernization of synagogue music that would eventually spread throughout Europe, Naumbourg was critical of the coloratura embellishments of old-style cantors and the musical illiteracy that had long plagued the cantorate.[10]

Naumbourg was commissioned by the French government to write a setting of the Shabbat service to be adopted in every French synagogue. In turn, Naumbourg commissioned several leading composers of his day to write pieces for the synagogue liturgy. His two-volume *Semiroth Yisrael* (Songs of Israel), published in 1847 and c. 1852, includes chants and melodies typical of Southern Germany (both unaccompanied recitatives and cantor-choir arrangements), original compositions for soloists and various choral ensembles, and pieces by other Jewish composers, most notably

Cantor Israel Lovy, Naumbourg's predecessor at the Paris synagogue, and opera composers Halévy and Giacomo Meyerbeer.[11]

The pursuit of new liturgical music from leading composers was the exception rather than the European norm. More prevalent was a conservative preservation of tunes and settings regarded as "traditional," along with an assortment of collections by trained cantors and synagogue composers that blended cleaned-up versions of cherished chants and melodies with Western choral harmonies and structural conventions, based on the Sulzer model. A number of cantor-choral settings for the liturgical year were produced, including those by German choir director Louis Lewandowski (1821–1894) and Russian cantor-composers Abraham Dunajewsky (1843–1911) and Elieser Gerovitsch (1844–1914).

In the United States, Sonderling witnessed a receptiveness to new Jewish liturgical music. During his years in New York City and the Northeast (1925–1934), he maintained strong ties to Temple Emanu-El, through which he was acquainted with the activities of its Russian-born musical director, Lazare Saminsky (1882–1959).

Before arriving in New York in 1920, Saminsky had been a member of the St. Petersburg Society for Jewish Folk Music (1908–1919), a short-lived but influential Jewish national movement.[12] A coterie of young Russian Jewish composers and intellectuals affiliated with the St. Petersburg Society collected and arranged Jewish folk songs from the Pale of Settlement and composed new pieces that blended folk, Romantic, and modernist styles—in the process inventing Jewish art song.[13] Spearheaded by Yo'el Engel and encouraged by Russian nationalist composer Nikolai Rimsky-Korsakov, Jewish musicians from the St. Petersburg Conservatory organized the society around four main areas: research, composition, performance, and publishing. The program attracted a number of prominent members, including Saminsky, Moses Milner, Solomon Rosowsky, Efrayim Shkliar, Aleksander Krein, Mikhail Gnesin, Alexander Veprik, and Joseph Achron.

The regular activities of the society, such as concert-lectures for members, occasional public concerts, and music publishing, were disrupted by World War I and the Russian Revolution. The society's mission continued in Palestine, where Engel and Rosowsky immigrated in the 1920s, and New York, where Saminsky, Leo (Lev) Zeitlin, and Achron settled. In New York, the society helped inspire the 1932 formation of Mailamm (Makhon Eretz Yisraeli le-Mada'ei ha-Musikah, or American-Palestine Music Association), and its successor, the Jewish Music Forum, which remained active into the 1960s.

Saminsky became musical director of Temple Emanu-El in 1924. Already a noted composer of secular and religious works, he wrote new settings of the Friday evening service (1926), the Saturday morning service (1926), and the High Holiday services (1927).[14] By 1930, he had begun commissioning new liturgical works from other composers, some on the rise and others already well established. These included a Friday evening service by Frederick Jacobi in 1930, another such service by Joseph Achron in 1932, and a Saturday morning service by Isadore Freed in 1938.[15]

Saminsky's influence was heightened by his platform at Temple Emanu-El, where the "historically elite social and economic status" of its board of directors and many of its members, along with its impressive cathedral-like sanctuary (completed in 1930), earned its popular reputation as the flagship of American Reform Judaism.[16] Sonderling was almost certainly aware of Saminsky's commissions and heard at least some of them during his New York years without a pulpit (1932–1934), when he visited different synagogues and formulated his "sense-appeal" theory.

Concurrent with Saminsky's development of new liturgical music in New York, Galician-born Cantor Reuben Rinder (1887–1966) was commissioning new works at San Francisco's major Reform synagogue, Congregation Emanu-El, where he served as cantor from 1913 to 1959 and continued as cantor emeritus until his death in 1966. In 1927, Cantor Rinder formed the Society for the Advancement of Synagogue Music, through which he sponsored an international competition for new settings of liturgical texts. In its first year, the winning rendition of *Adon Olam* was awarded $500, a significant amount in those days.[17] The contest rules reflected Rinder's high artistic standards and musical goals for the American synagogue:

1. The composition must be written to the Hebrew text of "Adon Olam" (The Lord of All), a liturgical poem contained in the Jewish Prayer Book.

2. The music must be unperformed and unpublished.

3. The composition must be written for Cantor (Baritone) and mixed choir, with accompaniment of organ and instruments, or a cappella. If a cappella or if with an arrangement of instruments, an ad libitum organ arrangement should accompany the manuscript.

4. A separate Soprano, Alto, Tenor, and Bass part should accompany the score.

5. Scores must be written in ink.

6. Time limit for the rendition of the entire composition should not exceed seven minutes.

7. Each manuscript must bear on its title page a nom de plume or motto. A sealed envelope containing the real name of the composer and bearing on the outside the same nom de plume or motto, must accompany the manuscript.

8. The judges will be subsequently announced. If no work of sufficient merit is submitted the contest may be postponed.

9. The winning manuscript shall become the property of the Society for the Advancement of Synagogue Music. Congregations designated by the Society will have the right of first performance. The composer will have the privilege of copyright and of collecting royalties from sources other than those mentioned above.

10. Manuscripts must be submitted no later than December 1st, 1927 to Cantor Reuben R. Rinder, care of Temple Emanu-El, Arguello Boulevard and Lake Street, San Francisco, California.[18]

Rinder also arranged for established composers to produce large-scale works. Most important was his commissioning of Ernest Bloch's *Avodath Hakodesh* (Sacred Service), widely considered the greatest achievement of twentieth-century synagogue song. Bloch (1885–1977), a Swiss-born composer of great renown, had been persuaded by Rinder to leave Cleveland, where he was founding director of the Cleveland Institute of Music, and take the post of director of the San Francisco Conservatory of Music. Rinder approached Bloch to compose the service in 1928. Bloch completed the score in 1932 during an extended stay in his home country of Switzerland. *Avodath Hakodesh*, written for cantor, choir, and orchestra, set the template for subsequent sacred services, many of which could only be performed as intended in well-heeled "cathedral-style" Reform synagogues, such as Congregation Emanu-El. In practice, selections from Bloch's service and other larger works of the era are still sometimes sung in services, especially during the High Holidays, with an organ arrangement replacing the orchestra.[19]

Another of Cantor Rinder's well-known contributions is Darius Milhaud's *Service sacré pour le samedi matin* (Sacred Service for Sabbath Morning), commissioned in 1947. The composition is unique for including texts in Hebrew, English, and French and is generally regarded as the second greatest Jewish sacred service of the twentieth century (after Bloch's). A Jew from Provence, Milhaud (1892–1974) left France at the onset of World War II. He eventually settled in Oakland, California, taking a position at Mills College. Rinder reportedly asked Milhaud to write the service after hearing the composer sing *Chad Gadya* in Provençal during a Passover *seder*. Milhaud accepted the offer immediately.[20]

Rinder, like Sonderling, was an ardent Zionist—an unpopular position in the Reform movement of the time. The Jewish community of San Francisco had a history of opposition to the impractical and politically problematic "wildest of all wild dreams."[21] Nevertheless, Rinder actively supported the Jewish National Fund and other Zionist causes. Attitudes shifted during Rinder's long tenure, which witnessed, among other things, the establishment of the State of Israel in 1948. Five years later, the congregation gave Cantor and Mrs. Rinder a trip to Israel in recognition of their four decades of service. While there, Cantor Rinder recruited Marc Lavry (1903–1967), then director of the Israel Broadcasting Authority, to write a Shabbat evening service, which premiered at Emanu-El in March 1955. During a visit to Israel seven years later, Rinder tracked down Paul Ben-Haim (1897–1984), the dean of Israeli composers, and contracted him to write three anthems using texts from the Book of Psalms (Pss. 4, 23, and 147).[22]

As noted, Sonderling was a frequent speaker on behalf of the Zionist Organization of America. Although we have no documentation of a meeting, it seems likely that Sonderling and Rinder would have crossed paths, perhaps even before Sonderling moved to California in 1934. In any event, given Sonderling's interest in aesthetics and Jewish music, he was almost certainly aware of

Rinder's Society for the Advancement of Synagogue Music and the commissions from Bloch, Milhaud, Lavry, Ben-Haim, and other leading composers.

Following Saminsky and Rinder, Sonderling commissioned new liturgical music from established classical composers living in Los Angeles' German-speaking émigré community. He encouraged composers Ernst Toch, Arnold Schoenberg, Erich Wolfgang Korngold, and Eric Zeisl to produce five works between 1938 and 1945. The four had widely varied aesthetic tendencies, stylistic approaches, and Jewish identities. It is a testament to Sonderling's artistic open-mindedness that he encouraged each to write works of personal meaning that freely expressed their individual voices.

Like all commissions, the pieces Sonderling initiated were the result of converging factors, both coincidental and intentional. Los Angeles in the 1930s became home to a close-knit community of German-speaking refugees. Sonderling, a German native who had immigrated to America a decade earlier, had arrived in Los Angeles in 1934. It was the right place and the right time to establish an independent liberal synagogue that catered to the needs of the new arrivals. His singular vision of Judaism—blending rationalism with Chassidism, particularism with universalism, and theology with humanism—was attractive not only to the mostly non-traditionally observant congregants but also to the composers themselves, whose Jewishness was more ethnic or cultural than synagogue-centered. Sonderling's artistic ideals, drawn from his "five-sense appeal," set a tone of openness, innovation, and creative vibrancy that attracted composers who may not have otherwise considered writing for Jewish liturgy, no matter how generous the commission. Moreover, as a congregation of *landsmen*, Fairfax Temple was a comfortable venue for debuting deeply personal concert-style pieces, particularly at a time when the city was largely unreceptive to new music.

The model set by Sonderling, Saminsky, and Rinder has evolved and spread in the decades since those commissions. Most immediately in Sonderling's wake was American-born Cantor David Putterman (1900–1979) of Park Avenue Synagogue in New York. Between 1943 and 1978, Putterman commissioned sacred works from seventy-two composers, all of which were premiered during services at his synagogue.[23] Many of the pieces originated from the annual Sabbath Eve Service of Liturgical Music by Contemporary Composers, which attracted composers as varied as Leonard Bernstein, Max Helfman, Kurt Weill, and Zavel Zilberts. Over the course of his career, Putterman commissioned more than forty sacred services, in addition to dozens of stand-alone pieces.[24]

Similar to Sulzer's *Schir Zion*, Putterman's project was open to Jews and non-Jews alike. A press release for the new music service of 1946 invited composers "regardless of color or creed," explaining: "Since music is the universal language of all mankind and ministers to human welfare, Cantor Putterman feels that it can be a most useful medium for better relations between peoples and faiths, because 'rhythm and harmony find their way into the inward places of the soul.'"[25] The inaugural service in 1943 featured an *Adonai Malakh* (Psalm 97) by Alexander Gretchaninoff (1864–1956), a non-Jewish Russian composer who had fled the Bolshevik Revolution and had composed numerous works for the Russian Orthodox Church. Other non-Jews commissioned during Putterman's tenure include Roy Harris, Douglas Moore, Henry Brant, McNeil Robinson, and William Grant Still, a prominent African American composer.

During a symposium of the Jewish Music Forum in June 1944, Putterman articulated his vision of expanding the horizons of Jewish music through commissioning liturgical pieces and encouraging gifted musicians to enter the cantorate:

Contemporary composers such as Ernest Bloch, Joseph Achron, Darius Milhaud, Mario Castelnuovo-Tedesco, Frederick Jacobi, David Diamond, Paul Dessau, and others, eager to profess Judaism by means of their creative art, or fired with a burning resentment toward the injustices, intolerances, and inhuman cruelties perpetrated upon our people in this world Holocaust, have recently poured out their hearts into new liturgical creations expressive of their own innermost feelings, heralding, as it were, a new era in the liturgical music of the synagogue. New forms of *hazzanic* [cantorial] art are now likewise in the process of development, due to the influx and influence of modern Americans into the profession of *hazzanut*.[26]

Cantor Putterman was joined by a host of cantors and synagogue musicians, some of whom were composers in their own right, who spearheaded the commissioning of new music during this Jewish musical renaissance. Among them were European-born composers who served as synagogue music directors in America, such as Isadore Freed, Herbert Fromm, Hugo Adler, Frederick Pickett, and Max Janowski.

In 1950, Harry Coopersmith (1902–1975), an influential Russian-born American musician and educator, published *The Songs We Sing*, a compendium of Hebrew, Yiddish, and English songs intended for Jewish religious schools.[27] Coopersmith acknowledged that Jewish music "ha[d], of late, experienced a real renaissance," but noted that the "resurgence" mostly manifested in elaborate synagogue services without meeting "the overall needs of the school and community."[28] The widely distributed book compiles music to supplement "a six-year curriculum, for the average home and community," including many songs and arrangements by synagogue and general composers commissioned specifically for the book.[29] Among them are Leonard Bernstein, Heinrich Schalit, Reuven Kosakoff, Herman Berlinski, Gershon Ephros, Julius Grossman, Robert Starer, and Eric Werner, to name just a handful.

In more recent years, commissions have continued from cantors, congregations, and individual congregants. New music is regularly commissioned for momentous events, such as synagogue anniversaries, sanctuary dedications, and bar and bat mitzvah ceremonies. For example, the one hundredth anniversary of Chicago's Congregation Anshe Emet in 1974 occasioned a joint Sabbath service from nine well-regarded composers: Samuel Adler, Charles Davidson, Herbert Fromm, Maurice Goldman, Shalom Kalib, Frederick Pickett, Heinrich Schalit, Sholom Secunda, and Lazar Weiner.[30] Similar projects of greater or lesser ambition have been carried out in succeeding decades.

In some respects, Rabbi Sonderling's dream of amplifying the aesthetic in Judaism has come to fruition in the years since his death. Although he might not recognize the current state of Jewish worship as a realization of his vision, he deserves a place among the pioneers who helped construct the American Jewish musical landscape we know today.

CHAPTER 3
ERNST TOCH'S *CANTATA OF THE BITTER HERBS*

E rnst Toch (1887–1964) was one of the best-known composers in Weimar Germany, often linked with Paul Hindemith
(1895–1963).[1] Toch was born into the family of a humble leath-
erer in Leopoldstadt, Vienna's Jewish district (in earlier times a
Jewish ghetto), which was also home to Arnold Schoenberg, Erich
Wolfgang Korngold, and Eric Zeisl. Possessed with abnormally
large ear canals, Toch was especially sensitive to musical as well as
environmental sounds, which would influence his inventive compositions.[2] Against the wishes of his family, Toch was compelled
to create music. A newspaper notice announcing the death of
Johannes Brahms in 1897 alerted him to the possibility of composition as a career. In 1902, at the age of fifteen, he became a pupil of
Vienna's top composition teacher, Robert Fuchs, whose students
included Gustav Mahler, Hugo Wolf, Alexander von Zemlinsky,

and Erich Wolfgang Korngold. Despite this and subsequent educational experiences, Toch would claim that his real teacher had
been pocket scores of Mozart quartets.[3] By age eighteen, Toch
had six string quartets to his credit. The sixth quartet, op. 12 in
A minor, was performed by Vienna's prestigious Rosé Quartet,
thanks to a schoolmate who had passed it along to Arnold Rosé,
the Jewish concertmaster of the Vienna Philharmonic Orchestra
and brother-in-law of Gustav Mahler. Toch's family refused to
attend the performance. Family lore attributes his father's early
death to Ernst's obsession with composing string quartets.[4]

Toch studied medicine in Vienna before transferring to
Frankfurt's Hochschule für Musik in 1909, the same year as Paul
Hindemith, his younger contemporary. Upon completing his
studies, Toch taught piano and composition at the conservatory
in Mannheim, with a brief interruption to serve in the Austrian
Army during World War I. Toch earned a PhD from Heidelberg
University in 1921 with a dissertation on the structure of melody, "Contributions to the Stylistics of the Melody" ("Beiträge
zur Stilkunde der Melodie"). He began composing with gusto in
the mid-1920s.

While Toch's music is sometimes referred to as "post-Expres-
sionism" or "New Objectivity," such labels do little to convey the
range of his styles and experimentation.[5] His diverse oeuvre has
been called "a fascinating blend of angular abstraction, tenderness
touched with sarcasm, and uproarious energy."[6] An early project
was conceived around 1920 with novelist Hermann Hesse. The
two were to collaborate on an opera dealing with the Far East. The
opera did not materialize, but it led Hesse to write the classic novel
Siddhartha (1922) and Toch to compose *Die Chinesische Flöte*, op.
29 (The Chinese Flute, 1923), an exotic song-cycle with text by
Hans Bethge.[7] Toch first gained national and international fame
with his Cello Concerto, op. 35 (1925), Concerto for Piano and

Orchestra, op. 38 (1926), and a humorous one-act opera based on Hans Christian Andersen's "The Princess and the Pea" (1927), with libretto by Benno Elkan, a German-Jewish sculptor whose works include an ornate menorah stationed in front of the Knesset building in Jerusalem.[8]

The year 1926 witnessed an unusual concert in Donaueschingen, a small German town in the Black Forest, featuring "original compositions for mechanical instruments."[9] The concert included three pieces by Toch, six by Gerhart Münch, and two by Hindemith—all written for an automatically playing piano called the Welte-Mignon, which operated by means of a pneumatic mechanism activated by a spinning paper roll. This was the beginning of a short-lived craze for new instruments that captivated the German musical intelligentsia in the mid-1920s. The introduction of mechanical instruments, in particular, threatened some musicians and aficionados, whose aesthetic and practical assumptions were defied by the separation of performer from instrument and musical sounds from human mediation. Others were unsure how to respond to such innovations. Music critic Erich Steinhard, who attended the Donaueschingen concert, described the scene:

> The piano began to play: music like an étude, toccatas with otherwise unplayable harmonic progressions, with a speed that could never be approached even by the most virtuosic of players, with an exactitude of which a human could never be capable, with a superhuman sonic force, with a geometrical clarity of rhythm, tempo, dynamics, and phrasing, which only a machine can produce. . . . The piano finished the composition and there was an uneasy pause. Should one applaud? There's no one sitting there. It's only a machine.[10]

Toch downplayed fears, stressing that music prepared for the Welte-Mignon was in a category of its own: "The music in question here is not just any music that is reproduced by a mechanical instrument; it is music *for* a mechanical instrument, just like 'music *for* violin and piano' or 'music *for* orchestra'; it is composed in or out of the spirit of the instrument."[11]

Toch moved to Berlin in 1929, where he premiered one of his most famous works, *Gesprochene Musik* (Spoken Music, 1930), at the New Music Festival. The suite features a chorus producing nonverbal sounds and isolated vowel and consonant sounds through two movements, gradually culminating in a chaotic roar that gives way in the third movement to a fugal recitation of geographical names. The third movement, known as *Fuge aus der Geographie* (Geographical Fugue), so impressed John Cage and Henry Cowell that they later created an English-language version with Toch's blessing. Years later, Toch returned to spoken-word composition with *Valse* (1961), which mocks the Los Angeles cocktail party chatter that aggravated his hypersensitive ears.[12]

With the rise of the Third Reich in 1933, Toch saw the writing on the German wall. During the next two years, he moved first to Florence, then to Paris, and finally to London. He immigrated to New York in 1935, where he accepted a teaching position at the New School for Social Research. George Gershwin pulled strings for Toch to become a member of the American Society of Composers and Performers (ASCAP), enabling him to profit from performances of his works in America. But Toch desperately needed more money in order to help friends and family trapped in Europe. He relocated to Los Angeles in 1936 in hopes of increasing his income by writing film scores.[13]

In California, Toch quickly secured a teaching position at Los Angeles City College and then at the University of Southern California (USC). He eventually grew weary of the American system of educating composers, which he felt favored technique and mechanistic rationalism over expressiveness and humanistic considerations—especially with many taking up Schoenberg's mathematically oriented twelve-tone system.[14] He infamously declared in a newspaper interview that composition, per se, could not be taught.[15] That statement, however artlessly expressed, was rooted in his 1945 essay, "The Credo of a Composer," which argues for a "reaction against the reaction" that overthrew nineteenth-century emotionalism:

> Technique of art may be learnable and teachable (though even it is learnable and teachable only to a very limited degree). The other part of art, the one of religion and naivety, is unlearnable and unteachable. This is the part that makes us love true art and stirs us to the depths of our soul. . . . [W]hile sentimentality has no place in true art, we must not confuse sentimentality with sentiment. . . . If music of our century has, so far, failed to compel general devotion, as in the past, the reasons for it should not be sought in technicalities. They most probably lie in the spiritual sphere.[16]

Toch found work in the film industry, although not of the type he had hoped for. Much like fellow émigré composers Hanns Eisler and Eric Zeisl, Toch expected Hollywood to afford a realization of *Gesamtkunstwerk*: a synthesis of the arts wherein music would play an integral role.[17] But, on the whole, film music proved to be exploitative "hack work," where unreasonable deadlines, formulaic writing, and a lack of recognition were the norm. For the most part, Toch provided cues and orchestrations for chase scenes, comic-horror scenes, and melodramatic moments, much of it uncredited. For example, he anonymously wrote sequences for the finale of Alfred Newman's score for *The Hunchback of Notre Dame* (1939) and orchestrated Erich Wolfgang Korngold's score for *Devotion* (1946). Nevertheless, Toch is credited with fifteen full scores, three of which received Academy Award nominations: *Peter Ibbetson* (1935), *Ladies in Retirement* (1941), and *Address Unknown* (1944).

It should be noted that, from 1934 to 1937, Academy Award nominations for Best Scoring went to the music department. Irvin Talbot, head of Paramount Studio's music department, was named in the nomination for *Peter Ibbetson*, even though Toch wrote the score. The category was changed in 1938 to honor individual composers, and initially had two sub-categories: Original Score and Scoring. Korngold was the first to win the Academy Award for Original Score with *The Adventures of Robin Hood* (1938).

Despite earning the respect of industry colleagues, Toch despised writing for films, which he considered "a prostitution of his talent."[18] Nevertheless, he worked steadily in the lucrative, if creatively frustrating, film medium until he quit in 1945. Throughout the 1940s, Toch battled depression and "creative paralysis" resulting from the devastation abroad and a feeling that American audiences were unresponsive to his music.[19] He published only two non-film works between 1938 and 1944. One of those serious pieces was the *Cantata of the Bitter Herbs*, commissioned by Rabbi Sonderling. (The other was *Poems to Martha*, 1943, for medium voice and string quartet, which sets poems by a young husband who had lost his wife. He also composed an unpublished piece, *Chansons sans paroles*, for voice and piano, in 1940.)

In 1948, following a massive heart attack, Toch left USC and devoted himself to composing works of personal import. To offset income lost from regular teaching and films, he took on courses at the Tanglewood Music Festival and occasional lecturing duties in Oregon and Minnesota. Although his post-film period was less imaginative than his earlier output, music poured out of him. Between 1945 and his death in 1964, he composed over forty works, including all seven of his symphonies. The symphonies have the distinction of not being structured in accordance with the established Austro-German idiom. Rather, as musicologist Michael Haas explains, they were akin to "Mahlerian tone-poems strung together with little that kept them from dissolving into chaos beyond transcendential [sic] ideas that drove Toch to write. By his own admission, it was now important that he put pencil to paper: 'someone else could edit them later.'"[20]

THE COMMISSION

In December 1937, Toch learned that his mother had died suddenly in Vienna. Although Toch himself had little involvement with Jewish religious observance, his mother was, as he described her, "a deeply religious being" who "adhered strongly to some of [Judaism's] rites," including the recitation of the Mourner's *Kaddish* in memory of the dead.[21] Because of the vast distance between them at the time of her death, Toch realized "all I could do [for her] was to dedicate myself to her way and spirit in reaction to my loss."[22] He thus attended a worship service, perhaps for the first time in his adult life, at Rabbi Sonderling's Society for Jewish Culture–Fairfax Temple in order to recite *Kaddish*. He likely knew of the temple through other members of the German émigré community—such as his close friend Alfred Leonard, whose brother Joseph was Sonderling's choir director—or through his contacts in the film industry, some of whom were Sonderling's congregants. More important, as a non-practicing universalist Jew, Toch felt at ease in the nonthreatening confines of Fairfax Temple. Grounded in Sonderling's ideals of aesthetic engagement, humanism, and spiritual arts, as well as the cultural heritage of German-speaking refugees, the community proved a welcoming environment for a composer whose Jewish identity was more familial than religious.

After the service, Toch spoke with Rabbi Sonderling, who urged him to return with his daughter for an upcoming Hanukkah celebration.[23] The precise date of this conversation is unknown, but it probably occurred after the Friday evening Shabbat service on December 3, 1937, since Hanukkah in 1937 fell between November 28 and December 6.

Even before his mother's death, Toch had been musically engaged in Jewish subjects. Earlier in 1937, he sent three arrangements of Palestinian folk songs to Hans Nathan, a musicologist and German émigré living in Boston. Nathan envisioned a collection of new arrangements to be called *Folk Songs of the New Palestine*, comprising songs of the *chalutzim, aliyot,* and *kibbutzim*—Jewish settlers and settlements of pre-state Israel. Most of the source material derived from songs printed on postcards issued by the Keren Kayemet L'Yisrael (Jewish National Fund). In addition to Toch, Nathan solicited arrangements from Paul Dessau, Darius Milhaud, Arthur Honegger, Stefan Wolpe, Aaron Copland, Erich Walter Sternberg, and Kurt Weill. Some of the arrangements were published as fascicles in 1938 and 1939, before the project was interrupted by the Holocaust and World War II. Some forty-five years later, after retiring from Michigan State University, Nathan resumed work on the collection, which was published posthumously in 1994 as *Israeli Folk Music: Songs of the Early Pioneers*, with editorial assistance and contextual essays by musicologist Philip V. Bohlman.[24]

Toch sent his arrangements to Nathan on May 26, 1937. The experience, coming months before his encounter with Sonderling, may have sparked his interest in Jewish music. A letter accompanying the songs explained:

> Enclosed are the arrangements of the songs [*She Ug'di* (A Lamb and a Kid), *Tapuach Zahav* (An Orange), and *Avatiach* (A Watermelon)]. I assume that aside from their artistic aspect (for which your suggestions were of value to me), they will also prove their usefulness. The encounter with this peculiar product of present Palestinian Israeli culture has touched me deeply, and, living far from its home, I am grateful for the encounter.[25]

Some have claimed that Sonderling asked Toch to "write some simple new music" for the Hanukkah celebration at Fairfax Temple.[26] Given the short timeframe before that celebration, such a request seems presumptuous and unreasonable, and neither Toch nor Sonderling mention it in their recollections of the conversation. In any event, Toch wrote no such Hanukkah music.

Toch did, however, return to Fairfax Temple with his daughter for the Hanukkah celebration. He later wrote that in participating in two religious events—one for the sake of his mother and one for the sake of his child—he was reminded of his old idea that the Passover Haggadah would be a good subject for an oratorio-like piece. Toch told "Dr. Sonderling about the recurrence of this old thought [and Sonderling] took it up with great enthusiasm and the resolve to make its realization possible."[27]

Reading between the lines of Toch's comment, it seems likely that part of Sonderling's "resolve" involved securing funds to pay Toch for the composition. We have no records indicating how Sonderling gathered such funds or how much was given to Toch, but it is possible that Boris Morros (1891–1963), one of Sonderling's wealthier congregants, funded the commission or secured funding from Jews working in the film industry.

Morros was born in St. Petersburg, where he received his music education and conducted opera in a local theater until 1918. He conducted at various opera houses throughout Europe between 1918 and 1922, when he immigrated with his family to the United States. They settled in Los Angeles in 1924. Morros rose quickly in the film industry, serving as music director at Paramount Studios from 1934 to 1939, and afterwards forming an independent production company.[28] His own success and Hollywood connections would have given him access to funds for the Toch commission. However, there is no paper evidence to support this speculation. Today, Morros is primarily remembered for his involvement in

Cold War espionage. He operated as a Soviet spy from 1934 until 1947, when he was arrested by the FBI, and thereafter worked as a double agent for ten years, passing misinformation to the Soviets. In 1957, he testified about Communists in Hollywood before the House Committee on Un-American Activities.[29]

Aside from arranging for the commission, Toch credited Sonderling with the conceptual framework of the piece: "It was his idea to have it fused with the actual Seder-Evening service in the temple, permitting the wording of the story and the musical numbers to intertwine with the actions of the service."[30] Sonderling recounted, "[T]he suggestion was made that we study the Hebrew text for the Passover ritual."[31] The study soon became a project involving Morros, Sonderling, Toch, and Leopold Jessner (1878–1945), who had been a successful director and producer of German theater and cinema, as well as an outspoken Socialist. Jessner fled to the United States in 1933 and landed in Hollywood, where he found work in low-level positions but never attained the recognition he enjoyed in Germany. Toch had little patience for the group's "theological debate" about permissible and impermissible texts. When asked his opinion on one of the contested subjects, Toch replied: "I could not help saying I had none, but was afraid that my music might evaporate in the heat of such discussions."[32]

Toch absented himself from the textual deliberations and "was presented with suggestions already cleared with which to forge the frame for what I needed as a musician."[33] Of his approach, Toch later wrote:

> Obviously, it was implicitly assumed that I would turn to the store of existing, traditionally established music in the Passover services and integrate some of it into mine. Strangely enough, that thought never occurred to me. My conception of the tale told in the Hagada was quite different, was non-denominational and broadly universal. It is the formula of a fate that men

have inflicted on men time and again. Whenever it happens it causes sufferings told and untold and calls upon powers of resistance, told and untold. It happened to the Jews and it has happened to others.

The simplicity of the Hagada story as I experienced it as a child, not as part of a religious ceremony but as part of a festive occasion, the reading of a breathtaking account of history, the impact of the strong emotions it carried along, stayed with me and made me welcome the task to convey with corresponding simplicity how this story had moved me at a time when we were as yet blissfully unaware of its pending revival in the fate of our generation. It appealed to me to address to children and to a community of religious people, whose privilege it is, as it is the privilege of all intrinsically religious men, to submit to, to accept, to reconcile the unfathomable with the assurance, the flooding, the ringing happiness of a faith.[34]

It is not clear to what extent, if any, Toch shared his composition in draft form with Sonderling, Morros, or Jessner. Sonderling recalled, "Toch refused to be guided by old traditional tunes. He composed how and what he felt without fear of contradiction."[35] The others may have recommended that Toch incorporate some of the old tunes (and he "refused"), but he was ultimately free to do as he felt best. In any event, Sonderling claimed that they were all pleased with the final product: "[W]hen we listened to his first climax 'Praised be Thee, O Lord, Thou hast kept us alive!' there was no doubt in us that the Jewish will to survive had found its most stirring expression."[36]

The work received its debut performance at Fairfax Temple as part of the Passover observance in 1938. The first *seder* was on Friday, April 15, 1938, likely the night of the premiere. According to Sonderling:

[W]e arranged the Passover festival in our modest Fairfax Temple. An orchestra, chorus and soloists were provided by

Boris Morros, and they played and sang Toch's work to an audience consisting of artists and musicians. It was accepted with such warmth that I was convinced that our new approach to old tradition was born.[37]

Toch was more circumspect, writing only, "At the first performance in the temple, our then 9-year-old daughter was one of the children who took an active part in the stage service."[38]

THE COMPOSITION

Cantata of the Bitter Herbs opens with an oboe solo over harp accompaniment in a three-beat meter, joined within a few bars by clarinet and flute.[39] The melodic movement is simple, in steps and small intervals, with frequent repetition. The texture thickens slightly with the addition of another clarinet and flute, and then a solo flute in its low register takes over from the oboe. The mood set by the winds and harp is tranquil, recalling the childhood home Toch had in mind more than the ancient setting of Egyptian bondage.

The strings take over in a lushly Romantic passage conveying a hint of bittersweet sentiment before building to a climax with brass and percussion, only to return to the oboe-harp passage that started the piece, followed by a fairly rapid cadence. The chorus enters abruptly in a classic chorale with which J. S. Bach would have been comfortable.

It is striking that Toch, a composer known for boundary-stretching modernism, would return to Baroque and Classical forms for the *Cantata*. These "old-fashioned" styles may be employed to support the piece's childlike character, or perhaps to convey the simplicity of Toch's childhood *seders*. As a boy, the budding composer was left to his own musical devices. "I am [trained] by Mozart, by Bach," he told his pupil, musicologist Robert Trotter. "How would anybody know? Nobody played an instrument with [me as a youth], nobody sang with [me], and I did all this in secrecy. These were my only masters. I never had any other."[40] The chorale is a fitting tribute to his early "masters."

Toch may have also intended to represent the timeless quality of the Passover narrative. Four years after composing the piece, he began writing *The Shaping Forces in Music*, which he would eventually finish in 1947. The book sought to "bring out and emphasize the timeless and permanent features of music as against the time-bound and transient ones. In doing so it attempts to reconcile the at-times-'classical' with the at-times-'modern.'"[41] *Cantata of the Bitter Herbs* satisfies that goal.

The chorale, despite its comfortable Baroque sound, is still a bit jarring to modern ears because of the English text that is sung:

> Fetters fell, the captive rose, Israel left Mitzrayim.
> "Home, home to Judah, back to our land!" And feet began to move.

Aside from the phrase "Israel left Mitzrayim [Egypt]," these words are not found in the Haggadah or in the Exodus account. The Hebrew slaves would never have referred to a land called "Judah," much less have called it home. According to the Bible, the Hebrews had been residing in Egypt for 430 years, and Egypt was the only home known to the generation of the exodus (Exod. 12:40–41). Even if they had a concept of a land of origin linked to the patriarchs Abraham, Isaac, and Jacob, that land would have been called Canaan. Judah was at that time merely one of the twelve Hebrew tribes. The Kingdom of Judah did not arise until the tenth century BCE, according to the biblical account (1 Kings 12:1–24), well after the Hebrews settled Canaan.

Perhaps we are hearing in this odd text the Zionist views of Rabbi Sonderling and a modern call for a return to Judaism's ancient homeland. Or, perhaps, Sonderling and his co-writers wished to echo the cries of "Juden" with the term "Judah." Whatever the thinking, we immediately feel that the present agenda is different from that of the traditional *seder*.

After the choral introduction, two lines from Psalm 114 are sung: the first by a mezzo-soprano soloist, and the second by a soprano soloist:

> The sea beheld them; terrified it fled.
> The Jordan sighted them, upstream it turned.
> The mountains skipped like rams, like lambs.
> The hills set to hopping.

The chorus then returns to repeat the initial chorale, this time singing the next two lines of Psalm 114:

> Why dost thou flee, O sea? Why turnest thou, O Jordan?
> Shake, shiver earth, thou facest Adonai.

Psalm 114 is customarily chanted during the Passover *seder* after the exodus tale has been recounted and just before the festive meal is introduced by the first taste of *matzah* (unleavened bread), bitter herbs, and *charoset* (a paste-like mixture of apples, nuts, cinnamon, and wine symbolizing the clay from which the Israelites made bricks for their Egyptian slave masters). It occurs near the beginning of the *Hallel* (Pss. 113–118),[42] psalms of praise recited on certain Jewish holidays, and marks a turning point in the *seder* from narrative to praise.[43] In contemporary family *seders*, the psalm is regularly sung to a bright melody to emphasize the triumphant aspect of the text.

The placement of Psalm 114 at the outset of Toch's *Cantata* raises the question of how the piece was interwoven with Fairfax Temple's Passover *seder*. Sonderling may have already performed the first part of the traditional meal before the *Cantata* began (although elements of that first part appear later in the *Cantata*). Or maybe the movement from tranquil to somber chords in Toch's setting was devised to first calm the audience and then introduce a note of awe before Sonderling told the story. Unfortunately, we have no detailed account of how the evening proceeded.

The *Cantata* continues with a narration attesting to the ancient tradition of reciting the Passover story, and concluding with the *Shehecheyanu* blessing, thanking God for enabling those assembled to reach this sacred moment. At a conventional *seder*, the *Shehecheyanu* is preceded by the blessing over wine. Sonderling may have used the narrative break to make that blessing, although it is not recorded in the *Cantata* text.

The *Shehecheyanu*, scored for chorus and orchestra, is a fanfare in a major key. It is announced by the brass (on scale degrees 5–1–3–2–1–3–5) and repeated by the chorus in unison, percussion, and strings. The section runs only about a minute and a half. To the extent that any of the triumphalism associated with Psalm 114 was missed, Toch makes up for it here in spades.

Next, a narrative break addresses the *pesach* (paschal lamb), *matzah*, and *maror* (horseradish). In the traditional Haggadah, these three items are discussed between the conclusion of the exodus story and the recitation of Psalms 113 and 114, prior to the eating of the meal. The items are usually introduced by recalling, "Rabbi Gamliel used to say, whoever did not explain these three things has not fulfilled his duty."[44] Whether Sonderling included this discussion out of deference to Rabbi Gamliel's legal ruling or because it served the dramatic arc, its placement relies on the congregation's knowledge of the exodus story from past tellings.

A two-minute orchestral interlude follows, entitled "Children's Dance." A group of children likely performed a dance at this juncture, especially given Toch's reference to his nine-year-old daughter's participation. Again, we have no description of that dance, so it is impossible to know whether it contributed to the narrative in some way or was simply an entertaining distraction for impatient children and their parents.

Following the orchestral interlude is a lengthy narration, beginning with Moses' birth and ending with the Ten Plagues. Curiously,
the text jumps chronologically in the middle to reference the part-
ing of the waters at the Red Sea. Moses is given a more heroic stat-
ure than in the Haggadah, which asserts that God, not Moses, was
responsible for the exodus. Moses is mentioned just once by name
in the traditional Passover Haggadah, shortly after the recounting
of the ten plagues: "By the sea—what does it say? 'Israel saw the
great hand of God wielded against Egypt, and the nation feared
Adonai and believed in Adonai and in Moses His servant.'" Moses'
role was presumably downplayed in order to combat tendencies
to deify him.[45] Sonderling's text has God lengthening Moses' staff
"so that the waters of the Nile, the creatures of the land, the wind
and the rain obeyed him [i.e., Moses]," and tells of Moses, in the
middle of the night of the last plague, "unlock[ing] the gates of the
slave encampments, calling his people forth." We can only specu-
late as to why Sonderling (and/or Morros and Jessner) elevated the
role of the human actor, thereby reducing the emphasis on divine
action. Perhaps Sonderling's theology was more humanistic than
theistic, or perhaps he felt the drama of the story was enhanced by
restoring human action, which plays a greater role in the biblical
account than in the rabbinic gloss of the traditional Haggadah.

The string accompaniment under the narrative of the Ten
Plagues is worthy of a Hollywood thriller from the 1930s. The
tremolo-laden melodic passages—augmented with each plague—
and the dramatic final climax dying away to nothing, may well
have thrilled listeners in 1938. Today, they seem a bit flat and
predictable.

The narration continues with the freeing of the people, recited
over a subdued string rendition of the chorale to come. That chorale, in the best tradition of Protestant hymnody, is sung softly by
the chorus with the simple lyrics: "And it was at midnight." The

text, drawn from Exodus 12:29, is the refrain of the first several stanzas of a seventh-century poem by Yannai, which is among the songs commonly sung at the end of the *seder*.[46]

The narrator picks up the story again with the universal message that "people in many lands and ages" have experienced nights of horror, agony, fear, and hope. There follows a brief allusion to Sinai, in which the revelation is reduced to "the commandment," namely, "Not tyranny but law; Law is light." While the traditional Haggadah contains references to Sinai—for instance, in the popular song *Dayeinu* (It Would Have Been Enough for Us)—Sonderling's message goes beyond the particularism of Sinai to assert a principle applicable to all humanity.

The insertion of the blessing of God as Giver of Torah further underlines the equation of Torah and Law. That text is normally recited prior to the story of the four sons, about midway through the first portion of the *seder*.[47] Here, it is sung in Hebrew by the mezzo-soprano soloist and is repeated five times (twice in an abbreviated form leaving out the words "in His holiness") with instrumental connectors of varying lengths. The aria itself is quite beautiful, and its repetition serves to further highlight the primacy of Torah.

Another narrative passage follows, this one alluding to Israel's exile from its land, forced wanderings in diaspora, and the relevance of the exodus story for all humanity.

Select phrases from Psalm 126 (verses 1–5) are next sung, first by the tenor and soprano soloists, then by the entire chorus. The phrases, which are isolated from their original context, erase any suggestion of Israel being the elect among the nations. Reference to restoring Israel's fortunes in the original text is translated as a present tense "free us from bondage." Sonderling, Morros, and Jessner presumably had in mind the bondage that was then descending upon European Jewry. Toch's slow, lyric setting stresses the pleading element of the text, with a greater flavor of tears and weeping than of joy and laughter. Psalm 126 is the first text in the Grace after Meals (*Birkat Hamazon*) and is customarily recited immediately after the festive meal.[48] Here, it functions as a prelude to a song of thanksgiving, not for food, but for deliverance from death. Again, there seems little doubt that Toch and the others were thinking of their own deliverance from Europe.

A narrative interlude describes a vision of a promised land of peace, which could equally be the Promised Land for the ancient Hebrews, the safety of America for European refugees, or the Zionist vision of a modern Jewish state. Toch follows with a choral piece, featuring a trio of soloists, which conveys a text derived from Psalms 115:17; 116:8–9; and (perhaps) 118:17—all of which are part of *Hallel*. The final line of that text—"I live and I shall sing Thy praise; Halleluyah"—may be a reworking of Psalm 118:17—"I shall not die but live, and praise the works of Adonai"—or may be drawn from Psalm 146:1–2 from the morning liturgy—"Halleluyah . . . I will praise the Lord all my life, sing hymns to my God while I exist." Whatever its source, it is not a central part of the Passover Haggadah. Its appearance in both the narration and the chorale seems to be geared toward the audience of European émigrés.

A dramatic flourish from the orchestra next introduces a recitative by the bass soloist, the text for which is a reworking of the blessing over the second cup of wine at the Passover *seder*.[49] Immediately after the recitative, a quartet of soloists sings the hymn-text "God of Right, God of Might." That text, written by Rabbi Gustav Gottheil (1827–1903) of Temple Emanu-El in New York, was a standard Passover hymn of the American Reform movement, normally sung to the simple, bright German folk-melody of *Addir Hu* (Mighty is He).[50] Toch's setting, however, is slow and lyrical, weaving the four voices into a complex tapestry reminiscent of a late-Romantic opera, rather than the familiar folksong.

A final narration reasserts the *Cantata*'s universalistic message, citing the many enslaved nations and "kindreds," and affirming that "Ours is one Father." Familiar texts from Psalm 121:1 ("From whence comes my help") and Isaiah 2:4 ("They shall beat their swords into ploughshares . . . ") plead for building a world of peace.

The triumphant final chorale, comprising selected verses of Psalm 113 (the first psalm of *Hallel*), suggests a coronation or martial victory. Lest one have any thought of a particularistic victory, the chorale is interrupted by a bass solo again declaring a universal vision. So broad is the text that it draws on Christian scripture, quoting from John 14:2—"our father's house" containing many "mansions"—and Matthew 11:28—"you who labor and are heavy-laden." Sonderling, Morros, and/or Jessner apparently used these sources to make their vision of universal brotherhood as explicit as possible.

The chorus concludes with a recapitulation of the passage from Psalm 113. Using brass and timpani, triangle and cymbals, full chorus and strings, the piece comes to a grand finale with a full-throated "Halleluyah."

Epilogue

After its Fairfax Temple premiere in 1938, the *Cantata* was performed at Los Angeles City College in 1941, New York's Town Hall in 1962, the Los Angeles Ernst Toch Festival in 1974, and a joint concert of the Los Angeles Zimriyah Chorale and the Los Angeles Jewish Symphony in 2002. The Milken Archive of Jewish Music recorded the work in 2000, with Gerard Schwarz conducting the Czech Philharmonic Orchestra and Prague Philharmonic Choir, and Theodore Bikel as narrator. Some of Rabbi Sonderling's descendants play recordings of the piece at their Passover *seders* each year.[51]

In 1945, Toch was again commissioned to write a work drawing on his Jewish heritage. This time, the instigator was Nathaniel

Shilkret, a noted conductor, music publisher, and composer for film, radio, and records.[52] Shilkret assembled the *Genesis Suite*, comprising seven movements for orchestra, choir, and narration based on the primordial history described in Genesis 1:1–11:9. Like Sonderling, Shilkret commissioned European refugees living in California, each of whom contributed a movement: Arnold Schoenberg (mvt. I: "Prelude—Earth was without form"), Alexandre Tansman (mvt. III: "Adam and Eve"), Darius Milhaud (mvt. IV: "Cain and Abel"), Mario Castelnuovo-Tedesco (mvt. V: "The Flood"), Ernst Toch (mvt. VI: "The Covenant"), and Igor Stravinsky (mvt. VII: "Babel"). Shilkret wrote the second movement, "Creation."

The Janssen Symphony Orchestra of Los Angeles premiered *Genesis Suite* at the Wilshire Ebell Theatre on November 18, 1945. Shilkret and Janssen recorded *Genesis Suite* at their own expense. Janssen expected RCA Victor to distribute the recording, but the company exercised its option to decline. The men turned down an offer from Capitol Records. Janssen and his business partners formed Artist Records, and the suite was issued under the Artist label as Album JS-10. It was released on December 11, 1945, with Werner Janssen conducting his orchestra and Hugo Strelitzer conducting the choral sections. (Naxos released a Milken Archive of Jewish Music recording in 2004.)

Shilkret intended the concert and album to appeal to "record buyers—not only music lovers of the ultramodern type but to all buyers and lovers of music and the bible." The goal was not fully realized, as Shilkret wrote defensively to his wife Anne:

> The critics didn't dare to criticize the 2 giants Stravinsky and Schoenberg because they didn't understand them. Schoenberg's music is so ultramodern and in the 12 tone scale that even you with all your experience will think that the cat is just jumping all over the piano—It is a great piece of music but oh—so new in sound . . . If you think that Shilkret, Tedesco, Tansman and

Toch wrote cheap music, you are mistaken—of course we used some dramatic tricks but you'll find them modern and beautiful—What is wrong in writing music to accentuate the scene or words—Wagner did it all the time. We do it in picture music because it is effective. For ordinary people even our music is strange and modern.[53]

The composite work is most remembered for bringing together Schoenberg and Stravinsky, bitter rivals who, despite living a few miles apart and socializing in the same circles, were insulated from one another by opposing camps of supporters. Dress rehearsals for *Genesis Suite* were arranged so that Schoenberg and Stravinsky would not meet. Still, they wound up being there at the same time, and repelled each other to opposite sides of the hall.[54]

Toch would return to Jewish themes thrice more during his final decade. Unlike the commissions from Sonderling and Shilkret, the later works were self-derived, suggesting that the *Cantata* and *Genesis Suite* had stimulated a deeper embrace of Judaic themes. Toch was especially attracted to biblical texts that resonated with existential uncertainties tied to post-Holocaust Judaism. Two pieces, derived from the Book of Ecclesiastes, address the fleetingness of life and the futility of human efforts: *There Is a Season for Everything* (1953) for mezzo-soprano, flute, clarinet, violin, and cello, and *Vanity of Vanities* (1954) for soprano, tenor, flute, clarinet, violin, viola, and cello. Toch's Symphony No. 5, titled *Jephta, Rhapsodic Poem*, published in 1965, dramatizes a troubling story from Judges 11:30–40, in which Jephthah vows that if he defeats the Ammonites, he will offer "whatsoever comes out of the door of my house to meet me" as a sacrifice to God (Jdgs. 11:31). Much to Jephthah's horror, the burnt offering would be his own daughter, who greets him with timbrel and dance. Toch initially intended the work to be an opera, but his impatience with the librettist led to its reconception as a programmatic tone poem.[55]

The vicissitudes of tastes and fickleness of musical audiences have placed Toch in the category of overlooked masters. Despite winning a Pulitzer Prize in 1956 for the third of his five symphonies, Toch called himself "the forgotten composer of the century."[56] Around him, partisans of Schoenberg were passionately espousing the merits of serialism, while Stravinsky's supporters were praising the virtues of neoclassicism. Toch's eclectic oeuvre, which evaded labels in vogue in those days, was largely neglected. In a lecture given at the University of Minnesota on November 9, 1954, Toch cautioned the audience against infatuation with technique, style, and timebound trends, and to instead explore music's "spiritual dimensions."[57] Although he had been among the most celebrated composers in Weimar Germany, he was not by nature a "schmoozer" or self-promoter, nor was he a fierce advocate of genres, such as serialism or neoclassicism. As a result, his career in Los Angeles was uneven and he suffered from bouts of depression.

Today, Toch's compositions are experiencing a modest revival through concerts, recordings, and broadcasts, especially in Europe. A notable performance was held on June 19–21, 2015, at Kings Place, an independently funded arts and conference venue in the Kings Cross area of London. The three-part concert, titled "Swept Away: Berlin in the Twenties," focused primarily on Toch, with Paul Hindemith, Kurt Weill, and other Weimar stars showcased as well. In 2014, Naxos released an anthology recording of five chamber works Toch composed between 1913 and 1950: Violin Sonata No. 1, op. 21; Divertimento, op. 37; *Adagio Elegiaco*; Cello Sonata, op. 50; and String Trio, op. 63. Academicians have also been drawn to his music in recent years.[58]

In late March 2018, several classical radio stations in the United States aired "A Musical Feast for Passover," a two-part showcase of Passover music narrated by Israeli American violinist Itzhak Perlman. Structured loosely around the *seder*, the program featured portions of thirty-four wide-ranging selections, including arrangements of European Jewish folksongs, such as *Ha Lachma Anya* (This is the Bread of Affliction) and *Addir Hu* (Mighty is He), George Frideric Handel's "He led them through the deep" (from *Israel in Egypt*), Paul Dessau's "*Knechte waren wir dem Pharao in Agypten*" (We Were Servants to Pharaoh in Egypt; from *Haggadah shel Pesach*), Paul Robeson's rendition of "Go Down Moses," "Miriam's Song" by contemporary Jewish songwriter Debbi Friedman, and another Sonderling commission, *A Passover Psalm*, by Erich Wolfgang Korngold. Two movements from Toch's *Cantata of the Bitter Herbs* were interspersed among the selections: "Children's Dance" and "The Ten Plagues."[59] Perlman introduced Toch as an "Austrian Jew who wound up in Los Angeles in the 1930s . . . and wrote [the *Cantata*] as Hitler's forces were triumphantly goose-stepping their way into Vienna."[60]

Chapter 4
Arnold Schoenberg's
Kol Nidre

A rnold Schoenberg (1874–1951) was one of the most influential figures in twentieth-century art music. His compositional system based on twelve-tone rows broke the bounds of Western harmony and shook the musical establishment in Europe and the United States to its foundations. His lasting influence has yet to be determined, but during the 1930s and '40s he was regarded as a prophet of modernism.[1]

Little is known of Schoenberg's Jewish upbringing. He was born to humble parents in the Jewish section of Vienna (Leopoldstadt). His mother, Pauline (née Nachod), was apparently "devoutly Jewish" and came from an Orthodox family of cantors. His father, Samuel, was an "idealistic freethinker."[2] This polarized home environment helped seed tensions between tradition and innovation in Schoenberg's work, as well as a lifelong interest in biblical themes and Jewish peoplehood, despite his ambivalence toward religion.[3]

Encouraged by his mother, a piano teacher, Schoenberg began violin lessons at age eight. As a child, he wrote duets for violin and taught himself cello, composing several string trios and quartets for an ensemble of schoolfellows with whom he performed.[4] In matters of harmony and composition, Schoenberg was largely self-taught. The budding composer was just sixteen when his father died, and he was forced to leave school to support his family. He worked in banking until age twenty-one and later earned a living orchestrating operetta. He studied counterpoint briefly with Alexander von Zemlinsky and within a few years debuted some of his early compositions.

Partly to strengthen his connection to the culture around him, and partly as a means of self-defense, Schoenberg converted to Christianity in the Lutheran church in 1898.[5] Bluma Goldstein cites other possible motivations for Schoenberg's conversion: "by the religious fervor of Protestant friend Walter Pieau, a singer who is inscribed as Schoenberg's godfather in the baptismal record; by cultural considerations as his wife Gertrud maintained; perhaps, as Alexander L. Ringer conjectures, by his close association with workers' choral groups during a time of animosity between labor and the Catholic church."[6] It was also a time of growing antisem-itism in Vienna. The disproportionate presence of Jews in finance, industry, law, medicine, and other fields aroused malicious envy and fed into antisemitic canards about usury, profiteering, and lurking Jewish power.[7] Moreover, as "the most culturally crea-tive of the Danube nationalities,"[8] Viennese Jews populated the intelligentsia with author Arthur Schnitzler, philosopher Ludwig Wittgenstein, psychoanalyst Sigmund Freud, and composer Gustav Mahler, among many others.

Karl Lueger had exploited antisemitism to become mayor of Vienna the previous year, and conversions increased accordingly.

Apostates were twice as likely as Jews generally to be in professions with public profiles, particularly in the arts.[9] Although Vienna was largely a Catholic city, only about half of Jewish apostates converted to Catholicism. Roughly a quarter declared themselves "without religious affiliation," while another quarter opted for Protestantism (Lutheran or Reformed), perhaps finding it a palatable alternative to ornate Catholic ritualism.[10] Schoenberg's choice of a less strenuous minority denomination suggests a compromise and, perhaps, the superficiality of the arrangement. In a letter to his cousin in May 1891, Schoenberg declared himself an "unbeliever."[11] Decades later, in a letter to soprano Marya Freund, Schoenberg added ambiguity to his earlier statement: "I have never at any time in my life been anti-religious, indeed have never really been unreligious either."[12]

In 1901, Schoenberg married Zemlinsky's sister, Mathilde, herself a Jewess, and moved to Berlin. There, Richard Strauss took Schoenberg under his wing and helped secure him a position at the Stern Conservatory. Still finding it difficult to make a steady living, Schoenberg went back and forth between Vienna and Berlin for the next fifteen years in search of better opportunities. Despite his economic straits, he produced several major works that generated significant debate in the music world, including *Verklärte Nacht* (Transfigured Night), op. 4 (1899), a one-movement string sextet in the late-Romantic style, and *Pierrot lunaire* (Moonstruck Pierrot), op. 21 (1912), an early atonal work comprising twenty-one songs for "speaking-voice" (*Sprechstimme*). Written around the time of Stravinsky's *Rite of Spring* (1913), and analogous in terms of the reaction it stirred, *Pierrot lunaire* lacks a central key and functional harmony as primary structuring elements, thereby abolishing the restrictive interplay of consonance and dissonance in tonal music. Schoenberg called it the "emancipation of the dissonance."[13] James Huneker, an American critic who attended the premiere, titled his *New York Times* review: "Schoenberg: Musical Anarchist Who Has Upset Europe." Huneker described this first encounter with Schoenberg's music, writing for himself and on behalf of the awestruck audience:

> What did I hear? At first, the sound of delicate china shivering into a thousand luminous fragments. In the welter of tonalities that brushed each other as they passed and repassed, in the preliminary grip of enharmonies that almost made the ears bleed, the eyes water, the scalp to freeze, I could not get a central grip on myself. It was new music, or new exquisitely horrible sounds, with a vengeance. The very ecstasy of the hideous! I say "exquisitely horrible," for pain can be at once exquisite and horrible; consider toothache and its first cousin, neuralgia. And the borderline between pain and pleasure is a territory hitherto unexplored by musical composers.[14]

In 1916–1917, Schoenberg served in the Austrian Army despite his relatively advanced age of forty-two. After the war, he began composing in the twelve-tone (dodecaphonic) method with which he is most closely associated. Giving structure to unfettered atonality, twelve-tone serialism employs tone rows to ensure that each note—or pitch-class, since the octave position is not specified—of the chromatic scale is sounded as often as each other within a piece, thus preventing an emphasis on any one note and eliminating any suggestion of a key. Aaron Copland, who at first avoided the technique and later experimented with it,[15] linked the system to Schoenberg's Germanic nature: "[A]s a good German, with the German passion for order and systematic thinking, Schoenberg was faced with the necessity of bringing logic and control to the disconcerting freedom of atonality."[16]

Others heard Schoenberg's music as a Jewish reaction against German tendencies. Musicologist and journalist Heinrich Berl attributed Schoenberg's system to an essentially "oriental" fascination with melodic-rhythmic forces in music, as opposed to the

European tendency toward the harmonic tradition.[17] Already in 1913, Huneker speculated that the strange expressiveness of Schoenberg's atonality stemmed from "the Hebraic strain in the composer's blood."[18] Eight decades later, Alexander L. Ringer, author of *Arnold Schoenberg: The Composer as Jew*, suggested that Schoenberg's *Sprechstimme* was inspired by the "logogenic [word-born] melodic heritage" of reform-minded cantors, such as Vienna's celebrated baritone Salomon Sulzer, who cleansed prayer chant of excessive flourishes and inflexions, resulting in a purified and "essentially rhetorical, non-metrical" means of textual delivery.[19]

Schoenberg seems to have confirmed these views in a letter to philosopher Jakob Klatzkin, dated June 13, 1933: "We [Jews] are Asians and nothing of real substance connects us to the West. We have our own destiny and no other temptation can honor us . . . our essence is not occidental; that is merely an exterior appearance."[20] This statement sharply contrasts with his earlier assertion that the twelve-tone method would secure Germany's hegemony in the musical realm and underscores his eventual rejection of German nationalism, which turned against Jews who had so significantly contributed to German culture. To some extent, Schoenberg seems also to have internalized the Aryan myth, which viewed Jews as a race wholly separate from Europeans and drew a dichotomy between "Asiatic Judaism" and "European Christianity."[21]

Schoenberg's compositions achieved increasing acclaim and opposition after World War I, reaching fever pitch in May 1930 when the *Musical Times* declared: "The name of Schoenberg is, as far as the British public is concerned, mud."[22] His personal life also went through turmoil with the death of his first wife in 1923 after a long illness, and his marriage to a second wife, Gertrud (née Kolisch), who was twenty-four years his junior. In 1925, he was appointed as a professor of music at the Prussian Academy of Arts in Berlin. Remarkably, in a country that prized "hierarchy and *Bildung*," one of the top academic positions went to a largely self-taught Jew with no university degrees.[23]

Schoenberg taught and composed for the next eight years in relative financial security. That ended with the Nazis' rise to power in 1933. He left the Prussian Academy before being officially terminated by its president, Max von Schillings, an early supporter of his work who later promised to eliminate Jewish influences from the institution.[24] Schoenberg relocated to Paris, where he engaged a rabbi to conduct a "return-to-Judaism" ceremony. The ceremony took place on July 24, 1933, at a Reform temple in Paris, with Rabbi Louis-Germain Levy presiding and artist Marc Chagall as his witness. Although Jewish law provides that one born Jewish can never leave Judaism, and thus does not have a ritual marking a return, Schoenberg felt the need to ceremonially reclaim his Jewish identity. The event was more a political statement than a religious affirmation. His wife, Gertrud, was a devout convert to Catholicism, and their children were raised Catholic.[25]

By the early 1920s, Schoenberg realized that racial antisemitism made true assimilation impossible. The ceremony marking his return to Judaism was the culmination of a process that began at least eleven years earlier. He wrote to his protégé Alban Berg on October 16, 1933, two weeks before the Schoenberg family arrived in the United States:

> As you have doubtless realized, my return to the Jewish religion took place long ago and is indeed demonstrated in some of my published work ("Thou shalt not . . . Thou shalt" [the second part of *Four Pieces* for mixed chorus, op. 27]) and in "Moses and Aaron," of which you have known since 1928, but which dates from at least five years earlier; but especially in my drama "Der biblische Weg"[26] [The Biblical Way] which was also conceived in 1922 or '23 at the latest, though finished only in '26–'27.[27]

Schoenberg declared his transition from free atonality to the twelve-tone system with his unfinished oratorio *Die Jakobsleiter* (Jacob's Ladder), which he began in 1914–1915 and mostly completed in 1926.[28] It seems no coincidence that the technique, which some view as a Jewish-Oriental rejection of Western musical conventions, was introduced through a piece drawn from the Hebrew Bible.[29]

After a failed attempt to immigrate to Great Britain, Schoenberg settled in the United States in November 1933. He taught for a year at the Malkin Conservatory of Music in Boston but found the cold climate damaging to his health. In September 1934, the family moved to Los Angeles. Initially, Schoenberg taught at both the University of Southern California and the University of California, Los Angeles (UCLA). In 1935, he was appointed to the faculty of UCLA, first as a visiting professor and then as a full professor in 1936. He retired from UCLA in 1944 at age seventy. Despite helping to develop a generation of important composers, from John Cage to Leon Kirchner, Schoenberg was dissatisfied with the American system of music education and the country's "commercial racket,"[30] which valued popular composers but routinely neglected contributions of "serious" composers, such as himself.[31] Shortly after retiring from UCLA, Schoenberg wrote: "[N]o serious composer in this country is capable of living from his *art*. Only popular composers earn enough to support oneself and one's family, and then it is not *art*."[32] While he continued teaching privately and composing his own music, a series of illnesses gradually reduced his ability to work. He died on July 13, 1951.

Jewish subjects consumed the final period of Schoenberg's life. In 1937, he sketched a programmatic Jewish symphony in four provocative movements: "1. Predominance (superiority) provokes envie [*sic*]. 2. Scherzo a) What they think about us, b) what we think about them, c) conclusion. 3. The sacred texts and costumes—Die heiligen Feste und Gebräuche. 4. The day will come."[33] The symphony was abandoned for *Kol Nidre*, op. 39, which he produced for Rabbi Sonderling in August 1938. Two months later, Schoenberg penned "A Four-Point Program for Jewry," a thirty-seven-page essay addressing the plight of European Jews. The essay advocates the formation of a United Jewish Party to "erect an independent Jewish state" and presents an eerily clear vision of the peril into which European Jewry was descending: "Is there room in the world for almost 7,000,000 people? Are they condemned to doom? Will they become extinct? Famished? Butchered?"[34] In 1945, Schoenberg wrote the prelude for Nathaniel Shilkret's *Genesis Suite*, which comprises movements written by émigré composers living in California, among them fellow Sonderling commissionee Ernst Toch.[35]

Schoenberg composed his last orchestrated work in 1947, *A Survivor from Warsaw*, for reciter, male chorus, and chamber orchestra. A dramatized first-person account of the Warsaw Ghetto Uprising, the piece climaxes with the condemned marching to gas chambers singing *Shema Yisrael* (Hear, O Israel), the affirmation of God's oneness and sovereignty. During 1949–1950, Schoenberg worked on several choral pieces on Jewish and biblical themes: *Israel exists again* (unfinished), *Who is like unto Thee, o Lord* (unfinished), *Dreimal tausend Jahre* (Three Times a Thousand Years) (1949), *De profundis* (Psalm 130) (1950), and *Moderne Psalmen* (unfinished).

THE COMMISSION

Rabbi Jacob Sonderling was first introduced to Schoenberg by their mutual acquaintance, Russian-born Jewish violinist and composer Joseph Achron.[36] Achron may have been a member of Sonderling's congregation. The two had known each other at least since their time in New York City. Achron resided there from 1925 to 1934—almost exactly the same period as Sonderling—and in 1932 composed a service for Lazare Saminsky at Temple Emanu-El, which Sonderling almost certainly heard. They also could have been acquainted in Germany, as Achron was in Berlin in 1922 when Sonderling was still in Hamburg.[37] The two men socialized together once they settled in California (1934 and 1935, respectively), and Achron knew of Sonderling's interest in new Jewish liturgical music.[38] Indeed, Sonderling may have asked Achron to compose Jewish liturgical music, although we have no record of such a request. Achron was surely aware that Sonderling's congregation attracted successful émigré artists and musicians and that Schoenberg was seeking affidavits from wealthy Americans to support immigration applications of friends and relatives stranded in Europe.[39] In any event, Achron brought the two together.

Sonderling suggested that Schoenberg write a new setting for a revised text of *Kol Nidre*, an Aramaic legal formula of unknown origin dating to the Geonic period (as early as the eighth century CE).[40] Schoenberg welcomed the opportunity to work with Sonderling, who was, in many ways, a kindred spirit. Their mutual respect is evident in the finished product. The two collaborated closely on the piece's interpretive text. Schoenberg accepted the rabbi's musical suggestions, while Sonderling allowed the composer to take those suggestions in any creative direction he wished. Sonderling was thrilled to secure a liturgical setting from one of the most important and well-known composers of his day. Schoenberg, in turn, was grateful to befriend a rabbi whose vision of Judaism and the Jewish people was so strongly centered on the arts. Schoenberg evidently received no compensation for the piece, later writing that he had composed and conducted it as a gift to the rabbi.[41] However, elsewhere it is reported that Sonderling arranged for Schoenberg to write the piece because the composer needed money.[42]

In the Ashkenazic rite, *Kol Nidre* is customarily chanted three times during the evening service of Yom Kippur (Day of Atonement), using loosely constructed standardized motifs that developed in the medieval Rhineland. In its classical formulation, the text metaphorically alludes to annulling vows made between humanity and God, and a desire to start the New Year with a clean spiritual slate:

> Every vow
> and bind, oath, ban, restriction, penalty,
> and every term that sets things out of bounds;
> all that we vow or swear, ban or bar from ourselves
> (from last Yom Kippur to this, and)
> from this Yom Kippur
> until that which will come—let it be for the good—
> each one, we regret.
> Let each be released,
> forgotten, halted, null and void,
> without power and without hold.
> what we vow is not vowed,
> what we bind is not bound,
> and what we swear is not sworn.[43]

Sonderling and Schoenberg apparently began their project with an examination of the customary text. Schoenberg later wrote in a letter to Paul Dessau: "When I first saw the traditional text I was horrified by the 'traditional' view that all the obligations that have been assumed during the year are supposed to be cancelled on the Day of Atonement," a belief he considered "truly immoral" and therefore "false."[44] The traditional text may have been altered at Schoenberg's request. However, Sonderling also struggled with the text and its implications, and may have handed Schoenberg an already revised version.[45] Whatever the case, Sonderling wrote a first draft of the English text, introducing themes not found in the customary version: God's creation of the universe and an eternal light, "which the 'humble, the meek and the modest' must rediscover in the year to come."[46]

The focus on light is not without liturgical precedent. *Kol Nidre* is traditionally preceded by the chanting of the Hebrew verse, "Light is sown for the righteous" (Ps. 97:11), which Sonderling translated as "light is sown for the pious." But Sonderling went further to incorporate portions of the creation myth from Genesis—a story absent from the traditional *Kol Nidre* service, although the creation of the world is a recurring theme of the Jewish High Holidays. Furthermore, he explored the theme of light in mystical and spiritual terms, tying the search for "our light" to repentance, atonement, and renewal. This interpretation resonated with Sonderling's interest in Chassidism, which draws many of its ideals from the mystical teachings of Kabbalah. According to the kabbalistic doctrine of creation, a primordial light broke the cosmic vessels that were meant to contain it, thus sowing the universe with sparks of light in impure shards or "husks." Humanity's ultimate purpose is to retrieve and restore these sparks, thereby repairing the universe (*tikkun olam*) and fulfilling the intended harmony of creation.[47]

Schoenberg made substantial revisions to Sonderling's draft, such that the final text should be seen as a genuine collaboration, bringing together the kabbalistic creation myth, Psalm 97:11, and elements of the original text dealing with the annulment of vows.[48]

> The Kabbalah tells a legend:
> At the beginning God said: "LET THERE BE LIGHT"
> Out of space a flame burst out.
> God crushed that light to atoms
> Myriads of sparks are hidden in our world, but not all of us behold them.
> The self-glorious, who walks arrogantly upright, will never perceive one;
> but the meek and modest, eyes downcast, he sees it,

"A light is sown for the pious."
In the name of God, that every transgressor,
be it that he was unfaithful to "Our People" because of fear,
or misled by false doctrines of any kind, out of weakness or
greed:
we give him leave to be one with us in prayer tonight.
A light is sown for the pious, a light is sown for the repenting
sinner.
All vows, oaths, promises and plights of any kind,
wherewith we pledged ourselves counter to our inherited faith
in God,
Who is One, Everlasting, Unseen, Unfathomable,
we declare these null, and void.
We repent that these obligations have estranged us from the
sacred task we were chosen for.
We shall strive from this day of atonement till the next to avoid
such and similar obligations,
so that the Yom Kippur to follow may come to us for good.
Whatever binds us to falsehood may be absolved, released,
annulled, made void and of no power.
Hence all such vows shall be no vows,
and all such bonds shall be no bonds,
all such oaths shall be no oaths.
We repent.
Null and void be our vows.
We repent them.
A light is sown for the sinner.
We give him leave to be one with us in prayer tonight.[49]

Sonderling, who was in awe of Schoenberg, was easily sold on
the composer's revisions. In a newspaper article he wrote about
the composition, he referred to Schoenberg as "that great master musician" and "this great master of our time," and quoted
Schoenberg at length rather than paraphrasing his thinking.[50]
Nevertheless, Schoenberg credited Sonderling with conceptu-
alizing the final text and almost certainly relied on the rabbi for

the kabbalistic elements, since Schoenberg would not have been acquainted with Jewish mysticism.

Novel though it is, the Sonderling-Schoenberg *Kol Nidre* was not the first to grapple with the language and implications of the original liturgical text. During the nineteenth century, a period that witnessed the emancipation of European Jewish communities for the first time since the Middle Ages, various efforts were made to update Jewish religious practices to conform with the Christian majority. "Enlightened" Jews abrogated a number of ritual laws, liturgical passages, and customs deemed outmoded and incompatible with their embrace of modern culture. Among them was *Kol Nidre*, a text historically cited by antisemites as proof that Jews could not be trusted, since they absolved themselves annually of promises made. The Reform *minyan* (quorum) of Berlin led the way by removing the text from its High Holiday prayer books in 1815 and 1817. The Hamburg Temple, where Sonderling would later serve, followed suit in 1819 and 1841. The omission of *Kol Nidre* from Isaac Noah Mannheimer's influential *Unity Prayerbook* of 1840 inspired other congregations to do the same. The practice continued in the United States, where the text was omitted from the major nineteenth-century Reform High Holiday prayer books of Isaac Mayer Wise, David Einhorn, and the Central Conference of American Rabbis.[51]

While the *Kol Nidre* text was generally regarded as dispensable, nostalgia for the age-old melody led to the practice of setting the melody to alternative texts—especially Psalm 130, which aptly concludes "redeem Israel from all its iniquities," and "Day of God," an English translation of a German hymn by nineteenth-century rabbi Leopold Stern—as well as playing the melody on the organ or another solo instrument.[52] "Day of God," which appears in the Reform movement's *Union Prayer Book* (1894, 1924, and 1945), bears little resemblance to the original *Kol Nidre*. With no mention of vows, the three-verse hymn ends by asking God to receive the prayers of the congregation:

> Lord God, see—
> See Thou our heart's contrition,
> And bow Thine ear.
> Hear, O hear, the voice of petition.
> Banish our fear,
> Blot out our evil ways,
> Open the door of grace,
> Bid us enter there.[53]

Kol Nidre did not officially return to American Reform liturgy until the *Union Prayer Book* was retired and replaced by *Gates of Repentance* in 1978, as part of a larger overhaul of Reform liturgy in response to Israel's victory in the Six-Day War (1967) and calls for Jewish particularism and traditionalism that followed.[54] Working with Schoenberg in 1938, Sonderling was no doubt familiar with the text's troubled history and various replacements. He presumably envisioned their creative rendering as another attempt to make *Kol Nidre* relevant for modern worshipers.

As for the music, Sonderling described the venerable Ashkenazi motifs as "old, known and cherished by all Jewry"[55] and likely asked Schoenberg to utilize some of them in his reimagining. As Schoenberg correctly observed in his correspondence with Paul Dessau, "there actually isn't [a single] melody, only a number of flourishes resembling each other to a certain degree, yet without being identical and without always appearing in the same order." Schoenberg "chose the phrases that a number of versions had in common and put them into a reasonable order."[56]

Schoenberg's stylized use of those "phrases" makes them generally unrecognizable to the average listener. His treatment of existing themes and motifs, masked by shifting tonality and countermelodies, caused cantor and scholar Sam Weiss to ask: "Is

Schoenberg quoting traditional variants, or is he varying selected motives traditionally? The answer, of course, is irrelevant, and merely points to the composer's skill in preserving an important facet of the chant within the contemporary musical idiom."[57] For Weiss and other keen listeners, something of the "cantorial flavor" is preserved in the piece, despite being set for reciter, chorus, and orchestra, and obscuring the old chant elements in a dense sonic fabric. *Kol Nidre* was not the last time Schoenberg would use a *cantus firmus*, or preexisting melody, derived from the synagogue. *A Survivor from Warsaw* (1947) similarly draws upon chant sources for its concluding declaration of the monotheistic mantra, *Shema Yisrael* (Hear, O Israel), sung defiantly by a male choir. As with *Kol Nidre*, the *Shema* is hidden by Schoenberg's technique—in the latter case the requirements of serialism, which prohibit an unaltered quotation.[58]

Kol Nidre received its first performance during a Yom Kippur service on the evening of October 4, 1938.[59] Fairfax Temple's small sanctuary could not accommodate the increased attendance on the High Holidays, so services were normally held in rented facilities. Services in 1938 took place at the Cocoanut Grove ballroom of the Ambassador Hotel. There is disagreement as to whether Schoenberg conducted a full orchestra, for which he had scored the piece, or had to settle for a reduced orchestration.[60] One source claims that the piece was performed by a chorus and orchestra recruited from the movie studios, and that Joseph Achron conducted.[61] It seems likely that an orchestra from the Twentieth Century Fox Studios did support the performance, since Schoenberg later thanked Louis Silvers, the studio's musical director at the time, for "putting all your power behind this dignified achievement."[62] Unfortunately, there is no record of the congregation's reaction to *Kol Nidre*, nor any further performances under the auspices of Fairfax Temple or anywhere else in Los Angeles during the composer's lifetime.[63]

Schoenberg intended to re-score the instrument parts for a single organ, acknowledging that a composition for a 27 to 37-piece orchestra was excessive for synagogues. He never took on that project, but many years later, Neal Brostoff, a Los Angeles-based pianist and musicologist, instigated such a score:

> Leonard Stein's new performance version of Schoenberg's *Kol nidre* came about via a phone conversation with Leonard in late 1991 or early 1992. In preparation for "Lebewohl Wien" in March '92, my concert of music by four exiled Viennese Jewish composers who all wound up in LA (Schoenberg, Zeisl, Toch, and Korngold), I called Leonard for some sage programming advice. He said that he had contemplated an organ reduction from AS's orchestral score and that my concert would be a perfect opportunity for its premiere. Leonard dove into his work and did not charge me for it—I've been grateful for the past 26 years.[64]

THE COMPOSITION

Schoenberg's *Kol Nidre* is a relatively brief 186 measures, taking approximately thirteen minutes in most recordings.[65] It is scored for two flutes, oboe, two clarinets, bass clarinet, bassoon, two horns, two trumpets, three trombones, tuba, two percussionists, at least ten string players, a four-part choir, and a rabbi-narrator performing *Sprechstimme* (speech-song). Most surprising for the listener who associates Schoenberg with twelve-tone music, the piece is emphatically tonal. Set in G minor and ultimately concluding on a G major triad, the composition is appropriately based on the modal character of the *Kol Nidre* chant variants Schoenberg studied, which, although diatonic, flow between major or minor keys and do not lend themselves to functional harmony. The piece also employs developing variation, a principle basic to both dodecaphonic music and to the customary *Kol Nidre* motifs, which likewise allow for variation and rotation within an overarching form.

The work opens with a 26-measure instrumental introduction. In the first measure, the lower strings establish the key with a G minor triad. In the second and third measures, the flute, horn, and second viola play a sustained Bb—a critical note that will rise to a B natural at the end of the piece, perhaps representing the sinner's transformation through atonement. In those same two measures, the first four tones of the familiar *Kol Nidre* melody are heard from the first cello (G–F#–D–F#) while the first viola plays a motif characteristic of the end of the first theme of that melody (D–Eb–F–Eb; the full traditional motif is D–Eb–F–Gb–F–Eb-D–F–Eb). The second cello echoes the signature descending major third of the familiar melody in measure 3 and again, transposed by a 4th, in measure 4.

The use of the cello in the opening is consistent with Schoenberg's stated intention of "vitriolizing out the 'cello-sentimentality of the Bruchs, etc."[66] Max Bruch's *Kol Nidrei*, op. 47 (1881), an adagio for cello and orchestra on two melodies—the second being Isaac Nathan's "O weep for those" (1815–1816), with text by Lord Byron[67]—became popular among Jewish audiences and is still performed in many liberal synagogues on Yom Kippur evening, despite the composer's antisemitic views.[68] Bruch conceived the piece as an exploration of folk themes, similar to his *Scottish Fantasy*, op. 46 (1880) for violin and orchestra, but acknowledged that its success was "assured, because all the Jews of the world are for it *eo ipso*."[69] For Schoenberg, Bruch's Romantic setting and its imitations obscured the text's legal essence. His treatment set out to restore *Kol Nidre* to "the dignity of a law, of an 'edict.'"[70]

After an ornamental-sounding motif in the flute in measure 4 (Bb–B–A–Bb–Ab–G), measures 5 and 6 feature the same melodic fragments as measures 2 and 3, now played in other instruments and registers: the flute plays the familiar four-note motif, the violins pick up the end motif previously played by the first violas, and bass clarinet and cellos repeat the pair of descending major 3rds—all against a backdrop of a sustained Bb from the clarinet and trumpet.

The flute motif from measure 3 returns in a number of instruments and variations in measures 7 through 10—first in its initial form in clarinet and viola, and then in inverted form in the first violins and clarinet. In measure 9, the cellos play an inversion of the familiar four-note motif (G–Ab–C–Ab) in thirty-second notes. In measure 10, the bass clarinet expands upon this by first playing the four-note theme in inversion and then playing it in its primary form (G–Ab–C–Ab/G–F#–D–F#), again in thirty-second notes. By measures 12 and 13, the first three tones of the primary motif have returned in the winds, now in a half note/whole note/quarter note pattern (B–A#–F#), as if to provide a touchstone in the storm of variations that Schoenberg employs.

Without analyzing every permutation of familiar *Kol Nidre* motifs that Schoenberg uses, the artistry of which largely escapes the ear of the average listener, one detects the build-up of sonic density through measure 20, followed by the thinning out of the texture up to measure 26. The familiar four-note theme returns in the horns in measure 23, the violins in measure 24, and the lower strings in measure 25. Measure 26 diminishes from an F# minor triad in the strings to an E minor seventh in the winds, and finally to an A in octaves in the violins. The rabbi-narrator then enters with "The Kabbalah tells of a legend . . . "

The kabbalistic story occupies measures 27 through 45. While the orchestral accompaniment continues to use motifs announced up to this point—for example, the primary four-tone motif appears in the flutes and bassoon in bar 28—there is a good deal of tone-painting to complement the text. The first five measures are *piano* or *pianissimo*, after which the divine declaration "Let there be light" triggers a brief *fortissimo* chord from the strings, an upward run of thirty-second notes in the clarinets and bass clarinet, and another *fortissimo* chord in the winds, trumpet, upper strings, and flexaton (a musical saw-like percussion instrument). The text "a flame burst out" in measure 33 results in two measures of high *pizzicato* in the strings and high *staccato* notes in the winds and trumpet. The text "God crushed that light to atoms" results in two beats of *fortissimo* trills in the winds, followed by a sharp *fortissimo* chord in the strings, horns, and tuba, succeeded by diminishing *spiccato* thirty-second notes in the strings as the atoms drift out into space. When the "meek and modest" one sees a hidden spark in our world in measure 44, the horn returns to the primary motif (D–C#–A); and when the section ends with the pronouncement that "a light is sown for the pious," the lower strings, bassoon, and bass clarinet answer with a sustained major triad (Db–F–Ab).

Over the sustained triad, the rabbi-narrator utters a portion of the legal formula that customarily precedes *Kol Nidre*. The full formula translates loosely: "With the agreement of God and of the community, in the heavenly council and the council of man, we give leave to pray with the transgressors among us." The rabbi-narrator recites the Hebrew for the middle clause, *"Bishiva shel mala u'vishiva shel mata"* ("By the authority of the heavenly court, and by the authority of the earthly court"), followed by an English text that idiosyncratically interprets the traditional formula. Permission is given to the transgressors to pray among the congregation, with the transgressor defined narrowly as one who has been unfaithful to the Jewish people, whether out of fear, weakness, greed, or being misled by false doctrines. The text here seems to be focusing on the unfounded myth that *Kol Nidre* originated in Spain to address the presence of *conversos*, who were forced to outwardly convert to Christianity during the Inquisition (est. 1478) but secretly remained Jewish, and whose public vow of Christianity was cancelled on Yom Kippur.[71] This story resonated with Schoenberg's own conversion to Christianity, which was largely superficial, and his later "re-conversion" to Judaism, which solidified his faithfulness to the Jewish people.

The orchestra accompanies lightly with three- and four-note groups moving in half-steps and whole steps, recalling the flute motif of measure 3. The section ends by connecting the earlier phrase, "a light is sown for the pious," with a new gloss: "a light is sown for the repenting sinner." To emphasize this positive ending, the orchestra holds a B major triad for one measure (56). But perhaps because the repentance is yet to come, the orchestra slips into a B minor triad in the next measure, immediately before the *Kol Nidre* text proper is declaimed.

Measures 58 through 69 have the rabbi-narrator reciting a text presaged by the definition of "transgressor" in the previous section. In keeping with the personalized interpretation of *Kol Nidre* that Schoenberg had fixed upon, the vows and oaths declared null and void are those "by which we pledged ourselves counter to our inherited faith in God." An expanded version of the primary four-note theme, now comprising the first five notes of the familiar melody (G–F#–D–F#–G), is played by the winds over the course of five measures. In the last of those measures, accompanying the text "inherited faith in God," the winds and brass sound a perfect 5th (G–D), which must have been an intentional play on the word "God." (Underneath, the strings play a syncopated figure that oscillates between Bb and B and C and A, although they, too, sound the perfect 5th G–D on the second beat of measure 63).

In measures 63 through 65, God is described as "One, Everlasting, Unseen, Unfathomable." To accompany that text, Schoenberg uses a familiar High Holiday motif, perhaps most closely associated with the *Avinu Malkeinu* prayer (Our Father,

Our King). Oboe, bass clarinet, and bassoon repeat the phrase twice (G–G–G–A–Bb–C–Bb–A–Bb–G–Bb) and even incorporate some of the traditional rhythm (eighth–quarter–quarter–triplet–half–four sixteenths–dotted quarter). In measures 65 to 67, there may be a quote of another High Holiday motif (Bb–Ab–G–Ab–B[b]–C), although the second Bb has been altered to a B natural.

Measures 68 and 69 assert "we declare these null and void." As if to signal the closure of this section of text, Schoenberg employs a concluding motif from the familiar *Kol Nidre* settings, G–F#–G–A–Bb–A–G–F#–A–Bb–G, initially omitting the last two notes when the motif appears in the winds, then omitting the first two notes but including the last two tones when the motif appears in the violas, and finally including only the middle seven tones when it appears in the cellos and clarinets.

A transition begins in measure 72, where the text is again the Schoenberg-Sonderling interpretation of *Kol Nidre* rather than the original language. "We repent that these obligations have estranged us from the sacred task we were chosen for," says the rabbi-narrator. Underneath this statement, Schoenberg employs a new motif from the familiar assortment of motifs comprising the *Kol Nidre* melody. Played most fully by the horn in measure 72, it is D–G–A–Bb–A–G–C–Bb–A–G.

In measure 74, the choir enters to the text "we repent." Yet another of the familiar motifs is sounded, this time by the cellos: D–C–D–Eb–D–C–Bb–A–Bb–C–Bb–A. The violas play a counter-pattern built around some of the same intervals (F–Eb–F–G–F–Eb–G). The oboe takes the primary motif in measure 77, with the clarinets playing the counter-pattern against it. Finally, trumpets and strings pick up the motif in measures 78 and 79, as the rabbi-narrator echoes the choir's "we repent," marked "very loud."

The choir again sings "we repent" in measure 80. Schoenberg brings another of the familiar *Kol Nidre* motifs to bear. The high winds play the motif in measures 80–81: E–B–E–D–C#–B. In measures 82–83, they add a companion motif: E–F#–G–F#–E–B–B–E–D–C#–B. All the while, the strings move the tempo forward and the volume higher through variations on the motif that they had played in 79, until reaching a *fortissimo* peak in measure 84, where they return to the ending motif that first appeared in measure 71 (A#–B–C#–D–C#–B–A#–C#).

A dramatic pause between measures 84 and 85 signals a new section, which opens with a slightly altered version of yet another *Kol Nidre* motif, an ascending scale pattern, played by the violas and cellos in eighth and sixteenth notes: E–F#–G#–A–B–C–D–D#–A#–B–C#–D. In the following measure, another motif is sounded by the oboe in a dotted-eighth/sixteenth note pattern: Bb–A–C–Bb–D–C–Eb–D–F. A number of motifs that were already introduced are woven into the thick texture accompanying the rabbi-narrator's statement: "We shall strive from this day of atonement till the next to avoid such and similar obligations, so that the Yom Kippur to follow may come to us for good." As the word "good" is spoken, the orchestra sounds a measure of accented quarter notes, some lines in ascending half-steps and others in descending half-steps, until reaching a B minor triad on the downbeat of measure 92. A dramatic quarter-note rest follows, after which the full orchestra moves through the dissonance of stacked 4ths (G#–C#–F#) to a C minor chord, a C major chord, and a unison Ab.

The chorus enters again at measure 94 for the second repetition of this *Kol Nidre* text. The dominant sound of the first five measures is the original familiar motif, played by the winds in unison and sung in unison by the chorus. The remainder of the repetition is accompanied by motifs already introduced, although often segmented, inverted, placed in retrograde, or otherwise varied.

The repetition ends in measure 130, and a brief transition by the orchestra concludes with an E minor triad in measure 135. The rabbi-narrator then begins a new section of text, echoed by the chorus: "Whatever binds us to falsehood may be absolved, released, annulled, made void and of no power." A three-bar transition, ending on an A major chord, takes the listener to a choral enunciation of some new text.

With a feeling of going in and out of C major and C minor, the chorus sings: "Hence all such vows shall be no vows and all such bonds shall be no bonds. All such oaths shall be no oaths." This is close to the traditional text of *Kol Nidre*. The chorus begins with the sopranos singing the primary motif (C–B–G) and the tenors chiming in with the last three notes of the motif (G–B–C). The phrase "Hence all such vows" is broken into four parts, progressing from C minor to C major, G major, F minor, and A minor chords. The phrase "shall be no vows" is then declaimed in unison. The conjunction "and" is sung on an E major triad, and "all such bonds" moves through C major, A major, B major, and G# major chords before "shall be no bonds" (and all of the remaining text) is again sung in unison.

The chorus recapitulates the basic theme of the text we have already heard: "We repent. Null and void be our vows. We repent them." The unison vocal line is a variant of the primary motif: Ab–G–Eb–Ab. The full orchestra builds to a loud climax at the end of measure 169, followed by a *caesura*. Winds, followed by chorus and strings, enter *pianissimo* with the text, "A light is sown for the sinner." Chromatic lines in the clarinet, bass clarinet, violin, and cello converge on a C minor triad as the rabbi-narrator speaks the last line: "We give him leave to be one with us in prayer tonight." A coda in measures 179 through 186 follows with the primary motif in the bass clarinet and violas. The chorus sings "we repent" on a unison figure moving from D to G, with a G minor chord on the final syllable. As the choir sustains that syllable for two more measures, the G minor transforms to a final G major chord; but the final chord is sounded *fortepiano*, suggesting some uncertainty in the resolution even at the end.

Epilogue

After its 1938 premiere, *Kol Nidre* was basically neglected for the remainder of the composer's lifetime. In a letter to one of his students, Schoenberg suggested that many synagogue musicians were uninterested in performing the piece.[72] This was an understatement. The work was evidently never again performed in a religious service.[73] Writing in 1954, composer and musicologist Albert Weisser reflected on *Kol Nidre*'s lackluster reception:

> How Schoenberg's solution can be reconciled with any of the existing institutions and forms of Jewish worship poses, of course, quite another and no less formidable problem. Yet this *Kol Nidre* impresses one as a work filled with an intense and personal religious devotion not easily found in liturgical pieces of a more accessible nature.[74]

Weisser's assessment addresses the twofold difficulty with Schoenberg's setting. First, it diverges greatly from the customary chant patterns, which date back to medieval Germany and have served as meaning-laden leitmotifs for generations. Second, it is an utterly personal piece, unable to capture the collective sentiments of synagogue-goers accustomed to unifying their hearts and minds around the more functional music. Additionally, the modernist aesthetic clashes with the conservative tendencies of Jewish religious worship, not to mention the improbability of cantors and choirs being able to tackle music at this level of difficulty and sophistication.

Schoenberg's setting of Psalm 130 (*De profundis*)—commissioned by Polish-born composer, conductor, and musicologist

Chemjo Vinaver and published posthumously in Vinaver's *Anthology of Jewish Music* (1953)—shared a similar fate.[75] Vinaver suggested that Schoenberg write music for Psalm 130, which, coincidentally, was once a popular replacement for the *Kol Nidre* text. For inspiration, Vinaver sent the composer his transcription of a Chassidic recitative of the psalm, which he heard in Poland in 1910 (also printed in the *Anthology*). In a series of letters to Vinaver from June 1950, Schoenberg apologized for delaying the work due to his "nervous eye trouble"—a lingering consequence of a heart attack he suffered in 1946—and shared that he "profited from the liturgical motif you sent me, in writing approximately a similar expression."[76] Schoenberg's setting adapts the Chassidic tune's eight-section structure and roughly approximates the melody using a twelve-tone system.[77]

The complicated piece would be Schoenberg's last. Psalm 130 was premiered in Cologne in 1954 and was sung two years later by Roger Wagner's UCLA a cappella choir at the opening of the university's Schoenberg Hall.[78] However, it has yet to be performed in a Jewish service and is conspicuously out of place in Vinaver's book, which mainly consists of folksongs and standards in conventional settings. Herbert Fromm, a prominent synagogue composer and music director, predicted its fate in a 1956 review:

> Arnold Schönberg's composition of Psalm 130 was written especially for this anthology. It is conceived for six-part a cappella chorus, partly sung, partly spoken in fixed rhythm. The work is a delicate maze of the most subtle, unsingable chromatic counterpoint. One stands in awe before this piece of paper-music that seems destined to remain buried within the pages of this expensive anthology as in a satin-lined coffin.[79]

Like *Kol Nidre*, Psalm 130 proved too modern, too difficult, and too personal to receive attention from cantors or synagogue musicians, a typically pragmatic bunch. A notable later performance came in 1974, on the occasion of the transfer of Schoenberg's ashes to a grave of honor in Vienna's Central Cemetery, near the memorials of Mozart, Beethoven, and Schubert. A newspaper reported: "[T]he sound of [Schoenberg's] last completed composition, Psalm 130, the a cappella chorus *De Profundis* (in the original Hebrew text) ascended to heaven, leaving us, the survivors, in deep contemplation, wondering whether the scene we had witnessed was dream or reality."[80]

Even in the concert hall, *Kol Nidre* was rarely performed until recent years. There is record of a performance in Israel in 1959,[81] and an arrangement for organ and chorus was premiered in Los Angeles in 1992.[82] The American Symphony Orchestra performed the orchestral version in New York in January 1996, as did the Israel Philharmonic Orchestra in October 2012 and the Salzburg Festival (Salzburger Festspiele) in July 2012. There were also performances by the Chicago Symphony in March 2012, the Los Angeles Zimriyah Chorale in 2013, and the Cleveland Symphony in September 2015. Despite this recent interest, the work remains largely unknown in both the classical and Jewish music worlds.

Understandably, Schoenberg was disappointed that the work failed to find an audience among Jewish clergy and congregations. Lazare Saminsky's reason for declining to use the piece is representative: "[T]he text [is] too far from the standard version of even the Reform Synagogue."[83] Schoenberg's response, recorded in a letter to Paul Dessau, captures his displeasure: "It is such a pity that people like Saminski [*sic*] decline to adopt the piece for use in the synagogue, on ritual and musical grounds. I believe it must be tremendously effective both in the synagogue and in the concert-hall."[84] That Schoenberg so failed to anticipate the reaction of religious Jews may be attributed to his inexperience with synagogue services and congregational attitudes. In any event, his optimism for the piece proved to be unfounded; it has made little impression in either synagogue or concert hall. Indeed, while there continues to be great interest in Schoenberg's music, both in performance and scholarship, his *Kol Nidre* has only attracted three brief stand-alone articles.[85]

Even so, the fact that Sonderling was able to secure a piece from such a high-profile composer did not go unnoticed. From the time of its commission until today, Schoenberg's *Kol Nidre* has been a source of inspiration for other patrons of synagogue song, as well as individuals and organizations who advocate aligning Jewish liturgical music with the standards of art music. More than the other pieces Sonderling commissioned, *Kol Nidre* showed that such a project was attainable and remains an aspirational model for those who seek to engage noted composers to write for the synagogue.

CHAPTER 5
ERICH WOLFGANG KORNGOLD'S *A PASSOVER PSALM AND PRAYER*

E rich Wolfgang Korngold (1897–1957) was born in Brünn (Brno), Moravia, the same town where Rabbi Sonderling had lived until about 1893.[1] Given the small Jewish community in Brünn, it seems likely that Rabbi Sonderling would have been acquainted with Korngold's grandfather Simon, a wine merchant, and/or Korngold's father Julius, an attorney in the late 1880s and early 1890s, and then a music critic for the *Brünner Tagesboten*. The Korngold family relocated to Vienna in 1901, where Julius, an accomplished musician who studied with Anton Bruckner, secured a job as assistant music critic to Eduard Hanslick at *Die Neue Freie Presse* (The New Free Press). Following Hanslick's death in 1904, Julius became chief critic at the paper and one of the most powerful voices in Austrian music.[2]

Die Neue Freie Presse was the leading progressive outlet in *fin de siècle* Vienna, attracting some of the greatest journalists and writers of the day, from Theodor Herzl to Winston Churchill. Reflecting the liberalism of the Hapsburgs' Austro-Hungarian Empire, the paper gave generous space to music, arts, and social commentary in the *Feuilleton* (feature) section, which could go on for pages.[3]

Jews, in particular, took advantage of Vienna's cosmopolitan atmosphere, flocking to the city from Hungary and from the Austrian provinces of Bohemia, Galicia, and Moravia, where the Korngold family originated. Assimilated Jews from bourgeois families gathered in the urban center, working as clerks, salespeople, and managers, contributing as artists and intellectuals, and attending *gymnasia*—all mostly in the company of other assimilated Jews.[4] Thus, despite the emergence of prominent Jewish families, Jews were nonetheless set apart by "typically Jewish" professions and rarely had close ties with their Gentile neighbors. For a time, baptism provided a "clean break" from Jewishness, prompting Viennese Jews to convert at a rate higher than anywhere else in the Austro-Hungarian empire. But the rise of racial antisemitism in the 1890s made total assimilation impossible, even for those who had been baptized.[5] For their part, the Korngold family dismissed confessional allegiance: they did not formally leave Judaism, but neither did they practice Jewish religious rites.[6]

Music was a popular means of "social entryism" for families of Jewish descent in nineteenth- and early twentieth-century Europe and often was a family affair.[7] As historian Ezra Mendelsohn observed, "[H]igh European art music held out the greatest prospects for successful acculturation and integration into European society."[8] This was certainly true for Julius and Erich Wolfgang Korngold, as it was for the family of Max Steiner, a fellow Viennese composer whose career similarly took him to Hollywood in the early days of sound films.[9]

A child prodigy described as the Mozart of his day, Erich Wolfgang Korngold began composing around age six. His well-connected father arranged lessons for him in harmony and composition from leading teachers, among them Robert Fuchs of the Vienna Conservatory and composer-conductor Alexander von Zemlinsky.[10] He received early encouragement from Gustav Mahler and was later mentored by Richard Strauss.[11] On October 4, 1910, his first work of consequence, *Der Schneemann* (The Snowman), orchestrated by Zemlinsky, was premiered at the Vienna Opera House to rave reviews. Several of his chamber works and a ballet were premiered by important musicians, including Bruno Walter and Artur Schnabel. Korngold's first operas were staged in Munich and Vienna in 1916 to resounding acclaim.[12]

Detractors accused Julius Korngold of using his position to hype an "artificially created 'child prodigy.'"[13] Speculation swirled that the boy received his middle name, Wolfgang, only after his musical talents were discovered. In fact, Erich Wolfgang and his older brother, Hans Robert, were so named for Julius' favorite composers, Mozart and Robert Schumann.[14] Some claim that Julius debated leaving *Die Neue Freie Presse* to allow his son's genius to flourish free of suspicion.[15] This seems unlikely, as Julius reveled in his role as chief defender of the Romantic tradition against the "subversion" of atonality, expressionism, and other modern innovations.

The vitriol with which Julius expressed his views ignited anti-semitic accusations. The "apartheid" situation in Vienna meant that elites of Jewish lineage tended to stick together and support each other professionally. This led Richard Strauss and others to accuse Julius of disproportionately promoting "fellow Israelites." Michael Haas refutes these charges:

> It was certainly true that Mahler, Schnabel, Selma Kurz, Richard Tauber and Bruno Walter suffered only the rarest and

mildest of occasional journalistic rebukes from Julius, though he would have defended himself by mentioning the many non-Jewish musicians he appreciated or the high-profile Jewish musicians he clearly loathed. These would have included Arnold Schoenberg, Egon Wellesz, Franz Schreker or the pianist Moritz Rosenthal, who thanks to reviews by Julius, brought charges of defamation against *Die Neue Freie Presse*. It didn't matter. To Weingartner, Strauss and their various supporters, it appeared that Julius had an agenda "based on race." Antisemitism was too ingrained in Catholic bourgeois Vienna to welcome without qualification the Jewish talent making positive contributions in every sector of local life.[16]

The controversy surrounding Julius was exacerbated by his obtrusive involvement in Erich's career. One of the most remarkable aspects of the wunderkind's early development is that he managed to express a unique musical language, even with Julius' overbearing attempts to "protect" him from the evils of modernism.[17]

Erich was no doubt exposed to a wide range of contemporary music, which his father played on the piano to prepare reviews for the paper. These included works with dissonances, expanded harmonies, and adventurous structures, which young Erich would synthesize with his predilection for melody.[18] As one critic notes, rather than "adapt[ing] his musically sweet tooth to his peer group's austere taste for modernism," Korngold used modernist elements to augment his lushly expressive music.[19] As such, he is sometimes called "the last Romantic," although he more accurately straddled Romanticism and Modernism without losing sight of melody. He composed lieder throughout his life and was one of the last composers of the genre. His penchant for melody, despite the seismic shifts in musical culture, is perhaps most strongly displayed in his lieder.[20] His three-act opera, *Die tote Stadt* (The Dead City, 1920), one of the great successes of the

1920s, fuses Puccini-like melodies with harmonies influenced by Zemlinsky, Strauss, Schoenberg, Schreker, and other modernists his father despised.[21]

Impressively, the young composer retained defenders from the ranks of Julius' enemies. Felix von Weingartner, who succeeded Mahler at the Vienna State Opera and was regularly subjected to Julius' wrath, nevertheless championed Korngold's music, conducting *Der Schneemann* in 1910. Weingartner remarked glowingly:

> Erich Korngold is an individuality. In vain I searched his compositions, even his earliest, for blunders. Nowhere did I find a point disclosing an inexperienced hand. His compositions never betray the composer's youth. No one would suspect that a little boy was the author. Erich's music is of a refinement which could almost frighten musical experts, but we must not forget that even a genius is a child of his time. He gives me an impression as though Nature has the caprice to sum up everything the art of music had produced in the last decades in order to give the sum total to a child in his cradle, who now plays with it.[22]

Despite Weingartner's being Erich's first prominent supporter, Julius wasted no opportunity to denigrate the former in the press. A devotee of fellow Moravian Gustav Mahler (Mahler was born in Kalischt, near the Moravian border of Bohemia),[23] Julius was devastated when the maestro left the Vienna State Opera in 1907 and died four years later. He mercilessly attacked Mahler's successors, Weingartner and then Richard Strauss, both of whom played important roles in Erich's career. Julius' ire was only heightened by Weingartner's support of the young composer, which he suspected was a plot to curry his favor.[24]

Erich met Richard Strauss at the premiere of Mahler's Eighth Symphony in Munich in September 1910. Several months earlier, Strauss had sent a congratulatory letter to Julius, expressing his admiration for the score of *Der Schneemann* and his desire to make "the personal acquaintance of this arch-musician."[25] At the time, Erich was just thirteen and Strauss was forty-six. They forged a decades-long friendship despite harsh reviews of Strauss' conducting published in *Die Neue Freie Presse.*[26]

Against his father's wishes, Erich married Luzi von Sonnenthal in 1924. Luzi's grandfather, Adolf von Sonnenthal, had been one of Vienna's most popular actors and was among the first Jews to receive ennoblement by Emperor Franz Joseph (1867). Luzi's sister, Helene, was a member of impresario Max Reinhardt's acting troupe, and Luzi herself had appeared in a few films. Julius' disapproval stemmed from both the fear of losing control over Erich's life and his distaste for popular culture. The latter frustration was heightened in the late 1920s, when Erich began supplying music for Reinhardt's theater, including arrangements of operettas by Johann Strauss Jr. and Jacques Offenbach. In additional to their professional relationship, Reinhardt became something of a surrogate father for Korngold, whose real father was agitated by his involvement in "lightweight" fare.[27]

The rise of the Third Reich and resulting loss of income forced Reinhardt, whose family was Jewish, to flee to Hollywood in 1934. His first project was a film adaptation of Shakespeare's *A Midsummer Night's Dream* (1935). In his contract with Warner Brothers, Reinhardt insisted that Korngold be hired to arrange incidental music by Felix Mendelssohn, which was customarily used for the staged production. Korngold accepted the job and worked on other Warner Brothers films over the next few years, dividing his time between Vienna and Los Angeles. Fortuitously, he was in Hollywood scoring *The Adventures of Robin Hood* when the Nazis annexed Austria in March 1938, and he managed to rescue his immediate family.

Korngold composed eighteen original film scores, two of which received Academy Awards: *Anthony Adverse* (1936) and *The*

Adventures of Robin Hood (1938). Prior to his arrival in Hollywood, no internationally known composer had been engaged to write for motion pictures. Early sound films had mostly been scored using snippets from public domain masterworks, a method carried over from the silent era. On rare occasions when the budget allowed for original music, the task went to an anonymous committee of studio composers whose roots in vaudeville and Tin Pan Alley usually translated into simple and sappy fare. Scores for smaller movies would often be pieced together from music written or arranged for earlier pictures.

Max Steiner, whose career began in theater and revue, wrote groundbreaking scores for *Symphony of Six Million* (1932) and *King Kong* (1933), in which the music was integral to the action on the screen. In so doing, he revolutionized the medium and laid the foundations for the "Hollywood sound." But Korngold's fame as a concert composer added prestige to the craft. Seizing the opportunity, Warner Brothers offered him generous short-term contracts, ownership of his music, the right to refuse projects, involvement in pre-production, the option to work at home, his own screen title, his name on advertisements, and only one or two films per year.[28] Contrastingly, Steiner's average output for two years equaled Korngold's total for his entire career.[29]

Relieved of the normal pressures faced by Steiner and other workhorses, Korngold had the luxury of writing his own orchestrations and treating his films as "operas without singing," especially through the use of leitmotifs (*à la* Wagner).[30] He was grateful for the unique arrangement:

> I am fully aware of the fact that I seem to be working under much more favorable conditions than my Hollywood colleagues who quite often have to finish a score in a very short time and in conjunction with several other composers. So far, I have successfully resisted the temptations of an all-year contract because, in my opinion, that would force me into factory-like

mass production. I have refused to compose music for a picture in two or three weeks or in an even shorter period.[31]

A number of serious composers wrote for films during the 1930s and '40s, including fellow émigrés Ernst Toch, Eric Zeisl, Hanns Eisler, Mario Castelnuovo-Tedesco, and Alexandre Tansman, and a few American-born masters, such as Virgil Thomson and Aaron Copland, dabbled in the medium. But Korngold stood alone as a Hollywood success. The other major film composers came from radio, theater, popular music, or European films, such as Steiner, Franz Waxman, Alfred Newman, Dimitri Tiomkin, Miklós Rózsa, and Bernard Herrmann.[32]

During the war years, Korngold refrained almost completely from writing art music, focusing instead on motion pictures. Like Reinhardt, Korngold did not consider himself "particularly Jewish," nor did he "take his ancestry as seriously as Hitler did."[33] Still, the war had a severe impact on him. He reportedly vowed not to compose serious music while Hitler was in power.[34] "Even if I wanted to," he told Luzi, "I could not compose on my own level."[35] The only exceptions are the two liturgical works he wrote for Rabbi Sonderling in 1941: *A Passover Psalm*, op. 30, and *Prayer*, op. 32.

After the war, Korngold attempted to reestablish a concert career and even hoped to return to Europe. However, by that time, interest in his late-Romantic style was waning and his reputation as a film composer tarnished his image among art music aficionados. The 1947 New York premiere of his Violin Concerto, op. 35, performed by Jascha Heifetz, was infamously deemed "more corn than gold."[36] In postwar Germany, where music was moving further into the avant-garde in an effort to escape Hitler's legacy, Korngold's nostalgic sound fell on cynical ears.[37] His film career even left a stain on works he composed before coming to Hollywood. According to critic Eric Myers, Korngold's music was "effective in a cheaply theatrical sort of way, and it is not surprising that [he] eventually went to Hollywood to ply his trade for The Bastard Art."[38] But Korngold's aesthetic was never schlocky or disingenuous. "The true creative artist," he stated, "does not wish to recreate for his fellow man the headlines screaming of atom bombs, murder, and sensationalism found in the daily paper. Rather . . . he will know how to take and uplift him into the purer realm of fantasy."[39]

Unhealthily overweight for years, Korngold suffered a heart attack in 1947, followed by a debilitating stroke in 1956. He died the following year at age sixty. Sources attribute his death to "sadness"[40] or "the stress of irrelevance."[41] Whatever the case, he was undoubtedly disappointed that Hollywood had suffocated his art music aspirations.

THE COMMISSIONS

Very little is known about how *A Passover Psalm* and *Prayer* came about. Neither Korngold nor his parents were "practicing" Jews in any sense of the term, and his father openly disdained religion. One of Korngold's biographers wrote: "By all accounts, he was not a religious Jew, nor does it appear that he had a bar mitzvah. Certainly, he did not attend synagogue, and the Korngold household was not kosher."[42] Another source posits that he was "so secular that his sons were not circumcised, nor did they celebrate bar mitzvahs."[43] It is therefore unlikely that Korngold would have met Rabbi Sonderling at a religious service, as had Ernst Toch. However, the German-speaking émigré community was very close-knit, and it is possible that the two met at a social gathering—perhaps, indeed, at the home of Arnold Schoenberg, who had befriended Korngold in their mutual exile.[44] Korngold was also involved in relief efforts for European Jews trapped by the Nazis and may have encountered Sonderling at a fundraising event.[45]

Korngold's reasons for accepting the commissions are likewise veiled in mystery. He had been suffering from deep depression over the war. Learning of the implementation of the Final Solution in 1941, he may have accepted the commissions as a personal tribute or as therapy.[46] A biographer offers a less emotional reason: "He was asked to write them; and he had not been formally commissioned to write anything other than film music for a very long time."[47] A third possibility is suggested by the fact that Korngold presented both works—along with *Narrenlieder* (Songs of the Clown), op. 29, and *Vier Shakespeare-Lieder* (Four Shakespeare Songs), op. 31—in a box marked: "My last four—or more optimistically my latest four works. For my dear parents on their Golden Wedding Anniversary, Hollywood, 27 September 1941."[48] Julius and Josephine, who had also settled in Los Angeles, struggled to acclimate to the new environment and were financially and socially dependent on their son. Julius never approved of Erich's film career and repeatedly urged him to return to art music.[49] Erich may have felt that composing the Sonderling pieces, together with the lieder, would help assuage his father's scorn and, perhaps, repair their strained relationship.

On an artistic level, the commissions provided Korngold an opportunity to write music from his own heart and soul. Although the texts he used were ancient—and certainly informed the compositions—the settings were as much about presenting the liturgy as presenting himself. In contrast to film scores, which accompany another's vision, these were self-revealing concert-style pieces. Sonderling's nurturing yet hands-off approach, combined with the captive and receptive audience of Fairfax Temple, was all the motivation Korngold needed to musically express himself at a time when Jewishness was very much on his mind.

Korngold turned out the pieces in relatively short order. *A Passover Psalm* was composed in March and April 1941 and performed at the Los Angeles Elks Temple, presumably rented for a Fairfax Temple Passover gathering on April 12, 1941.[50] The second piece, *Prayer*, was composed between June and September 1941 and first performed during Yom Kippur services on October 1, 1941.[51]

THE COMPOSITIONS

The text for *A Passover Psalm* is attributed to Rabbi Sonderling, who based it on passages from the Haggadah. As with the words for Toch's *Cantata of the Bitter Herbs* three years earlier, the traditional language receives an interpretative twist. However, whereas Toch's work was written in English and Hebrew, *A Passover Psalm* uses a German text. Sonderling likely chose German due to the increasing number of Fairfax Temple members who were not fluent in English.

The piece opens with three sentences based on the introduction to *Hallel*, which is customarily recited shortly before the festive meal.[52] The original text is usually translated:

> We are obligated to thank . . . to praise . . . to exalt . . . Him who performed all these miracles for our ancestors and for us. He took us from slavery to freedom, from suffering to joy, from mourning to celebration, from darkness to great light.[53]

Sonderling's interpretive translation reads:

> Let us praise . . . honor [and] sing praise to Him who did wonders for our fathers and us, their children. He broke open the prison, he led us out from slavery to freedom, from sorrow to joy. He broke open the prison, he led us out from grief to jubilation, from darkness to light.

As with *Cantata of the Bitter Herbs*, the repeated references to a prison break constitute Sonderling's own contemporary interpolation.

The final two paragraphs of the text appear to be largely original and must have resonated with a community of Jews who had personally experienced the Nazi threat:

> Baruch ata Adonay; praise to you O Lord. You have delivered us. Hear our pleading, deliver us once more, give peace to our souls, give joy to our hearts, give peace to the people that wanders from land to land, from hatred to hatred, from trouble to trouble. Rescue, rescue Israel, Your children, Your people!

> And when you have freed us as before, then from the depths of our souls a song full of thanks will ring out. Praise! Praise! Halleluyah!

This language bears some resemblance to the blessing over the second cup of wine in the traditional Haggadah:

> Baruch ata Adonai . . . who redeemed us . . . and brought us to this night. . . . So may Adonai . . . bring us to other festivals . . . may they come to us in peace, rejoicing in the building of Your city and delighting in Your worship . . . and we shall praise You with a new song about our redemption and the salvation of our souls.[54]

Sonderling raises the intensity of the passage by referring to "our pleading" and appealing for "deliverance" and "rescue," rather than "redemption" or "salvation." Furthermore, he focuses on the physical situation rather than the spiritual, and on the condition of diaspora Jewry, particularly émigrés, who wander "from land to land, from hatred to hatred, from trouble to trouble."

The musical setting begins with strings and harp under a classic German chorale. The melodic and dynamic arcs for the first line of text—"Let us praise . . . Him who did wonders for our fathers and us, their children"—gently rise to a peak with the words, "Him who did wonders," and gradually fall until reaching the word "children." A brief instrumental break follows the first statement of the text, in which the piano and harp ring out over the strings in ascending runs, introducing a repetition of the first line at greater volume.

The lower voices and lower strings introduce the next line with a new theme in a darker tonality: "He broke open the prison . . . from sorrow to joy." The higher voices begin the next line, "He broke open the prison . . . from darkness to light," with the lower voices answering. The overall volume increases to a peak on the word "jubilation," followed by a quick diminuendo on the last phrase, "from darkness to light."

Another brief instrumental break is played by the harp and solo strings, dominated by the suggestion of a new theme in the violin. A soprano soloist takes up that theme, singing the opening of the next paragraph: "Baruch ata Adonai, praise to You O Lord, You have delivered us." The theme climbs ever upward from "Baruch" to a peak at "Lord," and then falls to a lower ascending line for "You have delivered us."

Next, the full chorus and orchestra, including brass, enter with the words "hear our pleading." The music returns to the first melody of the piece, with the dynamic peak on the word "hearts," but the melodic peak on the repeated words, "peace to the people." The peak is identical to that which previously accompanied the text, "Him who did wonders." A tension-building extension underlies the text that follows, "wanders from land to land . . . trouble to trouble." Trumpet calls accompany the plea to "rescue, rescue Israel," and the full chorus and orchestra build to a false conclusion on "Your People."

After a dramatic pause, the soprano soloist sings the same theme as earlier (on "Baruch ata Adonai"), this time extended to accommodate the words, "and when You have freed us . . . a song . . . will ring out." The lower choral voices repeat the words and theme, with ascending piano runs and French horns providing accents in the accompaniment.

The full chorus and soloist then sing "Halleluyah" repeatedly to the same melodic theme. The full orchestra introduces a repetition of the entire final paragraph, "and when You have freed us . . . ," sung by the full chorus. The volume builds until the repetitions of "Halleluyah" are sung *fortissimo*, with timpani and brass driving all toward a final, Hollywood-esque ending.

Prayer, the second of Korngold's works for Rabbi Sonderling, is a short, 56-measure piece for tenor soloist, female voices (6 to 12), harp, and organ. The text purports to be a poem by Franz Werfel.[55] However, that claim seems questionable for a number of reasons. First, the text is in English (aside from a few words of Hebrew), and Werfel wrote almost exclusively in German. (It is unclear whether he wrote any poems or novels in another language.) Second, as demonstrated by the comparison below, the text is a fairly accurate, if stylized, translation of the liturgical Hebrew text for the *Kedushat Hashem* (Sanctification of the Name), found in the *Amidah* (Standing Prayer) for High Holidays.[56]

Kedushat Hashem

> And so place the fear of You,
> Lord our God,
> over all that You have made,
> and the terror of You over all You have created,
> and all who were made will stand in awe of you,
> and all of creation will worship You,
> and they will be bound together as one
> to carry out Your will with an undivided heart.
>
> For we know, Lord our God,
> all dominion is laid out before You,
> strength is in Your palm
> and might in Your right hand,
> Your name spreading awe over all You have created.

Korngold's *Prayer*

> Adonoy Elauhenu; Adonoy Elauhenu. [Lord our God; Lord
> our God]
> Pour awe into the hearts of all Thy creatures
> and dread upon all that Thou hast called into being,
> that all Thy works may fear Thee,
> that all may bend their knee
> and build one brotherhood of Man,
> united to do Thy will.

> Then father shall we know that Thine is dominion,
> Thine is all might and strength.
> Then we shall know that Thy name
> is to be feared above all that Thou hast created.
> Adonoy Elauhenu; Adonoy Elauhenu.

Franz Werfel was Jewish by birth but had renounced Judaism in 1929 in order to marry Alma Mahler, whose first husband, composer Gustav Mahler, died in 1911. He most likely lacked adequate knowledge of both Hebrew and English to create an original translation of the Hebrew prayer. Perhaps he agreed to have his name affixed to the text to attract a wider audience, or perhaps Sonderling wrote the text but was uncomfortable putting his own name on it. The language resonates with Sonderling's religious views. Like the author, Sonderling was unsure of God's dominion during the war and would only recognize that dominion in a future time of universal brotherhood.

The piece opens with a five-measure introduction, in which the meter alternates between 4/4 and 3/4, harmonies shift between minor and major, and the melody moves upward to emphasize the appeal to heaven that the prayer represents.[57] Starting on a C# minor triad, the first "Adonoy Elauhenu" (Lord our God) ends on a C# major triad. The second "Adonoy Elauhenu" begins with a C# minor triad and concludes with a G# major triad. Open 4ths and 5ths reinforce the "sacred sound" of the introduction, although they are more closely associated with music of the church than with the synagogue.

The English text continues in E major, but passing tones in the harmony create stacked 4ths, in which the tonality is ambiguous (e.g., D#–G#–C# on the second beat suggests chords based on G# and C#, without providing the 3rd for either root to indicate major or minor). The meter becomes even more irregular (e.g., 3/4–3/8–3/4–2/4–3/4–4/4–3/4 in the first ten bars). However, beneath all the passing tones and meter changes is the basic harmonic progression of I–IV–I–V–I for the first phrase, "Pour awe into the hearts of all Thy people," and I–V for the second phrase, "and dread upon all that Thou hast called into being." The third phrase, "that all Thy works may fear Thee," ends on stacked 4ths, B–E–A, which suggest both I and IV, and the fourth phrase, "that all may bend their knee," ends on a C# minor chord, recalling the beginning of the piece.

On the next phrase, "and build one brotherhood of man," the harmony modulates to B major. The following phrase, "united to do Thy will," ends melodically with a rising B–C#–D# reminiscent of the end of the introduction on "Adonoy Elauhenu." The harmony, too, follows the same progression as the introduction, ending on a G# major chord.

The piece then returns to the melody and harmony that began the English text. The organ accompaniment is set up an octave, the female voices are tacit for the first eight bars, and the meter is altered slightly to accommodate the new text; but, otherwise, it is a straightforward recapitulation up until the closing cadence. In the last four bars of the English text, "above all that Thou hast created," the music returns to E major rather than the B major heard in the melody's first statement.

Korngold ends the piece with a coda on the repeated phrase "Adonoy Elauhenu," duplicating the melody and harmony of the introduction, but extending both for an additional two measures to conclude on C# major instead of G# major, as at the end of the introduction. The entire piece can thus be understood as a movement from the opening C# minor chord to the closing C# major. The ascending line of the introduction, suggesting a prayer rising upward to God, now ascends one more step with an accompanying harp arpeggio, as if to give the prayer a final boost into heaven.

EPILOGUE

Korngold conducted the concert premiere of *A Passover Psalm* at the Hollywood Bowl on June 22, 1945, four years after the piece debuted at the Fairfax Temple Passover gathering.[58] In 1954, it was performed in Vienna at a concert sponsored by Gesellschaft der Musikfreunde (Society of the Friends of Music), during which Korngold dedicated the piece to that society.[59] More recently, *A Passover Psalm* was performed by the Los Angeles Master Chorale in February 1996, recorded by the Wiener Philharmoniker in Vienna in June 1997, and performed and recorded by the Munich Radio Orchestra in 2003. The Sarasota Opera in Florida included the piece on its November 2015 program. Recordings are sometimes heard on the radio during the Passover season, including on Itzhak Perlman's "A Musical Feast for Passover," which aired on several classical radio stations in March 2018.

Prayer was not published until 1995, despite debuting at Fairfax Temple on Yom Kippur in 1941.[60] There is no record of additional performances prior to a recorded concert in Linz, Austria, in January 2002.[61] Reports are not available for any performance since.

There can be no doubt of Korngold's skills as an orchestrator and creator of sonic effects. His Sonderling commissions bring together the same techniques he employed successfully as a film composer: the harp glissandi, the pointed use of brass and percussion, and instruments emerging elegantly from the orchestral fabric.[62] As Korngold admitted, he never "differentiated between my music for the films and that for the operas and concert pieces. Just as I do for the operatic stage, I try to give the motion pictures dramatically melodious music, sonic development, and variations of the themes."[63] The unity of his oeuvre is demonstrated in his Violin Concerto, op. 35 (1947), pejoratively referred to as the "Hollywood Concerto,"[64] which recycles music from scores for *Anthony Adverse* (1936), *Another Dawn* (1937), and *The Prince and the Pauper* (1937).[65] His only symphony, *Symphony in F-sharp*, op. 40 (1952), dedicated to the memory of Franklin D. Roosevelt, incorporates a theme from *The Private Lives of Elizabeth and Essex* (1939).[66] According to Haas, this seamless crossover raises questions not only about Korngold's music but also about "classical" music in general: "Is it elite, or is it populist? Is it high art or easy entertainment? Is it merely an application, like the use of colour in cinema or is it *l'art pour l'art*—a thing of purity and a bridge between the listener and a higher state? Is music a cultural cornerstone of European civilisation or is it merely 'disposable'?"[67]

Whereas Korngold's techniques are immediately effective in the visually dominant art form of film, in less visual settings, like the synagogue and concert hall, they can wear thin on repeated hearings. His sacred works somehow fail to echo the profundity of the sacred text. Perhaps for this reason, *A Passover Psalm* and *Prayer* have not found a place in Jewish ritual, even in reduced form for choir and keyboard. Musicologist Clayton Henderson opines:

> Music of the highest order seems never to divulge all its secrets from the beginning; rather, it leaves something yet to be discovered with frequent hearings. This is not true of the Korngold. Perhaps part of the problem is the sacred text. Korngold's movie scores succeed on one level because the music relies on untexted sound to reinforce dramatic movements. Korngold's music as a servant of words, of sacred text, however, doesn't seem

convincing at rehearing. The music here can sound repet-
itive, formulaic, less than convincing—bordering, at times,
on the trivial. Is it because Korngold's passionate musical
statements are at odds with the kind of passion expressed in
the psalm?[68]

During his lifetime, Korngold's sound had become anach-
ronistic in art music circles. Although he arrived in Hollywood
having written a ballet, operas, concerti, sonatas, lieder, and
other works, and returned to art music after the war, Korngold is
today most appreciated by film music scholars and fans. Whereas
concert audiences responded to discordant sounds reflecting the
traumas and uncertainties of the twentieth century, moviegoers
reveled—and continue to revel—in Korngold's lushly senti-
mental scores. He came to regret devoting so much energy to
films and the stigma of being a "film composer," but the escap-
ist medium was a perfect match for his approach. As he wrote:
"The genuine artist creates at a distance from his own time, even
for a time beyond."[69]

Nevertheless, recent years have brought renewed interest
in Korngold's non-film music. For instance, in October and
November 2017, he was the subject of a concert series marking
the fiftieth anniversary of his death. Held at London's South Bank
Centre, the series presented works spanning "an artistic galaxy
from Mahler's Vienna to Errol Flynn's Hollywood."[70] But most
attention is drawn to his film work, owing both to Hollywood's
broad appeal and to his significance as a film music pioneer. An
entire book is devoted to his music for *The Adventures of Robin
Hood*, which many consider among the finest film scores ever written.[71] In contrast, if Korngold is mentioned at all in musical ency-
clopedias or biographical dictionaries, his concert works are either
glossed over or neglected altogether. Even less likely to be mentioned are *A Passover Psalm* and *Prayer*, pieces rarely performed

for Jewish audiences, almost never used in Jewish services, and barely noticed by Korngold aficionados.

CHAPTER 6
ERIC ZEISL'S *REQUIEM EBRAICO*

E ric Zeisl (1905–1959) was born into a lower-middle class family of Czech background in Vienna's Jewish quarter (Leopoldstadt). His parents operated a café and maintained an identifiably Jewish, if not religious, household.[1] The Zeisls were not traditionally observant Jews; social and economic mobility outweighed whatever particularistic or ritual concerns they might have had.[2] Still, according to Eric's wife, lawyer Gertrud Zeisl (née Jellinek, 1906–1987), Eric learned to read Hebrew as a child (without understanding the meaning) and on Shabbat mornings would accompany his grandfather to a synagogue "in the backstreets."[3] These early experiences informed Zeisl's use of a "Hebraic element" in a number of compositions, which he integrated into a wide palette of musical vocabularies. Gertrud explained:

> The ancient melodies fell upon the heart of the listening child and evoked echoes from ages back, of sorrows and suffering and rapture in God. They mixed with the joyous sounds of

the Prayer, with the resounding hymns and masses that came through the open portals of the stately domes and churches, with the merry sounds of the city, with the delightful aroma of good food, that we deemed the essence of life in the city and especially in a restaurant-owner's house, with the lusty cries and yells of four boys of which he was the third.[4]

The four Zeisl boys and their parents lived in a cramped three-bedroom apartment. As an attention-starved budding composer, Eric's position in the family (third son) caused him to feel neglected at times. Like many middle-class Viennese Jewish families, the Zeisls viewed art music as a pathway to acculturation and integration into European society.[5] Piano lessons were a fixture in their home. The brothers each needed the piano for practice (two were singers), but Eric just wanted to "play."[6] Concerned that he would never make a living in music, Eric's parents discouraged him from following his passion. Undeterred, Eric reportedly sold his stamp collection in order to pursue advanced studies.[7] After a short time at the Academy of Music and Performing Arts, he continued learning privately with Richard Stöhr, a Viennese Jewish composer born in the same year as Schoenberg. In stark contrast to his better-known contemporary, Stöhr was a traditionalist who championed a nineteenth-century musical language. Zeisl would himself carry the traditionalist torch, favoring tonality and direct emotionalism over the cerebral systems fashionable at the time.

Much like Korngold, Zeisl's refusal to adapt his compositional voice to the dominant iconoclasm would eventually lose him performance opportunities. In a series of letters to Lawrence Morton, director of Los Angeles' avant-garde-leaning Monday Evening Concerts (1951–1974), Zeisl took umbrage with Morton's opinion of him as an uninteresting "lesser" composer: "I am very glad that you find my music *not* interesting! The word 'interesting' alone means the death sentence of every good and great music. . . .

Your public is a special one. It is a selected, discriminating and very educated crowd. Why don't you let *them* decide the issue!"[8]

By age sixteen, Zeisl had published his first set of songs. In the early 1930s, he studied with the conservative Joseph Marx and the progressive Hugo Kauder.[9] Zeisl internalized Kauder's infatuation with Gustav Mahler, bringing Mahlerian influence to the fore in the final movement of his *First String Quartet* (premiered in 1933), featuring a theme and variations on a Slovak melody, which he would later expand into *Variations on a Slovakian Folk Song* for string orchestra (1937).[10] Zeisl published several additional song collections, as well as chamber works, during that period. When avant-garde music was targeted in the early years of the Nazi regime, Zeisl's relatively conservative sound was more or less tolerated. It was therefore especially tragic when he and Gertrud were forced to flee to Paris in November 1938—narrowly escaping the events of Kristallnacht—leaving his parents behind in Austria.

Paris in the late 1930s was essentially a pass-through zone for European exiles. There, Zeisl became acquainted with the work of Austrian Jewish journalist and novelist Joseph Roth, who died in May 1939 at age forty-four, following years of alcoholism. Roth's novel, *Job: The Story of a Simple Man* (*Roman eines einfachen Mannes*, 1930), had been posthumously adapted to stage, and Zeisl was engaged to provide incidental music. The story follows Mendel Singer, a Jobian figure who flees the horrors of Tzarist Russia and immigrates to New York City, along the way losing his family, falling ill, suffering terrible abuses, and struggling with his Jewish identity. In Roth's story, Zeisl found a way to reconcile his own identity as a non-confessional, yet still self-identifying, Jew. Perhaps most musically significant are the "Hebraicisms" used in pieces for the Paris production, such as "Menuhim's Song" and "Cossack Dance," which have echoes of synagogal modes and Jewish folksong. Zeisl aimed to construct a musical language that was Jewish without being overtly religious. *Job* would captivate him for the rest of his life, although he ultimately failed to complete an opera adaptation with a libretto by Hans Kafka.

The Judaic sound continued to appear in Zeisl's works, including his Sonderling commission, *Requiem Ebraico* (1945), which weaves synagogal flavors into a Baroque fabric. This Jewish strain was but one aspect of Zeisl's richly textured approach. Like many Viennese composers, he was a master of many influences. Indeed, the so-called "Viennese style" is distinguished for its hybridization of multiple musical dialects, reflecting the city's cosmopolitan character. Gertrud explained:

> [The Austro-Hungarian] empire was far flung and powerful, yet it consisted of many small facets, each an individual development of its own, forever mixing and forever divided and limited, each to its own small realm; the Czechs, the Poles, the Slovaks and the Germans, the Hungarians, the Serbs and the Italian, the Celtic and the Jewish. The Viennese felt himself at the center of this humanity and he never quite knew "what" or "who" he was. It was most difficult to find himself, for he consisted of so many different pieces.[11]

Eric and Gertrud stayed in Paris for about a year, where they benefitted from the kindness of Darius Milhaud. Unable to find financial security in France, they arrived in the United States in September 1939, first stopping in New York. Their daughter, Barbara, who was born in New York the following May, described the shock of the new surroundings:

> [W]hat a transition it must have been: instead of living in Vienna's *Moelkerbastei*, opposite the Beethoven house, and rather than a little bird singing outside the window, as in 'Vor meinem Fenster,' they embraced their child while living in relative squalor in a New York tenement house with no heat, with no greenery, and windows which faced the endless rooftops.[12]

Zeisl had some success on the East Coast. His *Little Symphony* (1935) was included on Ernö Rapée's weekly national broadcast from Radio City Music Hall, and several of his compositions were performed and published. This allowed the family to move to a spacious rented house in Mamaroneck, Westchester, on the Long Island Sound.[13] While in New York, Zeisl befriended Hanns Eisler, a fellow Austrian who was teaching composition at the New School of Social Research. Eisler was preparing to leave for Hollywood to work in film and helped Zeisl secure an eighteen-month contract with MGM.[14] Both Zeisl and Eisler arrived in Southern California in 1942.[15]

Zeisl was among the youngest and least connected of Hollywood's émigré composers. A relative latecomer to the competitive film industry, he was limited to writing uncredited "moods" for short scenes and musical effects. Unable to secure a long-term contract from MGM or any other studio, he became a freelancer. Still, a busy schedule enabled him to support his family through the war years. He worked on background cues for more than twenty films between 1942 and 1958, ranging from *Lassie Come Home* (1943) to *Abbott and Costello Meet the Invisible Man* (1951). As Haas puts it, he was a highly competent "assembly line worker on the conveyer belts of the city's film studios."[16]

Zeisl found more stable employment after the war as an instructor of composition, first at the Southern California School of Music and Arts[17] and, beginning in 1949, at Los Angeles City College (LACC). The head of LACC's music department, Leslie P. Clausen, assigned Zeisl to the Evening Division, where he could teach without the usual credentials. Frustrated by his ineligibility for tenure and Clausen's habit of cutting his classes "without sense," Zeisl nevertheless enjoyed teaching theory and composition.[18] His students came from various walks of life. "There were window washers from Watts and mechanics from the aircraft industry," Gertrud recalled, "and there were musicians from the Philharmonic and young composers, and there was together the best and the most naïve and unschooled."[19] Zeisl's students included mega-film and television composer Jerry Goldsmith and concert composer Leon Levitch.

Zeisl was one of many émigré composers who took up teaching in Los Angeles, joining Ernst Krenek at the Southern California School of Music and Arts and LACC, Eisler at USC and UCLA, Toch at LACC and USC, and Schoenberg at USC and UCLA, among others. The 1941 edition of *Who Is Who in Music* noted the convenience of having these European teachers in Los Angeles:

> More and more it is to be noted that Americans are studying at home and this by preference. War conditions doubtless will limit still further and perhaps drastically the number of prospective artists who will still feel it necessary to put the European hallmark on their training. Many of the same teachers with whom they, or their fellow students, might have elected to study if they had gone abroad immediately after—or just before—the last war, now are established in America.[20]

From 1948 to 1950, Zeisl served as an instructor and composer-in-residence at the Brandeis Arts Institute for young Jewish artists, musicians, and performers in Simi Valley. The experience allowed him to further explore a "secular Jewish musical aesthetic,"[21] and inspired the "Brandeis Sonata" for violin and piano (1949–1950), perhaps his best-known chamber work. Max Helfman, music director of the Brandeis Institute and a noted synagogue composer, was drawn to Zeisl's incorporation of indigenous Jewish sounds and Middle Eastern-inspired flares. Helfman's own compositions and arrangements display a similar preference for modal melodies (using scales that are not strictly major or minor), pentatonic flavors, parallel fourths and fifths, rhythmic piano, and other vaguely Eastern (or Middle Eastern) elements meant to convey a "Jewish essence."[22] In Helfman's assessment, Zeisl's Hebraic sensibilities produced "compositions which spring strengthened and renewed from a base which unites East and West through the harmonies of the one and the techniques of the other."[23]

Zeisl's time at the Brandeis camp was bookended by compositions on Jewish themes, notably *Requiem Ebraico* for SAB soli, SATB choir, and organ (or orchestra), and the biblical ballets *Naboth's Vineyard* (1953) and *Jacob and Rachel* (1954), neither of which were performed during Zeisl's lifetime. The latter piece received its long-overdue world premiere by the Los Angeles Jewish Symphony, under Noreen Green, on May 9, 2009. The orchestra released a recording of *Jacob and Rachel* in early 2019.[24]

Never completely comfortable outside of Austria, Zeisl suffered from chronic depression. The hot sun of Southern California irritated his sensitive skin and aggravated his mental state. As Gertrud recounted, he longed for the rain and fog he left behind in Europe: "He has diaries where—every so often—every second day he writes down the temperature as the only event of the day—98, or something like this. And it was just terrible for him."[25] Still, the Zeisl home became a lively meeting place for luminary émigrés: the Tochs, the Korngolds, the Tansmans, Alma Mahler Werfel, and many others.[26] Zeisl apparently only met Schoenberg once, but their children, Barbara Zeisl and Ronald Schoenberg, were married after both composers had passed away.[27]

Zeisl died of a sudden heart attack after teaching an evening theory class on February 18, 1959. He was only fifty-three. Reflecting on his status as a "transplanted composer" several years earlier, Zeisl described himself as a homesick and tormented artist: "Longing, nostalgia, loneliness, and strife. I know of no better nourishment for the artist's soul."[28]

THE COMMISSION

Zeisl became acquainted with Rabbi Sonderling through his younger brother, baritone William Zeisl. The rabbi had hired William as cantor for Fairfax Temple on the recommendation of German émigré and voice teacher Hugo Strelitzer, who was on the faculty of LACC.[29] Strelitzer was the region's leading figure in vocal music, having founded the first opera workshop in Los Angeles at LACC.[30]

Sometime in 1944, Sonderling asked Zeisl to compose a setting of Psalm 92 for an interfaith concert that the rabbi was helping to organize. The psalm bears a superscription indicating its use on Shabbat, and it is customarily sung or chanted in synagogue on Shabbat evening. Sonderling apparently viewed the text as an appropriate representation of Judaism. Initially, Zeisl was hesitant to compose something of a liturgical nature, but he accepted the commission on the condition that his setting would blend the particular and the universal, much as Toch did with *Cantata of the Bitter Herbs*.[31]

As someone similarly drawn to Judaism's humanistic-universalistic tendencies, especially as expressed through the arts, Sonderling was not only agreeable to Zeisl's approach to the text, but enthusiastically in favor of it. Their collaboration was more than simply the result of the rabbi sharing a pulpit with the composer's brother. For Zeisl, Sonderling represented an intriguing brand of Judaism—one that combined aesthetic innovation, universalism, and a vibrant cultural identity, of which religious ritual was just one component.

While Zeisl was working on the commission, he received tragic news from Europe. His father, Sigmund, remained in Austria after the Anschluss, and Eric had received no word of his fate during the war. So long as there was no information to the contrary, Eric was hopeful that his father might have survived. But, as the war was winding down, he learned that his father had been murdered in the Treblinka extermination camp, along with his stepmother (his late mother's sister). The tragic news seeped into Zeisl's setting of Psalm 92, which, while best known for its praises, assumed the quality of a requiem, modeled on the Catholic requiem for mourning (*à la* Mozart, Berlioz, Verdi, and Brahms).[32]

Requiem Ebraico debuted at a Hollywood Inter-Faith Forum event, "The Message of Music and Religion," held at the First Methodist Church of Hollywood on April 8, 1945. In the program, the work is simply called *Psalm 92*. The piece was performed by organist Norman H. Wright, the Fairfax Temple Choir of about fifteen voices, and soloists William Zeisl, Lillian Fawcett, and Rece Saxon, with Strelitzer conducting. Also performed were an organ prelude by Zeisl and selections from Toch's Sonata in E Major for violin and piano, along with two hymns sung by the Crescent Heights Sigmatones and a Christian benediction. Sonderling and John H. Engle, minister of Crescent Heights Methodist Church, moderated the program.[33] Although some sources claim that the Santa Monica Symphony also participated,[34] that was not Gertrud's recollection.[35]

Zeisl composed another work for the concert, *Prayer*, for soprano and organ (or orchestra), dedicated to the United Nations. Unfortunately, it was set too high for the soprano soloist, and its premiere was postponed until the Festival of Modern Music held on May 26, 1945. There is no record of Sonderling commissioning *Prayer*, but the fact that it was written for the interfaith event strongly suggests the rabbi had a hand in its creation.

Psalm 92 was published as *Requiem Ebraico* later that year by Transcontinental Music Publications, a leading purveyor of synagogue music. In a letter to Transcontinental's founder, Josef Freudenthal, Zeisl addressed the company's earlier reluctance to publish the work due to its subject matter and costly orchestral arrangement:

I wrote this piece dedicated to the memory of my loving father and the other countless victims of the Jewish tragedy in Europe. ... [W]ith a heart full of tears [Jews] hold on to God and do not cease to thank Him and do not cease to hope. This is the message and the consolation which I found in the 92nd Psalm. ... I conceived the work as a requiem and it was generally accepted and liked that way. The Jews need a requiem, so let's try to give it to them. ... I wrote it from my heart and therefore it will find its way to their hearts.[36]

Zeisl's *Requiem* is among the first musical commemorations of the Holocaust and, because of its proximity to the event, one of the most effective. It was immediately successful, with more than 2,000 reportedly attending the premiere, and remains Zeisl's most popular work.[37] Praise from Toch and others encouraged Zeisl to write another Judaic choral piece, *Songs for the Daughter of Jephtha* (*Four Songs for Wordless Chorus*) (1948), completed while Zeisl was composer-in-residence at the Brandeis Camp Institute. In the biblical story, Jephthah's daughter is given two months to weep before her father carries out his promise to sacrifice her (Jdgs. 11:38). The four-movement piece explores that liminal timeframe, as Zeisl explained:

The cantata describes the difficult moods of the maiden in the mountains. "Lament" opens the tragedy. "Dance" brings a feeling of exhilaration, happy and sad simultaneously. "Evening Song" is a tender pastoral, like a farewell to life. "Halleluja," after a tragic introduction, leads to an agitated fugue which ends with a passionate expression of faith.[38]

THE COMPOSITION

Requiem Ebraico sets the Hebrew text of Psalm 92, which the Bible introduces as "A Psalm. A Song; for the sabbath day" (Ps. 92:1). Most scholars categorize the text as an individual thanksgiving psalm.[39] Of the 150 psalms of the Hebrew Bible, it is the only one ascribed to a specific day, and it holds a prominent place in the Friday evening *Kabbalat Shabbat* (Welcoming Shabbat) liturgy. Through the centuries, commentators have linked the psalm to Shabbat through its theme of thanksgiving. According to Israel Abrahams, a leading Jewish scholar of the late nineteenth century: "Its association with the Sabbath is found in its character as a thanksgiving psalm, eulogizing God's faithful providence and love in caring for our world, the marvelous works of His hands."[40] The psalm begins with a declaration, "It is good to give thanks to God," and recommends singing God's praises to the accompaniment of the *asor* and the *nevel*—ancient instruments often translated as "lute" and "harp" (although the precise instrument types are unknown) (vv. 2, 4).

The immediate question, then, is how Zeisl reinterpreted the text into a requiem. In his correspondence with Freudenthal at Transcontinental Music, Zeisl addressed the issue in some detail:

> I know that it is prominently the power of custom that want to see in [Psalm 92] a festive Sabbath song, but I could just as well argue that it would be bordering [on] the ridiculous [if] at the present time the Jews [were to] sing a festive song. With a heart full of tears, they nevertheless hold on to God and do not cease to thank Him and do not cease to hope. This is the message and consolation which I found in the 92nd Psalm. I can safely say that [over] the course of [the] ages the Jews have had . . . very [few] occasions for festive moods, countless for mourning, yet the 92nd Psalm has been sung every Sabbath. Could there be a timelier message than the passages sung by the cantor?[41]

In fact, the psalm is not as squarely focused on thanksgiving as most commentators contend. It is more properly understood as a mixed psalm, containing elements of thanksgiving (vv. 1–7), wisdom (vv. 7–9, 13–15), and petition (vv. 10–12). The petition sequence resonates very closely with Zeisl's reading and no doubt had special significance in the aftermath of the Holocaust and the defeat of the Third Reich: "Surely, Your enemies, O Lord, surely, Your enemies perish; all evildoers are scattered. . . . I shall see the defeat of my watchful foes, hear of the downfall of the wicked who beset me."

Requiem Ebraico builds on a modal, folk-like "Hebraic" melody in variation and fugue. Musical interest derives from the unconventional instrumentation, unpredictable harmonic movement, and frequent alterations between the instruments, chorus, and vocal soloists and duets. The piece opens quietly with a one-measure instrumental introduction of the primary theme played by a solo cello.[42] The meter is 6/4 and the tempo indication is "grave moderato." The chorus enters in the second measure with the melody carried by the sopranos. Beginning in B minor, the melody rises steadily in the first two bars from F# to B, and then by steps to F#, all set against a descending harmonic progression of B minor, A major, G# minor, and back to B minor. The soprano line in measure 2 is echoed by the tenors in measure 3, by the altos and tenors in measure 5, and by the basses in measure 7. The rising melodic line is typical of settings of sacred texts, as if directing the words to heaven, but the descending harmonic progression, combined with the minor tonality, produces a different color than might be expected.

This opening theme is a fairly simple eight-measure arc. Rising to an intermediate peak at the beginning of measure 3 (on the word "Adonai"), followed by a second peak at the end of measure 4 and the beginning of measure 5 (on the word "Elyon"), the line gradually descends through measures 5 to 9 as the chorus sings: "to relate your kindness each morning and your faithfulness each night." The dark tone is emphasized by the repetition of the words "each night" at the end of this first theme. The orchestration comprises a subdued string and wind accompaniment.

Next is a 17-measure repetition of the first words of the opening text, utilizing the same melodic theme. Basses, altos, and tenors trade off on the upward-moving first measure of the theme, "It is good to give thanks to *Adonai*," while the sopranos reinforce the downward movement of the harmony through a generally descending descant (F#–E–D/G–F#–E/F#–E–D/E–D–C#). The winds make their presence felt more strongly with echoes of the melody in the clarinet and oboe.

In the twelfth measure of this section (measure 21), a sudden change in dynamics from *piano* to *mezzo forte* accompanies a variation on the descending second half of the opening theme (from measures 5 to 9). The sopranos again carry the line while the other voices parallel the downward melodic drift, ending with a surprising cadence in B major.

From measures 26 to 40, an instrumental variation on the opening theme employs oboe, clarinet, flute, and English horn in melodic solos and duets over the strings. The lower strings repeat the ascending line of the first measure in octaves, and the section ends with a repeated downward motif in the winds (A#–G–F#) over a downward drift in the harmony (E major to D major), as the key ultimately modulates to G major in measure 41.

A second eight-measure theme begins in measure 41 and is first stated by an alto soloist singing, "to the music of the lute and the melody of the harp." Zeisl creates a pastoral feel with descending melodic lines in the flute and clarinet against softly weaving strings. The theme is distinguished by downward moving pitches followed by large upward leaps (a 4th, a major 9th, a minor 9th, and another major 9th).

The full chorus then enters *forte* for a ten-measure setting of "For you have gladdened me, Adonai with Your deeds; I will sing joyfully of the works of Your hands." The melodic material is again drawn from the first theme, but now in D major. The full orchestra accompanies, including timpani at the outset, French horns paralleling the female voices through the first phrase ("Your deeds"), and clarinet doing the same through the second phrase ("I will sing").

Another instrumental interlude follows, again employing the first theme. As the section concludes, the dynamics diminish and the texture thins with solo strings and clarinet. The key modulates from D major to E major, then abruptly moves to G# minor at measure 69. The meter also changes to 3/4 with the tempo indication *lento*.

Measures 69 through 112 comprise a baritone solo on the text:

> How great are Your deeds Adonai, how profound Your
> thoughts.
> The thoughtless cannot comprehend, the foolish cannot
> fathom:
> Though the wicked may flourish like grass and evildoers may
> blossom,
> they will be destroyed forever.

The basic melodic line begins with a simple eight-measure phrase (D#–D#–G#–D#, F–E–D#–D#), although it includes some *hazzanish* (cantorial) flourishes. The second phrase extends for twelve measures, starting with a four-measure climb (G#–C#–C#–D#–E) and then descending for eight bars (E–D#–C#–B, D–C#–B–A, C#–B–A–G#). The third phrase is expanded to nine measures by the repetition of the text, "doers of evil," accompanied by a harmonic progression from D diminished to C# minor, then B major to C augmented to C# minor. The final eight-measure phrase repeats the text, "will be destroyed forever," first in *forte* on a generally ascending pattern (G#–D#–E–G#), and then in *piano* at a slightly lower pitch (G#–C#–D#–G#). A six-measure instrumental interlude featuring cello and bass clarinet carries the piece to another choral section.

A new section is announced at measure 113 with chimes, brass, snare drum, and cymbals, leading to full orchestra and chorus. The text, "but You, Adonai, are exalted forever," is repeated three times, increasing in volume from *mezzo forte* to *fortissimo*. The melodic line climbs in pitch with each repetition, while the harmony progresses from D minor to D major in the first statement, Bb minor to F major in the second statement, and C# minor to G# minor in the final statement. From the climax at the end of the third statement, the chorus and orchestra gradually fade from *fortissimo* to *piano* over the course of measure 125 through 132, dissolving to a final chime.

At bar 133, the meter changes to 4/4 with the tempo marking "freely psalmodising." The baritone soloist resumes on the text:

> Your enemies, Adonai, Your enemies shall perish;
> All evildoers shall be dispersed.
> But me You have exalted; I am anointed with fresh oil.
> My eyes have seen the downfall of my foes;
> My ears have heard the destruction of those who would harm me.

The melodic line is again relatively simple, but the *hazzanish* flourishes increase. As the harmony progresses from G# minor to D# major, the phrasing expands from three two-measure phrases to a four-measure phrase and a final six-measure phrase.

At measure 150, the soprano soloist sings the initial theme for sixteen measures on the text:

> The righteous shall flourish like the palm tree,
> they will grow tall like a cedar in Lebanon.
> Planted in the house of Adonai,
> in the courtyards of our God, they will flourish.

The harmony starts in B major and progresses to F# major at bar 166, where the alto soloist joins and repeats the theme down a 4th while the soprano sings a new text, "they will be fruitful in old age, they will be robust and fresh," to melodic motifs culled from both the initial theme and the earlier alto solo.

Beginning at measure 185, the two female soloists repeat the text they had just sung alone, now in an extended duet. The melodic lines rise, and the dynamics increase as the harmony modulates to D major by measure 236. The last ten measures of the duet are *forte*, the rhythm slows through Zeisl's use of whole-note triplets, and a two-bar *rallentando* leads to a fugue in 3/4 beginning at measure 246.

The fugue subject is a seven-measure phrase recalling the initial theme of the piece. Like that initial theme, the first two intervals are a perfect 4th up, followed by a whole step up. Where the initial theme rose an octave in the first two measures, the fugue subject rises a 5th and then falls back to its starting pitch at the end of the second measure. The fugue also repeatedly uses the descending half-steps and whole steps that characterize the opening theme.

The text for the fugue is "Adonai is just, my Rock in whom there is no flaw." The basses deliver the first statement of the fugue subject, followed by tenors and altos. An eight-measure extension precedes the fugue statement by the sopranos, which starts at measure 276. Further alternating sections of development and fugue restatement occupy measures 277 through 368. At measure 369, the baritone soloist begins a restatement of the initial theme in whole notes, which spans another 40 measures. Against that solo, the chorus continues to sing the fugue theme and its development, initially in *piano* but gradually increasing until reaching *fortissimo* in measure 400. There, the tenors and basses restate the first two measures of the fugue subject, sopranos and altos do the same in the next two measures, followed by all voices in the last six measures repeating the motif of the second measure of the fugue in ever-accelerating rhythm (eighth and quarter notes, then all eighth notes, then eighth-note triplets) to a final cadence on D major.

EPILOGUE

Requiem Ebraico was a success from the outset. Norman H. Wright, the organist for the premiere, was reportedly so taken with the piece that he performed it with his church choir annually for several years thereafter.[43] The Canadian debut in Toronto on March 25, 1947, garnered enthusiastic reviews. The Santa Monica Symphony premiered the orchestral version on January 23, 1948.[44] The piece remains Zeisl's most popular and most frequently performed work. In recent decades, it has been performed by, among other ensembles, the Chicago Master Singers, the Cathedral Choral Society of Washington, DC, the Los Angeles Jewish Symphony and Los Angeles Zimriyah Chorale, the Israel Philharmonic Orchestra, the Vienna Philharmonic, and, most recently, the Moravian Philharmonic Orchestra during its 2017 tour of France.

Audiences continue to be drawn to the piece's clarity and message. As musicologist Michael Beckerman opines, the *Requiem* successfully straddles tradition and deviation, employing "unabashed directness, a penchant for rich textures, 'expressive' harmonies that sometimes recall the Baroque use of chords," and arriving at "some uncanny combination of the completely conventional with enough depth and subtlety to strike the listener as convincing and deeply moving."[45]

The most inventive aspect of the piece may be its demonstration of the fluidity of the Psalm 92 text. Synagogue-goers, accustomed to greeting Shabbat with energetic or uplifting settings of the psalm, would never view it as the appropriate basis for a requiem. But Zeisl stayed true to text, dramatizing its juxtapositions of hope, defeat, victory, mourning, and gratitude for continued life. His setting appropriately progresses from a temporary defeat of evil to a resilient faith in the triumph of righteousness. In exploring these textual themes, the piece exposes the multiple layers of emotion confronting those who survived the Holocaust, as well as those who mourn its victims. In doing so, Zeisl created a work that rewards multiple hearings.

The Zeisl family counts *Requiem Ebraico* among the composer's few successes on the American continent.[46] A prolific song composer in Vienna before the Anschluss, Zeisl was exiled before reaching professional maturation. His Hollywood career proved less glamorous or profitable than he had envisioned, and his tonal lyricism was out of sync with the modernist proclivities of the concert world. Like many émigré composers, he was frustrated by the lower status of composers in the United States—especially on the West Coast—compared to the celebrity they achieved in Austria and Europe more broadly. In the assessment of Ernst Krenek, a non-Jewish émigré whose music the Nazis deemed "degenerate," the composer was simply not a "living presence" in America.[47] Partly for this reason, Zeisl remained nostalgic for Europe and resisted complete cultural and social absorption in America.[48] It is, perhaps, no coincidence that *Job*, his unfinished projected *magnum opus*, was abandoned precisely when the story's protagonist arrives in America.[49]

In a 1950 interview with *Los Angeles Times* writer Albert Goldberg, Zeisl described feeling out of place in America, yet hopeful that his "foreign" voice might add something of value to the American public:

> I came to America in my early thirties, that is probably still young enough to undergo subtle changes in my personality. On the whole, however, I was a finished product of the old world. I could not change this even if I wanted to; it would only mean that I was trying to create from the surface rather than the core of my memories. America can find in my work . . . strong medicines against the ills of fate, to brew and which she may need one day. They are hers.[50]

CONCLUSION

More than eighty Hebrew services and 250 individual liturgical compositions were published in the United States
between 1925 and 1955, roughly three-fourths of them for the
Reform movement.[1] During that fertile period, tastes gradually shifted from the "Protestant" style enshrined in the *Union
Hymnal* and toward a consciously Jewish sonic vocabulary, which
blended age-old Ashkenazi signatures with twentieth-century
musical techniques. For the most part, the new compositions
retained the choir-organ model of the hymnal (albeit in a more
"ethnic" vein), but also restored the historic role of the cantor/
soloist. Eric Werner, an Austrian composer and musicologist who
immigrated to the United States in 1938, credited the modern
renaissance of synagogue music, as it came to be known, to émigré
musicians, scholars, and composers, many of whom were involved
with the New York-based Jewish Music Forum:

> When, in 1933, the first refugees from Germany arrived, the
> stage was set, the time was ripe, and the audience was ready
> for a new concept of synagogue music. It had formed itself, or

emerged, in three originally separate circles which gradually grew into one, albeit not quite homogeneous, group of musicians, composers and musical scholars committed to the revival of synagogue music in America.[2]

Central European émigrés built on the efforts of earlier immigrants from Eastern Europe, who had begun introducing indigenous Jewish sounds into the synagogue, drawn from Yiddish theater, folk tunes, modal liturgical chants, and nineteenth-century European synagogue composers. Most of their works were composed or published in New York, the center of American Jewish life. These included services by Lazare Saminsky, the Russian-born music director of New York's Temple Emanu-El. In 1929, Saminksy and his Choir Committee initiated a project for the "purification and performance of new choral synagogue services by representative composers of the United States—and then possibly also eminent Hebrew composers on the European continent," leading to the "revival of [new] Hebrew synagogue music in America."[3] In addition to writing liturgical music, Saminsky commissioned new settings from established and emerging composers of Jewish lineage.

Saminsky's mission was replicated on the West Coast by Cantor Rueben Rinder at Congregation Emanu-El in San Francisco and Rabbi Jacob Sonderling at the Society of Jewish Culture–Fairfax Temple in Los Angeles. Rinder commissioned Ernest Bloch's *Avodath Hakodesh* (1933) and Darius Milhaud's *Service sacré* (1947), widely regarded as the two crowning achievements of twentieth-century synagogue song, as well as shorter pieces from other renowned composers of Jewish descent. Rabbi Sonderling commissioned works from four refugee composers: Arnold Schoenberg's *Kol Nidre* (1938), Ernst Toch's *Cantata of the Bitter Herbs* (1938), Erich Wolfgang Korngold's *A Passover Psalm* (1941) and *Prayer* (1941), and Eric Zeisl's *Requiem Ebraico* (1945).

For a variety of reasons, including rehearsal demands, performance requirements, changing musical tastes of Jewish congregations, and the wealth of new synagogue music written since 1945, the Sonderling pieces never became a regular part of synagogue services. Unlike Bloch's *Avodath Hakodesh*, which included individual prayer settings that could be extracted and sung by choirs during services, Sonderling's commissions had little direct impact on the American synagogue. Only Zeisl's *Requiem Ebraico* and, to a lesser extent, Toch's *Cantata of the Bitter Herbs* and Korngold's *A Passover Psalm*, have enjoyed continued life in the concert hall or on the radio. Nevertheless, the high-profile commissions helped inspire others to pursue "cultured music" in the synagogue, bringing the artistic standards of concert music into the generally utilitarian arena of Jewish ritual. The existence of these works, if not the music itself, was well known among cantors, music directors, and synagogue musicians, and furthered the cause of elevating synagogue song to the status of art music.

In contrast to the practicality and accessibility of most Jewish liturgical music, the Sonderling commissions were as much an outlet for the composers' own emotions and conflicted Jewish identities as they were interpretations of sacred texts. The composers, all secular in orientation, were unlikely candidates for such commissions. Yet, they embraced the opportunity to explore musically the tensions they felt as exiled artists in a strange land and as universalists who could not escape their own Jewishness. Outsiders to the worship experience, their contributions added new insights to old texts and inventive sounds to the conservative worship environment.

Rabbi Sonderling was uniquely suited to commission liturgical works from these composers. As the German-born leader of a predominantly German-speaking refugee congregation, Sonderling offered a comfortable venue of shared language, culture, and aesthetic values. Rather than shocking congregants with their highly individualized musical styles and approaches to the texts, Toch, Schoenberg, Korngold, and Zeisl were speaking to their own. Music was also central to Sonderling's desire to appeal to the five senses—an experiential application of his idiosyncratic brand of Neo-Chassidism. His enthusiasm in this regard attracted the composers who, for the most part, had difficulty finding receptive audiences in Los Angeles. Moreover, the rabbi's rationalist background resonated with the composers, who were experientially and ideologically distanced from Jewish religious folkways. It is hard to imagine these Viennese artists collaborating with a traditionally observant rabbi or, for that matter, such a rabbi seeking commissions from them.

Los Angeles likewise played an important role in facilitating these commissions. Not only did Sonderling cultivate an audience at Fairfax Temple, but the city itself was something of a Jewish musical tabula rasa. Removed from the major spheres of Jewish influence, Los Angeles Jewry was less beholden to established standards than were Jews in Eastern or Midwestern cities. Jewish immigrants and migrants had historically come West to start anew, establishing an ethos of independence that persisted into Sonderling's day. Despite sociopolitical upheavals and the later arrival of more traditionalist Jews, the city remained a bastion of experimentation and innovation—attributes Sonderling exploited in commissioning the four composers.

Like all Jewish music (or, for that matter, all music), the pieces Sonderling commissioned are of their time and place. They represent an important step toward bringing artistic values into American Judaism and forging a distinctly Jewish musical path—one that was not as transparently dominated by music of the church. Additionally, the presence of Toch, Schoenberg, Korngold, Zeisl, and other refugee composers helped elevate the

Article by Rabbi Sonderling, *Los Angeles Times Sunday Magazine*,
October 2, 1938.

cultural reputation of Los Angeles, both Jewish and non-Jewish, and paved the way for future generations of gifted synagogue composers. Rabbi Jacob Sonderling was a pioneer in the development of modern Jewish liturgical music and a force whose influence is still felt today.

NOTES

Preface

1. Reinhold Brinkmann and Christopher Wolff, eds., *Driven into Paradise: The Musical Migration from Nazi Germany to the United States* (Berkeley: University of California Press, 1999).

2. David Wallace, *Exiles in Hollywood* (Pompton Plains, NJ: Limelight, 2006).

3. Ehrhard Bahr, *Weimar on the Pacific: German Exile Culture in Los Angeles and the Crisis of Modernism* (Berkeley: University of California Press, 2007).

4. Dorothy Lamb Crawford, *A Windfall of Musicians: Hitler's Émigrés and Exiles in Southern California* (New Haven, CT: Yale University Press, 2008).

5. See also Michael Haas' book, *Forbidden Music: The Jewish Composers Banned by the Nazis* (New Haven, CT:

Yale University Press, 2013), and a recent biographical study, Lily E. Hirsch, *Anneliese Landau's Life in Music: Nazi Germany to Émigré California* (Rochester, NY: University of Rochester Press, 2019).

INTRODUCTION

1. Max Vorspan and Lloyd P. Gartner, *History of the Jews of Los Angeles* (San Marino, CA: Huntington Library, 1970), 5. See also Robert M. Fogelson, *The Fragmented Metropolis: Los Angeles, 1850–1930* (Berkeley: University of California Press, 1993).

2. Ibid., 5–6; Norton B. Stern, "The Location of Los Angeles Jewry at the Beginning of 1851," *Western States Jewish Historical Quarterly* 5, no. 1 (1972): 25–32; Max Vorspan and Sheldon Teitelbaum, "Los Angeles," in *Encyclopedia Judaica*, vol. 13, eds. Fred Skolnik and Michael Berenbaum (New York: Macmillan, 2007), 195.

3. William M. Kramer, "The Founding of the Organized Jewish Community of Greater Los Angeles," in *The Jews of Los Angeles: Urban Pioneers*, ed. Norton B. Stern (Los Angeles: Southern California Jewish Historical Society, 1981), 9.

4. Stephen H. Norwood and Eunice G. Pollack, eds., *Encyclopedia of American Jewish History*, vol. 1 (Santa Barbara: ABC-CLIO, 2008), 132.

5. Vorspan and Teitelbaum, "Los Angeles," 196.

6. See Hyman B. Grinstein, *The Rise of the Jewish Community of New York, 1654–1860* (Philadelphia: Jewish Publication Society, 1947), 471; and Norton B. Stern, "Jews in the 1870 Census of Los Angeles," in *The Jews of Los Angeles: Urban Pioneers*, ed. Norton B. Stern

(Los Angeles: Southern California Jewish Historical Society, 1981), 129.

7.   "Historical Resident Population City & County of Los Angeles, 1850 to 2010," Los Angeles Almanac, http://www.laalmanac.com/population/po02.htm.

8.   Bruce A. Phillips, "Los Angeles Jewry: A Demographic Portrait," *American Jewish Yearbook 86* (1986): 160.

9.   Ibid.

10. Zubin Mehta, *The Score of My Life* (New York: Hal Leonard, 2009), 63.

11. Los Angeles' vaudeville theaters in 1906 included the Orpheum, Empire, Novelty, Unique, Star, Garnet, Chutes, and Fischer's. Anthony Slide, *The Encyclopedia of Vaudeville* (Jackson: University of Mississippi Press, 2012), 325.

12. For a biography of Walter Henry Rothwell, see Jonathan L. Friedmann, *A City Haphazard: Jewish Musicians in Los Angeles, 1887–1927* (Washington, DC: Academica, 2017), 73–91.

13. Edwin Schallert, "Philharmonic Makes Debut; New Orchestra Raises Tone of Local Music," *Los Angeles Times*, October 25, 1919.

14. Bruno David Ussher, "Los Angeles Philharmonic Makes Its Debut," *Pacific Coast Musical Review*, October 25, 1919.

15. Bruno David Ussher, "Philharmonic Orchestra of Los Angeles Plays to Packed Houses," *Pacific Coast Musical Review*, November 8, 1919.

16. The art collection of the Los Angeles County Museum of History, Science, and Art eventually outgrew the

capacity of the building. In 1963, the art department relocated to its own museum in Hancock Park, the Los Angeles County Museum of Art. The Exposition Park location became the Natural History Museum of Los Angeles County at that time. See Hunter Drohojowska-Philp, *Rebels in Paradise: The Los Angeles Art Scene and the 1960s* (New York: Henry Holt, 2011).

17. Kenneth H. Marcus, *Musical Metropolis: Los Angeles and the Creation of a Music Culture, 1880–1940* (New York: Palgrave MacMillan, 2004), 3.

18. Ibid., 9.

19. See Josh Kun, ed., *Songs in the Key of Los Angeles: Sheet Music from the Collection of the Los Angeles Public Library* (Santa Monica, CA: Angel City, 2013).

20. Neal Gabler, *An Empire of Their Own: How the Jews Invented Hollywood* (New York: Anchor, 1989), 5.

21. See Thomas Doherty, *Hollywood and Hitler, 1933–1939* (New York: Columbia University Press, 2015); Helga Schreckenberger, "Salka Viertel's Transnational Hollywood Network," in *Networks of Refugees from Nazi Germany: Continuities, Reorientations, and Collaborations in Exile*, ed. Helga Schreckenberger (Boston: Brill, 2016), 161–78; and Donna Rifkind, *The Sun and Her Stars: Salka Viertel and Hitler's Exiles in the Golden Age of Hollywood* (New York: Other Press, 2020).

22. Jonathan L. Friedmann, *Jews, Music and the American West* (Santa Fe, NM: Gaon Press, 2016), 117.

23. Jerome H. Bayer, "The Future of Jewish Music," *The Menorah Journal* 5, no. 2 (1919): 112.

24. Musicologist Judah M. Cohen challenges the negative

perception of American Jewish music and its dependency on European models during the nineteenth century, citing several music collections produced at that time on American soil. However, these initiatives were undertaken in Chicago and the East Coast and do not appear to have reached California. Judah M. Cohen, *Jewish Religious Music in Nineteenth-Century America: Restoring the Synagogue Soundtrack* (Bloomington: Indiana University Press, 2019).

25. Bayer, "The Future of Jewish Music," 114.

26. Phillips, "Los Angeles Jewry," 160.

27. Kurt Streeter, "At 93, Rabbi Leonard Beerman still stirs passions with pacifist views," *Los Angeles Times*, November 26, 2014.

28. See Karen S. Wilson, ed., *Jews in the Los Angeles Mosaic* (Los Angeles: Autry National Center of the American West, 2013), and Jonathan L. Friedmann, *Jewish Los Angeles* (Charleston, SC: Arcadia, 2020).

29. Joseph J. Cummins, "Buy Absolutely nothing 'Made in Germany,'" *B'nai B'rith Messenger*, April 7, 1933. See Leonard Leader, "The *B'nai B'rith Messenger*: Reviewing the First 74 Years of the Newspaper's Community Service, 1897–1971," *Western States Jewish History* 47, no. 1 (2014): 31–46.

30. "Untermyer Scores Hitler's New Move; Tells Los Angeles Audience the German Step is Challenge to Civilized World," *New York Times*, March 13, 1935. New York attorney Samuel Untermyer warned the mass meeting of the Los Angeles Americanization League at Philharmonic Hall of the dangers of Germany's abandonment of the Treaty of Versailles.

31. Vorspan and Gartner, *History of the Jews of Los Angeles*, 206, and Ferenc Morton Szasz, *Religion in the Modern American West* (Tucson: University of Arizona Press, 2000), 76.

32. Mordecai Kaplan, quoted in Marc Lee Raphael, "Beyond New York: The Challenge to Local History," in *Jews of the American West*, eds. Moses Rischin and John Livingston (Detroit: Wayne State University Press, 1991), 58.

33. Jacob Sonderling, Yom Kippur sermon at the Embassy Auditorium, Los Angeles, 1946, quoted in Deborah Dash Moore, *To the Golden Cities: Pursuing the American Jewish Dream in Miami and L.A.* (Cambridge, MA: Harvard University Press, 1994), 51.

34. This discussion of Hollywood and Vienna derives in part from Jonathan L. Friedmann, "Was Max Steiner a Jew?" presented at the symposium, "Max Steiner: Man and Myth," California State University, Long Beach, February 24–25, 2018. The topic of antisemitism in Hollywood, particularly during the McCarthy era, is outside the scope and timeframe of this volume. See Joseph Litvak, *The Un-Americans: Jews, the Blacklist, and Stoolpigeon Culture* (Durham, NC: Duke University Press, 2009), and Reynold Humphries, *Hollywood's Blacklists: A Political and Cultural History* (Edinburgh: Edinburgh University Press, 2008).

35. Gabler, *An Empire of Their Own*, 1–7.

36. Barry Rubin, *Assimilation and Its Discontents* (New York: Random House, 1995), 40.

37. See Haas, *Forbidden Music*. The Institut zur Erforschung der Judenfrage (Institute for the Study of the Jewish

Question) sponsored the publication of an encyclopedia, *Lexikon der Juden in der Musik* (*Encyclopedia of
Jews in Music*), compiled by Theo Stengel and Herbert
Gerigk, that listed musicians, musicologists, librettists,
composers, conductors, publishers, and others in the
music world whom the Nazis identified as "Juden." The
encyclopedia was republished in five expanding volumes
between 1940 and 1944.

38. Barbara Zeisl Schoenberg, "The Reception of Austrian
Composers in Los Angeles," *Eric Zeisl: Austrian-
American Composer*, http://www.zeisl.com/essays-and-ar-
ticles/the-reception-of-austrian-composers-in-los-angeles.
htm.

39. Isadore Lied Khan, letter of recommendation for Rabbi
Dr. Jacob Sonderling, Agudath Achim, Chicago, IL,
June 1932.

40. *Landsmanshaft shuls* were especially widespread in
New York City during the period of mass migration
from Eastern Europe (1882–1924). The phenomenon
paralleled ethnic churches established by other immigrant populations. See William I. Thomas and Florian
Znaniecki, *The Polish Peasant in Europe and America*
(New York: Alfred A. Knopf, 1927).

41. Mordecai Kaplan, *The Future of the American Jew* (New
York: Macmillan, 1948), 116. See Bob Gluck, "Mordecai
Kaplan on Art, Artists, and Creativity" (paper delivered
at "Architect of the Jewish Future: A Conference on the
Life, Work, and Legacy of Rabbi Mordecai M. Kaplan,"
Georgetown University, Washington, DC, 2014).

42. Michael Haas, "Hitler's Musical 'Tabula Rasa'—
Restitution—Restoration" (PhD diss., Middlesex

University, London, 2017), 43.

43. Aubin-Louis Millin, "Le Sublime" [from *Dictionnaire des beaux-arts* (1806)], in *Music and Aesthetics in the Eighteenth and Early Nineteenth Centuries*, eds. Peter le Huray and James Day (Cambridge: Cambridge University Press, 1988), 208.

44. This phrase is taken from Albert Weisser, *The Modern Renaissance of Jewish Music: Events and Figures, Eastern Europe and America* (New York: Bloch, 1954).

45. See Verena Bopp, *MAILAMM 1932–1941: Die Geschichte einer Vereinigung zur Förderung jüdischer Musik in den USA* (Weisbaden: Harrassowitz, 2007).

CHAPTER 1

1. Jacob Sonderling, "Five Gates: Casual Notes for an Autobiography," *American Jewish Archives Journal* 16, no. 2 (1964): 107–8.

2. Alfred Gottschalk, "Ordination Address" (HUC-JIR, Los Angeles, May 16, 2004).

3. Jacob Sonderling, "This Is My Life" (Sonderling Papers, Jacob Rader Marcus Center of the American Jewish Archives, HUC-JIR, Cincinnati, OH), 1.

4. Steven D. Sonderling, interview by author, Los Angeles, October 27, 2017.

5. Sonderling, "This Is My Life," 1; Sonderling, "Five Gates," 107.

6. S. D. Sonderling, interview by author.

7. Ibid.; Sonderling, "This is My Life," 1.

8. Sonderling, "This Is My Life," 1.

9. Ibid.; Natan Slifkin, "The Most Fascinating Rabbi You've Never Heard Of," *Rationalist Judaism*, July 20, 2011, http://www.ratiuonalistjudaism.com/2011/07/most-fascinating-rabbi-youve-never.html.

10. Ibid.; Isadore Singer and S. Funk, "Placzek, Baruch Jacob," in *The Jewish Encyclopedia*, vol. 10, ed. Cyrus Adler (New York: Funk and Wagnalls, 1906), 69.

11. Sonderling, "This Is My Life," 1.

12. Ibid., 2; "Chief Rabbi Feuchtwang of Vienna Dies at 71," Jewish Telegraphic Agency, July 6, 1936.

13. Sonderling, "This Is My Life," 2.

14. Sonderling, "Five Gates," 107.

15. Sonderling, "This Is My Life," 2; Bibliothèque nationale (France), "Catalogue des Dissertations et écrits Académiques" (1905): 264.

16. Michael A. Meyer, *Response to Modernity: A History of the Reform Movement in Judaism* (Detroit: Wayne State University Press, 1995), 193.

17. Isaak Noah Mannheimer was not permitted to use the title of preacher or rabbi but was inducted in June 1825 as Direktor der Wiener K. K. Genehmigten Oeffentlichen Israelitischen Religionsschule (Director of the Vienna K. K. Approved Public Jewish Religious School).

18. The spread of the Vienna Rite was aided by the publication of Mannheimer's prayer book and Sulzer's *Schir Zion* (c. 1840).

19. Meyer, *Response to Modernity*, 193.

20. Sonderling, "This is My Life," 2.

21. Ibid.

22. Ibid.

23. "Rabbi Sonderling, Zionist Aided Herzl," *New York Times*, October 1, 1964.

24. See, for instance, Yoram Mayorek, "Herzl and the Dreyfus Affair," *The Journal of Israeli History* 15, no. 1 (1994): 83–89; and Shlomo Avineri, *Herzl: Theodor Herzl and the Foundation of the Jewish State* (London: Weidenfeld and Nicolson, 2013).

25. Marvin Perry and Frederick M. Schweitzer, *Antisemitism: Myth and Hate from Antiquity to the Present* (New York: Palgrave Macmillan, 2002), 146.

26. "Unsigned and Undated Notes" (Sonderling Papers, Jacob Rader Marcus Center of the American Jewish Archives, HUC-JIR, Cincinnati, OH), 1.

27. "Rabbi Jacob Sonderling, Herzl Co-worker, Dead on Coast at 85," Jewish Telegraphic Agency, October 2, 1964; "Rabbi Sonderling, Zionist Aided Herzl."

28. Mel Scult, ed., *Communings of the Spirit: The Journals of Mordecai M. Kaplan, vol. 1: 1913–1934* (Detroit: Wayne State University press, 2001), 207–8.

29. "Unsigned and Undated Notes," 1.

30. Jacob Sonderling, "Unpublished Notes," March 16, 1961 (Sonderling Papers, Jacob Rader Marcus Center of the American Jewish Archives, HUC-JIR, Cincinnati, OH), 4.

31. The New Israelite Temple Association, "Constitution of the Hamburg Temple (December 11, 1817)," in Paul R. Mendes-Flohr and Jehuda Reinharz, eds., *The Jew in the Modern World: A Documentary History* (New York: Oxford University Press, 1980), 145.

32. Max Nordau, quoted in Sonderling, "This is My Life," 3.

33. "Unsigned and Undated Notes," 1.

34. Ibid.

35. Sonderling, "Unpublished Notes," 8.

36. Ibid., 1.

37. Letter from Israelitischer Tempel-Verband in Hamburg, no addressee, January 12, 1923 (Sonderling Collection, Jewish Museum, Berlin).

38. For an early treatise on the beginnings of Reform Judaism, see Emmanuel Schreiber, *Reformed Judaism and Its Pioneers: A Contribution to Its History* (Spokane, WA: Spokane Printing, 1893).

39. Aleinu begins: "It is our duty to praise the master of all, to ascribe greatness to the author of creation, who has not made us like the nations of the lands, nor placed us like the families of the earth; who has not made our portion like theirs, nor our destinies like all their multitudes." See David Ellenson, "The Israelite Gebetbücher of Abraham Geiger and Manuel Joël: A Study in Nineteenth-Century German-Jewish Communal Liturgy and Religion," *Leo Baeck Institute Yearbook* 44 (1999): 143–64, and Ruth Langer "The Censorship of Aleinu in Ashkenaz and its Aftermath," in *The Experience of Jewish Liturgy: Studies Dedicated to Menahem Schmelzer*, ed. Debra Reed Blank (Boston: Brill, 2011), 147–66.

40. Sonderling, "Five Gates," 109.

41. Ibid.

42. Sonderling, "Unpublished Notes," 1–2.

43. Ibid., 2.

44. Ibid.

45. Joshua Leib Ne'eman, "Henle, Moritz," in *Encyclopedia Judaica*, vol. 8, eds. Fred Skolnik and Michael Berenbaum (New York: Macmillan, 2007), 808.

46. Sonderling, "This is My Life," 3–4.

47. Ibid., 3.

48. Leora Batnitzky, *How Judaism Became a Religion: An Introduction to Modern Jewish Thought* (Princeton, NJ: Princeton University Press, 2011), 5.

49. Ibid.

50. Ibid., 7.

51. Ibid., 49.

52. "Unsigned and Undated Notes," 3.

53. David Engel, "World War I," in *The YIVO Encyclopedia of Jews in Eastern Europe*, vol. 2, ed. Gershon David Hundert (New Haven, CT: Yale University Press, 2008), 2032.

54. "Unsigned and Undated Notes," 3; "Unsigned Biographical Summary" (Sonderling Papers, Jacob Rader Marcus Center of the American Jewish Archives, HUC-JIR, Cincinnati, OH), 1–2.

55. Sonderling, "This Is My Life," 4–5.

56. Scult, *Communings of the Spirit*, 208.

57. Jacob Sonderling, "Shalvi," unpublished manuscript (Sonderling Papers, Jacob Rader Marcus Center of the American Jewish Archives, HUC-JIR, Cincinnati, OH).

58. Ibid.

59. Sonderling, "This Is My Life," 5.

60. Scult, *Communings of the Spirit*, 208. Hermann Cohen was largely responsible for founding orthodox neo-Kantianism, which dominated academic philosophy in Germany from the 1870s until the end of World War I.

61. "Unsigned Biographical Summary," 2; "Unsigned and Undated Notes," 4.

62. See Nadine M. Marks, Heyjung Jun, and Jieun Song, "Death of Parents and Adult Psychological and Physical Well-Being: A Prospective U.S. National Study," *Journal of Family Issues* 28, no. 12 (2009): 1611–38.

63. Another explanation for Sonderling's departure from Hamburg is posited in Ruben Maleachi, "Die Synagogen in Hamburg," *Mitteilungen des Verbandes ehemaliger Breslauer und Schleiser in Israel* 45 (April–May 1979).

64. Sonderling, "Five Gates," 108.

65. Ibid., 113.

66. Ibid., 112.

67. Ibid.

68. Ibid., 111–12.

69. A letter of reference from Agudath Achim president Isadore Lied Khan, dated June 1932 and held in the Sonderling Collection at the Jewish Museum in Berlin, states that Sonderling was rabbi of the congregation "during the years 1924 and 1925." Written seven years after the fact, this is likely inaccurate. The history of the congregation, posted on its website, and Sonderling, "Five Gates," assert that his tenure was 1923–1925.

70. "History of Agudas Achim," Agudas Achim, https://www.agudasachimnsc.org/history/index.html.

71. Sonderling, "Five Gates," 112.

72. Ibid., 113.

73. "History of Agudas Achim"; Sonderling, "Five Gates," 112–13.

74. Scult, *Communings of the Spirit*, 207–9.

75. Ibid.

76. Sonderling, "Five Gates," 113.

77. "History," Temple Beth El of Manhattan Beach, http://templebethelmb.org/history.

78. Sonderling, "Five Gates," 114; untitled article, *Jewish Daily Bulletin*, May 26, 1927, 2.

79. "Temple Israel of Washington Heights," New York City Organ Project, https://www.nycago.org/Organs/NYC/html/TempleIsraelWHts.html.

80. Sonderling, "Five Gates," 116.

81. "Temple Israel of Washington Heights."

82. Sonderling, "Five Gates," 116.

83. I. Berger, Letter to Jacob Sonderling, June 4, 1931 (Sonderling Collection, Jewish Museum, Berlin).

84. Eleanor F. Horvitz, "Temple Beth-Israel 1921–1981," *Rhode Island Jewish Historical Notes* 9 (1983): 30–67, 34–36.

85. Sonderling, "Five Gates," 118; Berger, letter to Jacob Sonderling.

86. Horvitz, "Temple Beth-Israel 1921–1981," 34.

87. Sonderling, "Five Gates," 118.

88. Ibid., 119.

89. Ibid.

90. Ibid.

91. "Aesthetic Judaism," *Daily Jewish Courier*, January 6, 1924.

92. Sonderling, "Five Gates," 120.

93. "To Hold New Religious Service in Full Dress," Jewish Telegraphic Agency, August 30, 1932.

94. Rabbi Jacob Rader Marcus (1896–1995) was the first American-born trained historian of Judaism and the founder of the American Jewish Archives (est. 1947). He was a professor at HUC-JIR in Cincinnati, which houses the Jacob Rader Marcus Center of the American Jewish Archives.

95. Jacob Sonderling, letter to Jacob R. Marcus, June 4, 1961 (Sonderling Papers, Jacob Rader Marcus Center of the American Jewish Archives, HUC-JIR, Cincinnati, OH).

96. The two-page program is held in the Sonderling Collection of the Jewish Museum in Berlin.

97. Murray Phillips (1889–1942) was an actor, agent, and producer of many plays for the New York stage. Joseph Yasser (1893–1981) was organist at Rodeph Shalom from 1929 through 1960 and a musicologist whose most important work is *A Theory of Evolving Tonality* (New York: American Library of Musicology, 1932).

98. It is unclear whether the Ma'ariv included the Bar'chu and/or Ma'ariv Aravim.

99. "To Hold New Religious Service in Full Dress."

100. Ibid.

101. Henry Beckett, "Rabbi to Appeal to All 5 Senses,"

purportedly from the *New York Evening Post*, according to a handwritten notation (Sonderling Collection, Jewish Museum, Berlin).

102. Ibid.

103. See Arthur Green, "Renewal and Havurah: American Movements, European Roots," in *Jewish Renaissance and Revival in America: Essays in Memory of Leah Levitz Fishbane*, eds. Eitan Fishbane and Jonathan D. Sarna (Waltham, MA: Brandeis University Press, 2011), 147–48.

104. Compare, for instance, Jacob Sonderling, "A Rabbi Tells of God," *New Outlook* (September 1954): 15–19, which shares stories of the Baal Shem Tov, founder of Chassidic Judaism, and Martin Buber's anthologies of Chassidic lore, including *The Legend of the Baal-Shem*, trans. Maurice Friedman (Princeton: Princeton University Press, 1955).

105. See Judah M. Cohen, "A Holy Brother's Liberal Legacy: Shlomo Carlebach, Reform Judaism and Hasidic Pluralism," *American Jewish History* 100, no. 4 (2016): 485–509.

106. Sonderling, Letter to Jacob Marcus.

107. "Rabbi Sonderling in Town Hall Services," Jewish Telegraphic Agency, September 10, 1933.

108. Ibid.

109. "Raise $65,000 at Los Angeles Jewish Appeal," Jewish Telegraphic Agency, July 18, 1934.

110. Sonderling, "This Is My Life," 5.

111. "Unsigned and Undated Biographical Summary," 2.

112. "Unsigned and Undated Notes," 5.

113. See George Sanchez, "'What's Good for Boyle Heights Is Good for Jews': Creating Multiculturalism on the Eastside During the 1950s," *American Quarterly* 56, no. 3 (2004): 633–61.

114. Richardo Romo, *East Los Angeles: History of a Barrio* (Austin: University of Texas Press, 2010), 95.

115. Daniel Katter, "Los Angeles, West Side and San Fernando Valley Jewish Enclaves (California)," in *America's Changing Neighborhoods: An Exploration of Diversity through Places*, vol. 2, ed. Reed Ueda (Santa Barbara, CA: Greenwood, 2017), 807–11. For postwar developments in Los Angeles' Jewish communities, see Moore, *To the Golden Cities*.

116. Vorspan and Gartner, *History of the Jews of Los Angeles*, 209.

117. Ibid.

118. Ibid., 209, 212.

119. Ibid., 215.

120. Jacob J. Meltz, ed., *Mount Sinai Yearbook of 1946* (Los Angeles: Associated Organizations of Los Angeles, 1946), 60.

121. Ibid.

122. Lynn C. Kronzek, "Fairfax: A Home, A Community, A Way of Life," *Legacy: Journal of the Jewish Historical Society of Southern California* 1, no. 4 (1990): 26.

123. Amos Elon, *The Pity of It All: A Portrait of the German-Jewish Epoch, 1743–1933* (New York: Henry Holt, 2003), 110–12.

124. Mordecai M. Kaplan, *Judaism as a Civilization* (New York: Macmillan, 1934).

125. "Unsigned and Undated Notes," 5; "Unsigned Biographical Summary," 2.

126. The Carthay Circle Theatre was used by a number of embryonic Jewish organizations, including Temple Beth Am.

127. Zemach worked as a choreographer, director, and acting teacher in Los Angeles from 1932 through 1935, and again from 1948 to 1971. Many of his dance pieces involved Jewish themes (e.g., *Fragments of Israel*, *Ruth*, and *Farewell to Queen Sabbath*) and were performed in major venues, such as the Hollywood Bowl and Carnegie Hall. Zemach collaborated with Zeisl on the ballet *Jacob and Rachel* (1954).

128. Brecher was a Czech actor and director of Vienna's Stadttheater before moving to Hollywood in the late 1920s. He appeared in a number of classic horror films, including *Mark of the Vampire* (1935) and *So Dark the Night* (1946).

129. Kronzek, "Fairfax," 23.

130. Ibid., 26.

131. The Sonderling Papers, housed at the Jacob Rader Marcus Center of the American Jewish Archives at HUC-JIR in Cincinnati, include sermons from 1946 to 1947. A list of contents is found at http://collections.americanjewisharchives.org/ms/ms0582/ms0582.html.

132. Max Nussbaum, "Jacob Sonderling," *Proceedings of the Central Conference of American Rabbis* 75 (1965): 158.

133. Ibid.

134. "Orchestra Tickets from Society for Jewish Culture, 1944 and 1946," Los Angeles Museum of the Holocaust, http://www.lamoth.info/?p=digitallibrary/ digitalcontent&id=3138.

135. Meltz, *Mount Sinai Yearbook of 1946*, 60. Fairfax Temple may have actually been affiliated with the Conservative Movement at some point. A January 9, 1948, *Los Angeles Times* article lists the temple among the "Conservative Jewish congregations allied with the United Synagogue of America."

136. Kronzek, "Fairfax," 26.

137. "Finding Aid for the Alfred Leonard and Joseph Leonard Collection, 1902–2001," Online Archive of California, https://oac.cdlib.org/findaid/ark:/13030/tf18700458/. Collection housed at UCLA: Special Collections, Performing Arts.

138. "The Oriental and Occidental Beliefs, Expressed through the Arts," Hollywood Inter-Faith Forum, newspaper advertisement, April 1946.

139. "Finding Aid for the Alfred Leonard and Joseph Leonard Collection, 1902–2001."

140. Sonderling, Letter to Jacob R. Marcus.

141. Alfred Sendrey authored four books: *David's Harp: The Story of Music in Biblical Times*, with Mildred Norton (New York: New American Library, 1964), *Music in Ancient Israel* (New York: Philosophical Library, 1969), *The Music of the Jews in the Diaspora (up to 1800): A Contribution to the Social and Cultural History of the Jews* (New York: T. Yoseloff, 1971), and *Music in the Social and Religious Life of Antiquity* (Rutherford, NJ: Farleigh

Dickinson University Press, 1974), and compiled the still valuable *Bibliography of Jewish Music* (New York: Columbia University Press, 1951).

142. The Brandeis Camp Institute opened in 1947 and was named for Supreme Court Justice Louis D. Brandeis (1856–1941). The camp was renamed Brandeis-Bardin Institute in 1977 to honor its founder, Shlomo Bardin (1898–1976). In 2007, the campus was acquired by the American Jewish University (formerly University of Judaism).

143. "Announcement of Courses," 1957–'58, 1958–'59, 1959–'60, 1960–'61, and 1961–'62 (HUC-JIR Archives, Los Angeles).

144. Gottschalk, "Ordination Address."

145. "Rabbi Jacob Sonderling," unpublished (Sonderling Collection, Jewish Museum, Berlin), 2.

146. "Brandeis Camp Institute Flyer 1960," Online Archive of California, https://oac.cdlib.org/ark:/13030/kt0b69r60k/?brand=oac4.

147. See Philip Moddel, *Max Helfman: A Biographical Sketch* (Berkeley, CA: Judah L. Magnes Memorial Museum, 1974), 39; Jonathan L. Friedmann, "Max Helfman in California: Creating Jewish Music, 1947–1963," *Western States Jewish History* 42, no. 1 (2009): 33–44; Friedmann, *Jews, Music, and the American West*, 121–23; and Bruce J. Powell, "Shlomo Bardin's 'Eretz' Brandeis," in *California Jews*, eds. Ava F. Kahn and Marc Dollinger (Hanover, MA: Brandeis University Press, 2003), 171–84.

148. "Rabbi Sonderling, Zionist Aided Herzl."

149. Nussbaum, "Jacob Sonderling," 158.

CHAPTER 2

1. Salomon Sulzer, *Schir Zion* (Wien: Artaria and Co., c. 1840).

2. Tina Frühauf, *Salomon Sulzer: Reformer, Cantor, Icon* (Berlin: Hentrich and Hentrich, 2012), 30–31. Discussion of Sulzer's commissioning of Franz Schubert's *Tov L'hodos* is drawn from Jonathan L. Friedmann, "Groping for the Greats: The Strange Musical Claims of Nathan Ausubel," *Journal of Modern Jewish Studies* 15, no. 1 (2016): 444.

3. Neil W. Levin, liner notes to *Vol. 7: Masterworks of Prayer*, Milken Archive of Jewish Music (2011), digital album; Frühauf, *Salomon Sulzer*, 40.

4. Frühauf, *Salomon Sulzer*, 30.

5. Eduard Birnbaum, "Franz Schubert als Synagogenkomponist," *Allgemeine Zeitung des Judentums* 61 (1897): 6. This assessment is perhaps overstated, as Eduard Birnbaum was a noted synagogue music purist.

6. For Sulzer's impact on synagogue music in Europe and the United States, see Jonathan L. Friedmann, "Sulzerism, Sulzermania, and the Shaping of the American Cantorate," *American Jewish History* 101, no. 2 (2017): 287–306.

7. See, for instance, Frances Milton Trollope, *Vienna and the Austrians: With Some Account of a Journey through Swabia, Bavaria, the Tyrol, and the Salzbourg* (London: R. Bentley, 1838), 373, 379; Franz Liszt, *The Gipsy in*

Music, Vol. 1, trans. Edwin Evans (London: W. Reeves, 1926), 52–53; Benjamin Franklin Peixotto, "Solomon Sulzer: Reminiscences of Vienna," *Menorah Journal* 8 (1890): 260–64; and Adolph Guttman, "The Life of Salomon Sulzer," *Year Book of the Central Conference of American Rabbis* 13 (1903): 227–36.

8.   Frühauf, *Salomon Sulzer*, 63.

9.   The Consistoire Israélite was established as part of the Imperial Decree of March 17, 1808, which prescribed measures for the regulation of the Jewish communities of France.

10. See Eliyahu Schleifer, *Samuel Naumbourg: The Cantor of French Jewish Emancipation* (Berlin: Hentrich and Hentrich, 2012).

11. Ibid, 19–27.

12. Russian: Obshchestvo Evreiskoi Narodnoi Muzyki; Yiddish: Gezelshaft far Yidisher Folks-Muzik.

13. See James Loeffler, "Society for Jewish Folk Music," in *The YIVO Encyclopedia of Jews in Eastern Europe*, vol. 2, ed. Gershon David Hundert (New Haven, CT: Yale University Press, 2008), 1170–71; and James Loeffler, *The Most Musical Nation: Jews and Culture in the Late Russian Empire* (New Haven, CT: Yale University Press, 2010).

14. Saminsky was also a prolific speaker and writer on musical topics. He published a collection of essays: *Music of the Ghetto and the Bible* (New York: Bloch, 1934).

15. Hugo D. Weisgall, "Jewish Music in America," *Judaism: A Quarterly Journal of Jewish Life and Thought* 3, no. 4 (1954): 427–36.

16. Neil W. Levin, "Lazare Saminsky," Milken Archive of Jewish Music, http://www.milkenarchive.org/artists/view/lazare-saminsky/.

17. The figure exceeded $7,000 in today's value.

18. "Contest Announcement," *Musical Leader*, July 7, 1927.

19. Benjie-Ellen Schiller, "The Hymnal as an Index of Musical Change in the Reform Synagogue," in *Sacred Sound and Social Change: Liturgical Music in Jewish and Christian Experience*, eds. Lawrence A. Hoffman and Janet R. Walton (Notre Dame, IN: Notre Dame University Press, 1992), 201–2.

20. Friedmann, *Jews, Music and the American West*, 60.

21. Rabbi Jacob Voorsanger of Temple Emanu-El, San Francisco, quoted in Fred Rosenbaum, *Cosmopolitans: A Social and Cultural History of the Jews of the San Francisco Bay Area* (Berkeley: University of California Press, 2009), 104.

22. Friedmann, *Jews, Music and the American West*, 60.

23. Irene Heskes, *Passport to Jewish Music: Its History, Traditions, and Culture* (New York: Tara, 1994), 306.

24. One hundred twenty-five pieces commissioned by Putterman are anthologized in David Putterman, comp., *Mizmor L'David: An Anthology of Synagogue Music* (New York: Cantors Assembly, 1979).

25. Levin, liner notes to *Vol. 7*.

26. David Putterman, "The Academy's Place in Jewish Life," *The Jewish Music Forum Bulletin* 5, no. 1 (1944): 23–24.

27. Harry Coopersmith, comp., *The Songs We Sing* (New

York: The United Synagogue Commission on Jewish Education, 1950).

28. Ibid., vii.

29. Ibid. *The Songs We Sing* received six printings through 1965. A second volume was published in 1970: Harry Coopersmith, comp., *More of the Songs We Sing* (New York: The United Synagogue Commission on Jewish Education, 1970).

30. Heskes, *Passport to Jewish Music*, 307.

CHAPTER 3

1. Michael Haas, "The 'Geographical' Journey of Dr. Ernst Toch," *Forbidden Music*, June 11, 2014, https://forbiddenmusic.org/2014/06/11/the-geographical-journey-of-dr-ernst-toch/.

2. Crawford, *A Windfall of Musicians*, 135.

3. Haas, "The 'Geographical' Journey of Dr. Ernst Toch."

4. Ibid.

5. Neil W. Levin, "Ernst Toch," Milken Archive of Jewish Music, https://www.milkenarchive.org/artists/view/ernst-toch.

6. Ivan Hewitt, "Swept Away, Kings Place, review," *The Telegraph*, June 21, 2015, https://www.telegraph.co.uk/culture/music/classicalconcertreviews/11685727/Swept-Away-Kings-Place-review-astonishingly-ambitious.html.

7. Haas, "The 'Geographical' Journey of Dr. Ernst Toch."

8. Benno Elkan's menorah was donated to Israel by members of the British Parliament on April 5, 1956. The seven branches depict symbols, figures, and events of

Jewish history and traditions.

9.   Thomas Patterson, *Instruments for New Music: Sound, Technology and Modernism* (Berkeley: University of California Press, 2016), 18.

10. Erich Steinhard, "Donaueschingen: Mechanisches Musikfest," *Der Auftakt* 6, no. 8 (1926): 183.

11. Ernst Toch, "Musik für mechanische Instrumente," *Musikblätter des Anbruch* 8, nos. 8–9 (1926): 346–47.

12. Crawford, *A Windfall of Musicians*, 138.

13. Michael Haas, "The 'Geographical' Journey of Dr. Ernst Toch."

14. Alan Lessem, "The Refugee Composer in America: A Topic for Twentieth-Century Music History," *Canadian University Music Review* 6 (1985): 229. Like many composers of the era, Toch could not entirely avoid the twelve-tone system, which he employed in his 1953 String Quartet, op. 74.

15. Albert Goldberg, "The Sounding Board," *Los Angeles Times*, January 24, 1954.

16. Ernst Toch, "The Credo of a Composer," *Deutsche Blätter*, April 1945.

17. Lessem, "The Refugee Composer in America," 231.

18. Crawford, *A Windfall of Musicians*, 139. Upon learning that Aaron Copland had listed him as a "film composer" in his book, *Our New Music: Leading Composers in Europe and America* (New York: McGraw-Hill, 1941), Toch wrote Copland an angry letter demanding that he correct the error in the next edition. Ernst Toch, letter to Aaron Copland, April 9, 1942.

19. Lessem, "The Refugee Composer in America," 232.

20. Haas, "The Geographical' Journey of Dr. Ernst Toch."

21. Ernst Toch, "How *Cantata of the Bitter Herbs* Was Created," *The Amor Artis Bulletin* 2, no. 1 (December 1962). Despite his secular orientation, Toch carried a Jewish prayer book from his youth with him through his various migrations. Haas, "Hitler's Musical 'Tabula Rasa,'" 41.

22. Ibid.

23. Ibid.

24. Hans Nathan, *Israeli Folk Music: Songs of the Early Pioneers* (Madison, WI: A-R Editions, 1994).

25. Ibid., xii.

26. Neil W. Levin, liner notes to *Ernst Toch: Cantata of the Bitter Herbs* and *Jephta, Rhapsodic Poem*, Naxos American Classics 8.559417, 2004, compact disc. Dorothy Lamb Crawford writes that the *Cantata* "was first performed at a Hanukkah celebration for children," presumably confusing the initial discussions of new Hanukkah music with the *Cantata* itself, which deals with and premiered during Passover. Crawford, *A Windfall of Musicians*, 140.

27. Ernst Toch, "How Cantata of the Bitter Herbs Was Created."

28. Isaac Landman, ed., *The Universal Jewish Encyclopedia in Ten Volumes*, vol. 7 (New York: Universal Jewish Encyclopedia, 1947), 656.

29. See Boris Morros, *My Ten Years as a Counterspy: As Told to Charles Samuels* (New York: Viking, 1959).

30. Toch, "How *Cantata of the Bitter Herbs* Was Created."

31. Jacob Sonderling, "The Jews Are Changing Their Music," *Los Angeles Times Sunday Magazine*, October 2, 1938.

32. Toch, "How *Cantata of the Bitter Herbs* Was Created."

33. Ibid.

34. Ibid.

35. Sonderling, "The Jews Are Changing Their Music."

36. Ibid.

37. It is surprising that the orchestra, chorus, and congregants sitting at *seder* tables could all fit in the small Fairfax Temple, but writings from both Sonderling and Toch indicate that they did.

38. Toch, "How *Cantata of the Bitter Herbs* Was Created."

39. The analysis that follows is an aural one based on the Milken Archive of Jewish Music's Naxos American Classics recording by the Czech Philharmonic Orchestra and the Prague Philharmonic Choir, with Gerard Schwarz conducting and Theodore Bikel as narrator. Gerard Schwarz, *Cantata of the Bitter Herbs*, Naxos American Classics 8.559417, 2004, compact disc.

40. Crawford, *A Windfall of Musicians*, 136.

41. Ernst Toch, *The Shaping Forces in Music: An Inquiry into the Nature of Harmony, Melody, Counterpoint, Form* (New York: Criterion, 1948), ii.

42. The "full" *Hallel*, consisting of Psalms 113–118, is customarily chanted in synagogue on Sukkot, the first day of Passover, Shavuot, and (in some synagogues) Rosh Chodesh. The "half" *Hallel*, excluding Psalms 115:1–11

and 116:1–11, is more typically chanted on Rosh
Chodesh and on the other six days of Passover.

43.   Joseph Tabory, *JPS Commentary on the Haggadah*
(Philadelphia: Jewish Publication Society, 2008), 102.

44.   Ibid., 99.

45.   Lawrence A. Hoffman and David Arnow, eds., *My
People's Passover Haggadah: Traditional Texts, Modern
Commentaries, Volume 2* (Woodstock, VT: Jewish Lights,
2008), 48.

46.   Tabory, *JPS Commentary on the Haggadah*, 122.

47.   Ibid., 86. The Passover Haggadah includes four questions
told by four archetypal sons (or children): the wise son,
the wicked son, the simple son, and the son who doesn't
know how to ask.

48.   Ibid., 105.

49.   Ibid., 102.

50.   See Eric Werner, "The Tunes of the Haggadah," *Studies
in Bibliography and Booklore* 7 (1965): 77.

51.   Diane Sonderling Gray, interview by author, Los
Angeles, August 9, 2017.

52.   Neil W. Levin, "Nathaniel Shilkret," Milken Archive of
Jewish Music, https://www.milkenarchive.org/artists/
view/nathaniel-shilkret/.

53.   Nathaniel Shilkret, letter to Anne Shilkret, November
26, 1945. On May 29 and 31, 2008, *Genesis Suite* had its
first complete performance since 1945. Gerard Schwarz
conducted the Seattle Symphony Orchestra and the
University of Washington Chorale. The concert used a
reconstructed score, as the original had been lost in a fire.

54. Neil W. Levin, liner notes to *Genesis Suite, Volume 17: Odes and Epics*, Milken Archive of Jewish Music, https://www.milkenarchive.org/music/volumes/view/odes-and-epics/work/genesis-suite/.

55. German-Jewish writer Lion Feuchtwanger, who had settled in Los Angeles in 1941, turned the story of Jephthah's daughter into a novel in 1957, *Jefta und seine Tochter* (*Jephthah and His Daughter*).

56. Crawford, *A Windfall of Musicians*, 134.

57. Lessem, "The Refugee Composer in America," 225.

58. For example, Mark Katz, "Hindemith, Toch, and Grammophonmusik," *Journal of Musicological Research* 20, no. 2 (2001): 161–80; Carmel Raz, "From Trinidad to Cyberspace: Reconsidering Ernst Toch's 'Geographical Fugue,'" *Zeitschrift der Gesellschaft für Musiktheorie* 9, no. 2 (2012): 227–73; C. Nichole Grass, "The Wind Chamber Works of Ernst Toch: A History and Comparative Analysis" (D.M. diss., University of South Carolina, 2013); and Carmel Raz, "The Lost Movements of Ernst Toch's Gesprochene Musik," *Current Musicology* 97 (2014): 37–59. Two earlier studies should also be noted: Diane Peacock Jezik, *The Musical Migration of Ernst Toch* (Ames: Iowa State University Press, 1989), and Miriam Susan Zach, "The Opera Works of Ernst Toch" (M.M. thesis, University of Florida, 1990).

59. The selections were played from the Milken Archive's Naxos recording, with Gerard Schwarz conducting the Czech Philharmonic Orchestra and Prague Philharmonic Choir, and Theodore Bikel narrating.

60. "Itzhak Perlman celebrates Passover with a 'Musical

Feast,'" Classical MPR, March 28, 2018, https://www.
classicalmpr.org/story/2018/03/27/a-musical-feast-for-
passover-with-itzhak-perlman.

CHAPTER 4

1. For a recent biography and critical assessment, see Mark
   Berry, *Arnold Schoenberg* (London: Reaktion, 2019).

2. Pamela Cynthia White, *Schoenberg and the God-Idea: The
   Opera* Moses und Aron (Ann Arbor, MI: YMI Research,
   1985), 51.

3. See Boaz Tarsi, "*Moses and Aaron* as a Reflection of
   Arnold Schoenberg's Spiritual Quest," *Musica Judaica*
   12 (1991–1992): 52–64.

4. Edwin Evans, "Schönberg, Arnold," *Grove's Dictionary
   of Music and Musicians*, vol. 5, ed. H. C. Colles (New
   York: Macmillan, 1939), 571.

5. Malcolm MacDonald, *Schoenberg*, 2nd ed. (Oxford:
   Oxford University Press, 2008), 93.

6. Bluma Goldstein, *Reinscribing Moses: Heine, Kafka,
   Freud, and Schoenberg in a European Wilderness*
   (Cambridge, MA: Harvard University Press, 1992), 138.

7. By the first decade of the twentieth century, Viennese
   Jews, who accounted for less than 10 percent of the city's
   population, comprised 71 percent of its financiers, 63
   percent of its industrialists, 65 percent of its lawyers,
   and 59 percent of its physicians. Perry and Schweitzer,
   Antisemitism, 84–85.

8. Bruce F. Pauley, *The Habsburg Legacy: 1867–1939* (New
   York: Holt, Rinehart and Winston, 1972), 169.

9. Marsha L. Rozenblit, *Jews of Vienna, 1867–1914:*

Assimilation and Identity (Albany: SUNY Press, 1984), 137–38.

10. Ibid., 136.

11. White, *Schoenberg and the God Idea*, 51.

12. Arnold Schoenberg, letter to Marya Freund, December 30, 1922, reprinted in Erwin Stein, ed., *Arnold Schoenberg Letters* (Berkeley: University of California Press, 1987), 82.

13. See Arnold Schoenberg, "Opinion or Insight?" (1926). Republished in Leonard Stein, ed., *Style and Idea: Selected Writings of Arnold Schoenberg*, trans. Leo Black (New York: St. Martin's, 1975), 258–264. Despite Schoenberg's objections to the term "atonal" on semantic grounds, the term is regularly used to describe his music from this period. Aaron Copland, *The New Music, 1900–1960* (New York: W. W. Norton, 1968), 43–44.

14. James Huneker, "Schoenberg: Musical Anarchist Who Has Upset Europe," *New York Times*, January 19, 1913.

15. Copland's use of the twelve-tone system is perhaps best represented in *Connotations*, commissioned by Leonard Bernstein to commemorate the opening of Philharmonic Hall in New York in 1962. Copland wrote that the technique enabled him to express "something of the tensions, aspirations and drama inherent in the world today." Aaron Copland, quoted in Emily Abrams Ansari, *The Sound of a Superpower: Musical Americanism and the Cold War* (New York: Oxford University Press, 2018), 138.

16. Copland, *The New Music*, 45.

17. Heinrich Berl, *Das Judentum in der Musik* (Stuttgart:

Deutsche Verlags-Anstalt, 1926), 172.

18. Huneker, "Schoenberg."

19. Alexander L. Ringer, *Arnold Schoenberg: The Composer as Jew* (Oxford: Clarendon, 1990), 12.

20. Arnold Schoenberg, letter to Jakob Klatzkin, June 13, 1933. Quoted in Alexander Ringer, "Arnold Schoenberg and the Politics of Jewish Survival," *Journal of the Arnold Schoenberg Institute* 3, no. 1 (1979): 26.

21. Perry and Schweitzer, *Antisemitism*, 94.

22. Nicolas Slonimsky, ed., *Lexicon of Musical Invective: Critical Assaults on Composers Since Beethoven's Time* (Seattle: University of Washington Press, 1965), 162.

23. Kenneth H. Marcus, *Schoenberg and Hollywood Modernism* (Cambridge: Cambridge University Press), 9.

24. Steven Joel Cahn, "Variations in Manifold Time: Historical Consciousness in the Music and Writings of Arnold Schoenberg" (PhD diss., State University of New York, Stony Brook, 1996), 209.

25. Haas, "Hitler's Musical 'Tabula Rasa,'" 41.

26. Schoenberg would later use *Der biblische Weg*, a three-part play dealing with Zionist themes, to promote the idea of the United Jewish Party. The work fictionalizes Theodor Herzl's negotiations with the British regarding the establishment of a temporary Jewish colony in Uganda and Herzl's failure to gain general support for the plan among fellow Zionists. David Michael Schiller, *Bloch, Schoenberg and Bernstein: Assimilating Jewish Music* (New York: Oxford University Press, 2003), 83–84. Schoenberg laments the failure of the Uganda

plan in "A Four-Point Program for Jewry" (October 1938), *Journal of the Arnold Schoenberg Institute* 3, no. 1 (1979): 56.

27. Arnold Schoenberg, letter to Alban Berg, October 16, 1933. Reprinted in Stein, *Arnold Schoenberg Letters*, 184.

28. Schoenberg began the libretto for *Die Jakobsleiter* in 1914–1915, published it in 1917, and began the music in 1915, finishing most of it in 1926. He added a small amount of orchestration in 1944. Seven hundred measures were completed by the time of his death.

29. Tarsi, "*Moses and Aaron* as a Reflection of Arnold Schoenberg's Spiritual Quest," 57–58.

30. Arnold Schoenberg, letter to Rudolf Kolisch, April 12, 1949, in Stein, *Arnold Schoenberg Letters*, 170.

31. For an in-depth examination of Schoenberg's life and career during this period, see Dorothy Lamb Crawford, "Arnold Schoenberg in Los Angeles," *The Musical Quarterly* 86, no. 1 (2002): 6–48. While in Los Angeles, Schoenberg worked on four textbooks to counter what he perceived as an impoverished system of educating composers, the most important being *Structural Functions of Harmony*, ed. Leonard Stein (New York: W. W. Norton, 1954). The book begins: "I had been constantly dissatisfied with the knowledge of harmony of my students of composition at the University of California, Los Angeles."

32. Arnold Schoenberg, letter to Henry Allen Moe, January 22, 1945, in Stein, *Arnold Schoenberg Letters*, 232.

33. Jan Maegaard, "Schoenberg: The Texts He Used," *Danish Yearbook of Musicology* 25 (1997): 33.

34. Schoenberg, "A Four-Point Program for Jewry," 49.

35. For the *Genesis Suite*, Shilkret commissioned Arnold Schoenberg, Igor Stravinsky, Ernst Toch, Darius Milhaud, Mario Castelnuovo-Tedesco, and Alexander Tansman.

36. Sabine Feisst, *Schoenberg's New World: The American Years* (New York: Oxford University Press, 2011), 99–100.

37. Neil W. Levin, "Joseph Achron," Milken Archive of Jewish Music, https://www.milkenarchive.org/artists/view/joseph-achron.

38. Marcus, *Schoenberg and Hollywood Modernism*, 130.

39. Crawford, *A Windfall of Musicians*, 106–7; Marcus, *Schoenberg and Hollywood Modernism*, 138; Feisst, *Schoenberg's New World*, 99–100.

40. Reuven Hammer, *Entering the High Holy Days: A Complete Guide to the History, Prayers and Themes* (Philadelphia: Jewish Publication Society, 2005), 115.

41. Mike Boehm, "Rarely Heard Yom Kippur Music by Schoenberg Set for New Release," quoting Schoenberg's letter to Louis Silvers, November 22, 1938.

42. Michael Berenbaum, "Sonderling, Jacob," *Encyclopedia Judaica*, vol. 19, eds. Michael Berenbaum and Fred Skolnik (New York: Macmillan, 2007), 13.

43. Jonathan Sacks, trans. and comm., *The Koren Yom Kippur Mahzor: The Rohr Family Edition* (Jerusalem: Koren, 2012), 72. The *Kol Nidre* text exists in numerous variations found in Yom Kippur prayer books through the centuries.

44. Arnold Schoenberg, letter to Paul Dessau, November

22, 1941, reprinted in Stein, *Arnold Schoenberg Letters*, 212–13. Paul Dessau—a German composer who had fled to Paris (1933–1939), immigrated to the East Coast of the United States (1939–1943), and settled in Los Angeles (1943–1948)—had himself explored Jewish themes in his music. In Paris he composed a dramatic oratorio, *Haggadah shel Pesach* (1936), with text by Max Brod, based on the Passover narrative. Other Jewish works followed.

45. Levin, liner notes to *Vol. 7*.

46. Ibid.

47. Charles Heller, *What to Listen for in Jewish Music* (Toronto: Ecanthus, 2006), 52–53.

48. Levin, liner notes to *Vol. 7*; Marcus, *Schoenberg and Hollywood Modernism*, 168.

49. Text reproduced from Arnold Schoenberg, *Kol Nidre*, op. 39, for Speaker (Rabbi), Chorus and Orchestra, reduction for organ by Leonard Stein, registration by Mark Robson (Pacific Palisades, CA: Belmont Music, 1997). Repetitions omitted.

50. Sonderling, "The Jews Are Changing Their Music."

51. Stuart Weinberg Gershon, *Kol Nidrei: Its Origin, Development, and Significance* (Northvale, NJ: Jason Aronson, 1994), 97–116; Lawrence A. Hoffman, "Kol Nidre from Union Prayer Book to Gates of Repentance," in *All These Vows: Kol Nidre*, ed. Lawrence A. Hoffman (Woodstock, VT: Jewish Lights, 2011), 99–108.

52. The third edition of the Reform movement's *Union Hymnal* includes the *Kol Nidre* tune without any text. *Union Hymnal: Songs and Prayers for Jewish Worship*

(New York: CCAR, 1932), 318.

53. *The Union Prayer Book for Jewish Worship, Part II* (New York: CCAR, 1945), 127.

54. Hoffman, "Kol Nidre from Union Prayer Book to Gates of Repentance," 106.

55. Sonderling, "The Jews are Changing Their Music."

56. Schoenberg, letter to Paul Dessau, November 22, 1941, in Stein, *Arnold Schoenberg Letters*, 213.

57. Sam Weiss, "The Cantus Firmus of Arnold Schoenberg's 'Kol Nidre,'" *Journal of Synagogue Music* 9, no. 2 (1979): 8.

58. Charles Heller, "Traditional Jewish Material in Schoenberg's *A Survivor from Warsaw*, op. 46," *Journal of the Arnold Schoenberg Institute* 3, no. 1 (1979): 69–74. Heller compares Schoenberg's setting of the *Shema* with one from Samuel Naumbourg's *Zmirot Yisrael* (1847) and one from Abraham Baer's *Baal T'fillah* (1883).

59. Marcus, *Schoenberg and Hollywood Modernism*, 168.

60. Compare Levin, liner notes to *Vol. 7*, and Mike Boehm, "Rarely Heard Yom Kippur Music by Schoenberg Set for New Release," *Los Angeles Times*, October 7, 2011.

61. Weisser, *The Modern Renaissance of Jewish Music*, 158.

62. Schoenberg, letter to Louis Silvers, November 22, 1938, quoted in Marcus, *Schoenberg and Hollywood Modernism*, 168.

63. Marcus, *Schoenberg and Hollywood Modernism*, 169.

64. Neal Brostoff, email to author, December 11, 2018. Cantor William Sharlin was the "rabbi/speaker" for the 1992 performance.

65. The analysis that follows is based on a review of the orchestral score, published by Belmont Music Publishers, Los Angeles, catalogue no. 1027, and the recording by Robert Craft and the Philharmonia Orchestra, Naxos 8.557525, 2007, compact disc.

66. Schoenberg, letter to Paul Dessau, in Stein, *Arnold Schoenberg Letters*, 213.

67. Isaac Nathan and Lord Byron, *A Selection of Hebrew Melodies, Ancient and Modern*, eds. Frederick Burwick and Paul Douglas (Tuscaloosa: University of Alabama Press, 1988), 25–26.

68. Bruch's antisemitism was of an "ordinary nineteenth-century social character," akin to the prejudices of Robert Schumann and Franz Liszt. Leon Botstein, "A Mirror to the Nineteenth Century: Reflections on Franz Liszt," in *Franz Liszt and His World*, eds. Christopher H. Gibbs and Dana Gooley (Princeton: Princeton University Press, 2010), 556.

69. Max Bruch, letter to Emil Kamphausen, January 3, 1882. Quoted in Christopher Fifield, *Max Bruch: His Life and Works* (New York: George Braziller, 1988), 169. This affection morphed into Bruch's misidentification as a Jew, including briefly by the Third Reich.

70. Schoenberg, letter to Paul Dessau, in Stein, *Arnold Schoenberg Letters*, 212.

71. Schoenberg, letter to Paul Dessau, in Stein, *Arnold Schoenberg Letters*, 212. In a 1945 letter to Cantor David J. Putterman, Schoenberg called the piece "my own idea of what the persecuted Jews of Spain [during the Inquisition] might have prayed." Leonard Stein, introduction to Schoenberg, *Kol Nidre*, op. 39. For an

analysis of the myth and its history, see Marc Saperstein, "Sermons and History: The 'Marrano' Connection to *Kol Nidre*," in *All These Vows: Kol Nidre*, ed. Lawrence A. Hoffman (Woodstock, VT: Jewish Lights, 2011), 31–38.

72. Marcus, *Schoenberg and Hollywood Modernism*, 170.

73. Boehm, "Rarely Heard Yom Kippur Music by Schoenberg Set for New Release."

74. Weisser, *The Modern Renaissance of Jewish Music*, 158.

75. See Mary Hannah Klontz, "The Heart and Mind of Arnold Schoenberg's '*De Profundis*,' Op. 50B" (PhD diss., George Mason University, 2015).

76. Chemjo Vinaver, ed., *Anthology of Jewish Music* (New York: Edward B. Marks, 1953), 203.

77. Feisst, *Schoenberg's New World*, 110.

78. Ibid.

79. Herbert Fromm, "Vinaver's Anthology," *Menorah Journal* (Spring–Summer 1956). Reprinted in Herbert Fromm, *On Music: A Composer's View* (New York: Bloch, 1978), 129–30.

80. Ena Steiner, "Schoenberg the Jew: On the 110th Anniversary of his Birth," *American Jewish Refugee Information*, October 10, 1984, 4.

81. Marcus, *Schoenberg and Hollywood Modernism*, 338, n.31.

82. Boehm, "Rarely Heard Yom Kippur Music by Schoenberg Set for New Release."

83. Lazare Saminsky, letter to Arnold Schoenberg, April 20, 1941.

84. Schoenberg, letter to Paul Dessau, in Stein, *Arnold Schoenberg Letters*, 213.

85. Weiss, "The Cantus Firmus of Arnold Schoenberg's 'Kol Nidre'"; Hans H. Stuckenschmidt, "Arnold Schoenberg's 'Kol Nidre' and the Jewish Elements in His Music," *Journal of Synagogue Music* 11, no. 1 (1981): 51–57; and Charles Heller, "The Traditional Jewish Sources of Schoenberg's *Kol Nidre*, op. 39," *Journal of Synagogue Music* 24, no. 1 (1995): 39–48. Paul Dessau's lecture on the piece was published as "Arnold Schoenberg's *Kol nidre*," *Jewish Music Forum* 3, no. 1 (1942): 10–12.

CHAPTER 5

1. Brendan G. Carroll, *The Last Prodigy: A Biography of Erich Wolfgang Korngold* (Portland, OR: Amadeus Press, 1997), 27.

2. Eduard Hanslick is perhaps most remembered for his rivalry with Richard Wagner. In contrast to Wagner, who believed music could make direct and unambiguous emotional appeals, Hanslick argued that music could only express musical ideas. Jonathan L. Friedmann, *Musical Aesthetics: An Introduction to Concepts, Theories, and Functions* (Newcastle: Cambridge Scholars, 2018), 3. Hanslick was immortalized as the stuffy, rule-obsessed critic Beckmesser (originally Veit Hanslich) in Wagner's *Die Meistersinger* (1868).

3. Michael Haas, "The False Myths and True Genius of Erich Wolfgang Korngold," *Forbidden Music*, July 18, 2015, https://forbiddenmusic.org/2015/07/18/the-false-myths-and-true-genius-of-erich-wolfgang-korngold/.

4. Rozenblit, *The Jews of Vienna*, 48–49.

5. Apostates from Judaism in Vienna numbered 110 in 1880, 302 in 1890, 559 in 1900, and 512 in 1910—a pattern showing that conversions increased in proportion to the spread of racial antisemitism, even as apostasy itself became increasingly futile. Ibid., 132.

6. Haas, "The False Myths and True Genius of Erich Wolfgang Korngold."

7. David Conway, *Jewry in Music: Entry to the Profession from the Enlightenment to Richard Wagner* (Cambridge: Cambridge University Press, 2012), 13.

8. Ezra Mendelsohn, "On the Jewish Presence in Nineteenth-Century European Musical Life," in *Modern Jews and Their Musical Agendas: Studies in Contemporary Jewry*, vol. IX, ed. Ezra Mendelsohn (New York: Oxford, 1993), 6.

9. See Peter Wegele, *Max Steiner: Composing, Casablanca, and the Golden Age of Film Music* (Lanham, MD: Rowman and Littlefield, 2014).

10. Carroll, *The Last Prodigy*, 29–34. Gustav Mahler recommended to Julius Korngold that Erich study with Zemlinsky, rather than the dry theoretician Robert Fuchs, who was Mahler's own teacher.

11. Ibid., 34, 43–44.

12. Ibid., 109–16.

13. Gdal Saleski, *Famous Musicians of Jewish Origin* (New York: Bloch, 1949), 89.

14. Hans Robert Korngold did not attain any musical significance and was thus all but forgotten by Julius. For more on the Korngold family tree, see Guy Wagner, *Korngold:*

Musik ist Musik (Berlin: Matthes and Seitz, 2008).

15. Saleski, *Famous Musicians of Jewish Origin*, 89.

16. Haas, "The False Myths and True Genius of Erich Wolfgang Korngold."

17. Ibid.

18. Ibid.

19. Jessica Duchen, "Erich Korngold: The Last Romantic," *The Independent*, October 17, 2017, https://www. independent.co.uk/arts-entertainment/music/features/ erich-korngold-the-last-romantic-394920.htmlGeorgia.

20. See Georgia Jamieson Emms, "Is Romance Dead?: Erich Korngold and the Romantic German Lied" (M.M. thesis, Victoria University of Wellington, 2017).

21. Haas, "The False Myths and True Genius of Erich Wolfgang Korngold."

22. Felix Weingartner, quoted in Saleski, *Famous Musicians of Jewish Origin*, 89.

23. Gutav Mahler and Julius Korngold both had fathers who were lower-middle class wine traders from the Czech province of Moravia.

24. Haas, "The False Myths and True Genius of Erich Wolfgang Korngold."

25. Richard Strauss, letter to Julius Korngold, January 3, 1910. Quoted in Carroll, *The Last Prodigy*, 31.

26. Emms, "Is Romance Dead?," 15.

27. Haas, "The False Myths and True Genius of Erich Wolfgang Korngold."

28. Brian Gilliam, "A Viennese Opera Composer in

Hollywood: Korngold's Double Exile in America," in *Driven into Paradise: The Musical Migration from Nazi Germany to the United States,* eds. Reinhold Brinkmann and Christopher Wolff (Berkeley: University of California Press, 1999), 228; Crawford, *A Windfall of Musicians,* 178. Korngold was also the highest-paid composer in Hollywood, earning $12,500 per film—around $200,000 in today's money.

29. Wegele, *Max Steiner,* 210.

30. Ibid.; Marcus, *Musical Metropolis,* 176.

31. Erich Korngold, quoted in Wegele, *Max Steiner,* 210.

32. Haas, "The False Myths and True Genius of Erich Wolfgang Korngold."

33. Crawford, *A Windfall of Musicians,* 179.

34. Jessica Duchen, *Erich Wolfgang Korngold* (London: Phaidon, 1996), 194.

35. Crawford, *A Windfall of Musicians,* 179.

36. Irving Kolodin, writing for the *New York Sun.* Quoted in Emms, "Is Romance Dead?," 19.

37. Haas, "The False Myths and True Genius of Erich Wolfgang Korngold."

38. Eric Myers, quoted in William Cheng, "Opera *en abyme*: The Prodigious Ritual of Korngold's *Die tote Stadt,*" *Cambridge Opera Journal* 22, no. 2 (2010): 123.

39. Erich Korngold, "Foreword," in Ulric Devaré, *Faith in Music* (New York: Comet, 1958). Cited in Carroll, *The Last Prodigy,* 358.

40. Jessica Duchen, "Composer of the Month: Erich Korngold, Post Romantic Film Music Pioneer," *BBC*

Music Magazine (November 2007): 50.

41. Haas, "The False Myths and True Genius of Erich Wolfgang Korngold."

42. Carroll, *The Last Prodigy*, 71.

43. Haas, "Hitler's Musical 'Tabula Rasa,'" 39.

44. Carroll, *The Last Prodigy*, 289–93.

45. A major share of contributions made to the United Jewish Welfare Fund came from people in the movie industry, many of whom had friends and family in Europe impacted by the Nazi regime. Gabler, *An Empire of Their Own*, 289.

46. Crawford, *A Windfall of Musicians*, 179–80.

47. Duchen, *Erich Wolfgang Korngold*, 194.

48. Carroll, *The Last Prodigy*, 301.

49. Julius Korngold was the only major Austrian music critic to immigrate to Los Angeles during this period. Although disappointed by Erich's involvement in film, he did write that his son "raised and enriched the style of musical film accompaniment through the melodic-symphonic elements inherent in his dramatic compositions." Julius Korngold, *Child Prodigy: Erich Wolfgang's Years of Childhood* (New York: Willard, 1945), 79.

50. Carroll, *The Last Prodigy*, 398.

51. Ibid.

52. The aural analysis that follows is based on Riccardo Chailly's recording with the Wiener Philharmoniker and the Slovak Philharmonic Choir, Decca Recording Co. LON 460213, 1998, compact disc, and the accompanying liner notes.

53. Tabory, *JPS Commentary on the Haggadah*, 101.

54. Ibid., 102.

55. Carroll, *The Last Prodigy*, 398; Duchen, *Erich Wolfgang Korngold*, 194; Crawford, *A Windfall of Musicians*, 179.

56. Sacks, *The Koren Yom Kippur Machzor*, 96.

57. The analysis that follows is based on the score published by B. Schott's Söhne (Mainz 1994), catalogue number ED 8203.

58. Carroll, *The Last Prodigy*, 320.

59. Ibid.

60. Ibid., 398.

61. Ian Lace, "Review of Erich Wolfgang Korngold (ASV CD 1131, 2002, compact disc)," Music Web International, http://www.musicweb-international.com/classrev/2002/Dec02/KORNGOLD_Concert.htm

62. See Adrianus Jacobus Lek, *Diegetic Music in Opera and Film: A Similarity Between Two Genres of Drama Analysed in Works by Erich Wolfgang Korngold (1897–1957)* (Amsterdam: Rodopi, 1991).

63. Paul Chihara, "'A Steppe is a Steppe': How Hitler Helped to Create Hollywood Music," The OREL Foundation, October 19, 2011, http://orelfoundation.org/journal/journalArticle/a_steppe_is_a_steppe_how_hitler_helped_to_create_hollywood_music

64. *New York Times*, quoted in Carroll, *The Last Prodigy*, 330.

65. Emms, "Is Romance Dead?," 21.

66. Ibid.

67. Haas, "The False Myths and True Genius of Erich Wolfgang Korngold."

68. Clayton Henderson, "Review of PARADISI GLORIA: Psalms," *Opera Today*, October 13, 2005, http://www.operatoday.com/content/2005/10/

69. Korngold, "Forward," in Devaré, *Faith in Music*. Cited in Carroll, *The Last Prodigy*, 358.

70. Duchen, "Erich Korngold."

71. Ben Winters, *Erich Wolfgang Korngold's* The Adventures of Robin Hood (Lanham, MD: Scarecrow, 2007).

CHAPTER 6

1. Michael Haas, "Eric(h) Zeisl: The One Who Nearly Got Away," Forbidden Music, March 24, 2014, https://www.forbiddenmusic.org/2014/03/24/erich-zeisl-1905-1959-the-one-who-nearly-got-away/.

2. Michael Beckerman, "Eric Zeisl," The OREL Foundation, http://orelfoundation.org/composers/article/eric_zeisl

3. Malcolm S. Cole, "Eric Zeisl: His Life and Music," interview with Gertrud S. Zeisl (Los Angeles: UCLA Oral History Program, 1978), 297; Gertrud Zeisl, "Biographical Essay," Eric Zeisl: Austrian-American Composer, http://www.zeisl.com/essays-and-articles/biographical-essay-gertrud-zeisl.htm

4. G. Zeisl, "Biographical Essay."

5. Mendelsohn, "On the Jewish Presence in Nineteenth-Century European Musical Life," 6.

6. G. Zeisl, "Biographical Essay."

7. Cole, "Eric Zeisl," 15.

8. Eric Zeisl, Letter to Lawrence Morton, October 14, 1956. Quoted in Crawford, *A Windfall of Musicians*, 210. Lawrence Morton's "Monday Evening Concerts" (1954–1971) were preceded by Peter Yates' "Evenings on the Roof" (1939–1954). The Los Angeles County Museum of Art continues "Monday Evening Concerts" to the present. See Dorothy Lamb Crawford, *Evenings on and Off the Roof: Pioneering Concerts in Los Angeles, 1939–1971* (Berkeley: University of California Press, 1995).

9. Malcolm S. Cole and Barbara Barclay, *Armseelchen: The Life and Music of Eric Zeisl* (Westport, CT: Greenwood Press, 1984), 8.

10. The theme in the fourth movement of Zeisl's *First String Quartet* and *Variations on a Slovakian Folk Song* originated from a book titled *Slowakisch*. Cole and Barclay, *Armseelchen*, 416, n.5.

11. G. Zeisl, "Biographical Essay."

12. Barbara Zeisl Schoenberg, "Biographical Essay," Eric Zeisl: Austrian-American Composer, http://www.zeisl.com/essays-and-articles/biographical-essay-barbara-zeisl.htm

13. Cole, "Eric Zeisl," 219.

14. Cole and Barclay, *Armseelchen*, 37–48.

15. Dorothy Lamb Crawford has 1941 as Zeisl's year of arrival in Los Angeles. Crawford, *A Windfall of Musicians*, 206.

16. Haas, "Eric(h) Zeisl."

17. According to Richard Drake Saunders, ed., *Music and*

Dance in California and the West (Hollywood, CA:
Bureau of Musical Research, 1948), 160: "Southern
California School of Music and Arts, founded in 1945
by Lily D. and Hal D. Grain and Walter H. Chase, is
devoted to serious purposes in music from beginning
to fully developed artistry, and offers graded courses,
diplomas, certificates and degrees through affiliation with
Fremont University. Its teaching staff includes Ernst
Krenek, composer; Simon R. Stein, pianist; Erik [*sic*]
Zeisl, composer and conductor; Charles Follett, Ruth
Widenham, pianists; and others. It is approved under the
G.I. Bill of Rights."

18. Cole, "Eric Zeisl," 346–47.

19. Ibid., 262–63.

20. Lee Stern, *Who is Who in Music: A Complete
Presentation of the Contemporary Musical Scene, with a
Master Record Catalogue* (New York: Lee Stern, 1941),
26.

21. Haas, "Eric(h) Zeisl."

22. To some extent, these "Hebraic" propensities mirror
those of the Eastern Mediterranean style of composition,
which flourished in Israel among European immigrants
and native-born Israelis in the 1930s–1940s.

23. Max Helfman, quoted in *B'nai B'rith Messenger*,
October 6, 1950. The quotation appears in Cole and
Barclay, *Armseelchen*, 95.

24. *Naboth's Vineyard* and *Jacob and Rachel* were written
in collaboration with Russian-born dancer and choreographer Benjamin Zemach (1902–1997), Zeisl's col-
league at the Brandeis Institute. The performance and

recording of *Jacob and Rachel* were underwritten by E. Randol Schoenberg (grandson of Eric Zeisl and Arnold Schoenberg) and his wife, Pamela Lynn Schoenberg. Los Angeles Jewish Symphony, *The Music of Eric Zeisl: Jacob and Rachel; Variations on a Slovakian Folk Song*, Albany TROY1756, 2019, compact disc.

25. Cole, "Eric Zeisl," 4.

26. Beckerman, "Eric Zeisl"; Zeisl Schoenberg, "Biographical Essay."

27. Barbara Zeisl and Ronald Schoenberg were married in 1965. According to Barbara, Hanns Eisler had prepared a letter of introduction for Zeisl to study with Schoenberg in Los Angeles, but Zeisl never followed up because he could not afford the lessons and did not want to compromise his unique compositional voice. Crawford, *A Windfall of Musicians*, 207.

28. Albert Goldberg, "The Transplanted Composer," *Los Angeles Times*, May 28, 1950.

29. Cole, "Eric Zeisl," 427.

30. Hugo Strelitzer premiered Zeisl's long-delayed opera, *Leonce und Lena*, in a student workshop production in 1952. Haas, "Eric(h) Zeisl."

31. Haas, "Eric(h) Zeisl."

32. Cole, "Eric Zeisl," 249.

33. Program for "The Message of Music in Religion," Hollywood Inter-Faith Forum, First Methodist Church of Hollywood, Sunday, April 8, 1945.

34. Crawford, *A Windfall of Musicians*, 209.

35. Cole, "Eric Zeisl," 249.

36. Eric Zeisl, letter to Josef Freudenthal, November 16, 1945. Randol Schoenberg, program notes to "Music of Arnold Schoenberg and Eric Zeisl," Los Angeles Zimriyah Chorale, Sinai Temple, Los Angeles, August 22, 2013.

37. Ibid.

38. Ibid.

39. T. F. Williams, "A Form-Critical Classification of the Psalms According to Hermann Gunkel," *Resources for Biblical, Theological, and Religious Studies* (October 2006): 3.

40. Israel Abrahams, *A Companion to the Authorized Prayer Book* (New York: Sepher-Hermon, 1966), 127.

41. R. Schoenberg, program notes to "Music of Arnold Schoenberg and Eric Zeisl."

42. The analysis that follows is based on the score published by Transcontinental Music, catalogue no. 266, and the recording by Lawrence Foster with the Rundfunk-Sinfonieorchester Berlin and the Rundfunkchor Berlin, Deca 289 460 211-2, 1998, compact disc.

43. Cole and Barclay, *Armseelchen*, 51.

44. Ibid., 53.

45. Beckerman, "Eric Zeisl."

46. Crawford, *A Windfall of Musicians*, 211.

47. Ernst Krenek, quoted in Lessem, "The Refugee Composer in America," 232. Krenek was often misidentified as a Jewish composer, and was a target of the Third Reich until his emigration in 1938.

48. Lessem, "The Refugee Composer in America," 234.

49. Ibid., 233.

50. Goldberg, "The Transplanted Composer."

CONCLUSION

1. Eric Werner, *From Generation to Generation: Studies on Jewish Musical Tradition* (New York: American Conference of Cantors, 1967), 151.

2. Ibid., 152.

3. Levin, "Lazare Saminsky."

BIBLIOGRAPHY

Abrahams, Israel. *A Companion to the Authorized Prayer Book.*
  New York: Sepher-Hermon, 1966.
"Aesthetic Judaism." *Daily Jewish Courier,* January 6, 1924.
Ansari, Emily Abrams. *The Sound of a Superpower: Musical
  Americanism and the Cold War.* New York: Oxford University
  Press, 2018.
Avineri, Shlomo. *Herzl: Theodor Herzl and the Foundation of the
  Jewish State.* London: Weidenfeld and Nicolson, 2013.
Bahr, Ehrhard. *Weimar on the Pacific: German Exile Culture in
  Los Angeles and the Crisis of Modernism.* Berkeley: University
  of California Press, 2007.
Batnitzky, Leora. *How Judaism Became a Religion: An
  Introduction to Modern Jewish Thought.* Princeton, NJ:
  Princeton University Press, 2011.
Bayer, Jerome H. "The Future of Jewish Music." *The Menorah
  Journal* 5, no. 2 (1919): 109–14.
Beckerman, Michael. "Eric Zeisl," The OREL Foundation.
  http://orelfoundation.org/composers/article/eric_zeisl

Berenbaum, Michael. "Sonderling, Jacob." In *Encyclopedia Judaica*, vol. 19, edited by Michael Berenbaum and Fred Skolnik, 13. New York: Macmillan, 2007.

Berger, I. Letter to Jacob Sonderling, June 4, 1931. Sonderling Collection, Jewish Museum, Berlin.

Berl, Heinrich. *Das Judentum in der Musik*. Stuttgart: Deutsche Verlags-Anstalt, 1926.

Berry, Mark. *Arnold Schoenberg*. London: Reaktion, 2019.

Birnbaum, Eduard. "Franz Schubert als Synagogenkomponist." *Allgemeine Zeitung des Judentums* 61 (1897): 5–7.

Boehm, Mike. "Rarely Heard Yom Kippur Music by Schoenberg Set for New Release." *Los Angeles Times*, October 7, 2011.

Bopp, Verana. *MAILAMM 1932–1941: Die Geschichte einer Vereinigung zur Förderung jüdischer Musik in den USA*. Weisbaden: Harrassowitz, 2007.

Botstein, Leon. "A Mirror to the Nineteenth Century: Reflections on Franz Liszt." In *Franz Liszt and His World*, edited by Christopher H. Gibbs and Dana Gooley, 517–68. Princeton, NJ: Princeton University Press, 2010.

"Brandeis Camp Institute Flyer 1960." Online Archive of California. https://oac.cdlib.org/ark:/13030/kt0b69r60k/?brand=oac4

Brinkmann, Reinhold, and Christopher Wolff, eds. *Driven into Paradise: The Musical Migration from Nazi Germany to the United States*. Berkeley: University of California Press, 1999.

Buber, Martin. *The Legend of the Baal-Shem*. Translated by Maurice Friedman. Princeton: Princeton University Press, 1955.

Cahn, Steven Joel. "Variations in Manifold Time: Historical Consciousness in the Music and Writings of Arnold Schoenberg." PhD diss., State University of New York, Stony Brook, 1996.

Carroll, Brendan G. *The Last Prodigy: A Biography of Erich Wolfgang Korngold*. Portland, OR: Amadeus Press, 1997.

Catalogue des Dissertations et Écrits Académiques Provenant des Échanges avec les Universités Etrangères et Reçus par la Bibliothèque Nationale in 1904. Paris: Librairie C. Klincksieck, 1905.

Chailly, Riccardo. *Passover Psalm*. Decca Recording Co., LON 460213, 1998, compact disc.

Cheng, William. "Opera *en abyme*: The Prodigious Ritual of Korngold's *Die tote Stadt*." *Cambridge Opera Journal* 22, no. 2 (2010): 115–46.

"Chief Rabbi Feuchtwang of Vienna Dies at 71." Jewish Telegraphic Agency, July 6, 1936.

Chihara, Paul. "'A Steppe is a Steppe': How Hitler Helped to Create Hollywood Music." The OREL Foundation, October 19, 2011. http://orelfoundation.org/journal/journalArticle/a_steppe_is_a_steppe_how_hitler_helped_to_create_hollywood_music

Cohen, Judah M. "A Holy Brother's Liberal Legacy: Shlomo Carlebach, Reform Judaism and Hasidic pluralism." *American Jewish History* 100, no. 4 (2016): 485–509.

———.*Jewish Religious Music in Nineteenth-Century America: Restoring the Synagogue Soundtrack*. Bloomington: Indiana University Press, 2019.

Cole, Malcolm S. "Eric Zeisl: His Life and Music," interview with Gertrud S. Zeisl. Los Angeles: UCLA Oral History Program, 1978.

Cole, Malcolm S., and Barbara Barclay. *Armseelchen: The Life and Music of Eric Zeisl*. Westport, CT: Greenwood Press, 1984.

"Contest Announcement." *Musical Leader*, July 7, 1927.

Conway, David. *Jewry in Music: Entry to the Profession from the*

Enlightenment to Richard Wagner. Cambridge: Cambridge University Press, 2012.

Coopersmith, Harry, comp. *More of the Songs We Sing*. New York: The United Synagogue Commission on Jewish Education, 1970.

———. *The Songs We Sing*. New York: The United Synagogue Commission on Jewish Education, 1950.

Copland, Aaron. *The New Music, 1900–1960*. New York: W. W. Norton, 1968.

———. *Our New Music: Leading Composers in Europe and America*. New York: McGraw-Hill, 1941.

Craft, Robert. *Kol Nidre*. Naxos 8.557525, 2007, compact disc.

Crawford, Dorothy Lamb. "Arnold Schoenberg in Los Angeles." *The Musical Quarterly* 86, no. 1 (2002): 6–48.

———. *Evenings on and Off the Roof: Pioneering Concerts in Los Angeles, 1939–1971*. Berkeley: University of California Press, 1995.

———. *A Windfall of Musicians: Hitler's Émigrés and Exiles in Southern California*. New Haven, CT: Yale University Press, 2008.

Cummins, Joseph J. "Buy Absolutely Nothing 'Made in Germany.'" *B'nai B'rith Messenger*, April 7, 1933.

Dessau, Paul. "Arnold Schoenberg's *Kol nidre*." *Jewish Music Forum* 3, no. 1 (1942): 10–12.

Devaré, Ulric. *Faith in Music*. New York: Comet, 1958.

Doherty, Thomas. *Hollywood and Hitler, 1933–1939*. New York: Columbia University Press, 2015.

Drohojowska-Philp, Hunter. *Rebels in Paradise: The Los Angeles Art Scene and the 1960s*. New York: Henry Holt, 2011.

Duchen, Jessica. "Composer of the Month: Erich Korngold, Post Romantic Film Music Pioneer." *BBC Music Magazine* (November 2007): 46–50.

———. "Erich Korngold: The Last Romantic." *The Independent,* October 17, 2017. https://www.independent.co.uk/arts-entertainment/music/features/erich-korngold-the-last-romantic-394920.htmlGeorgia

———. *Erich Wolfgang Korngold.* London: Phaidon, 1996.

Ellenson, David. "The Israelite Gebetbücher of Abraham Geiger and Manuel Joël: A Study in Nineteenth-Century German-Jewish Communal Liturgy and Religion." *Leo Baeck Institute Yearbook* 44 (1999): 143–64.

Elon, Amos. *The Pity of It All: A Portrait of the German-Jewish Epoch, 1743–1933.* New York: Henry Holt, 2003.

Emms, Georgia Jamieson. "Is Romance Dead?: Erich Korngold and the Romantic German Lied." M.M. thesis, Victoria University of Wellington, 2017.

Engel, David. "World War I." In *YIVO Encyclopedia of Jews in Eastern Europe*, vol. 2, edited by Gershon David Hundert, 2032–37. New Haven, CT: Yale University Press, 2008.

Evans, Edwin. "Schönberg, Arnold." *Grove's Dictionary of Music and Musicians*, vol. 5, edited by H. C. Colles, 571–74. New York: Macmillan, 1939.

Feisst, Sabine. *Schoenberg's New World: The American Years.* New York: Oxford University Press, 2011.

Fifield, Christopher. *Max Bruch: His Life and Works.* New York: George Braziller, 1988.

"Finding Aid for the Alfred Leonard and Joseph Leonard Collection, 1902–2001." Online Archive of California. https://oac.cdlib.org/findaid/ark:/13030/tf18700458/

Fogelson, Robert M. *The Fragmented Metropolis: Los Angeles, 1850–1930.* Berkeley: University of California Press, 1993.

Foster, Lawrence. *Requiem Ebraico.* Decca Recording Co. 289 460 211-2, 1998, compact disc.

Friedmann, Jonathan L. *A City Haphazard: Jewish Musicians in*

Los Angeles, 1887–1927. Washington, DC: Academica, 2017.

———. "Groping for the Greats: The Strange Musical Claims of Nathan Ausubel." *Journal of Modern Jewish Studies* 15, no. 1 (2016): 436–50.

———. *Jewish Los Angeles.* Charleston, SC: Arcadia, 2020.

———. *Jews, Music and the American West.* Santa Fe, NM: Gaon Press, 2016.

———. "Max Helfman in California: Creating Jewish Music, 1947–1963." *Western States Jewish History* 42, no. 1 (2009): 33–44.

———. *Musical Aesthetics: An Introduction to Concepts, Theories, and Functions.* Newcastle: Cambridge Scholars, 2018.

———. "Sulzerism, Sulzermania, and the Shaping of the American Cantorate." *American Jewish History* 101, no. 2 (2017): 287–306.

———. "Was Max Steiner a Jew?" Paper delivered at symposium, "Max Steiner: Man and Myth." California State University, Long Beach, February 24–25, 2018.

Fromm, Herbert. *On Music: A Composer's View.* New York: Bloch, 1978.

Frühauf, Tina. *Salomon Sulzer: Reformer, Cantor, Icon.* Berlin: Hentrich and Hentrich, 2012.

Gabler, Neal. *An Empire of Their Own: How the Jews Invented Hollywood.* New York: Anchor, 1989.

Gershon, Stuart Weinberg. *Kol Nidrei: Its Origin, Development, and Significance.* Northvale, NJ: Jason Aronson, 1994.

Gilliam, Brian. "A Viennese Opera Composer in Hollywood: Korngold's Double Exile in America." In *Driven into Paradise: The Musical Migration from Nazi Germany to the United States,* edited by Reinhold Brinkmann and Christopher Wolff, 223–42. Berkeley: University of California Press, 1999.

Gluck, Bob. "Mordecai Kaplan on Art, Artists, and Creativity." Paper delivered at "Architect of the Jewish Future: A Conference on the Life, Work, and Legacy of Rabbi Mordecai M. Kaplan." Georgetown University, Washington, DC, 2014.

Goldberg, Albert. "The Sounding Board." *Los Angeles Times,* January 24, 1954.

———. "The Transplanted Composer." *Los Angeles Times,* May 28, 1950.

Goldstein, Bluma. *Reinscribing Moses: Heine, Kafka, Freud, and Schoenberg in a European Wilderness.* Cambridge, MA: Harvard University Press, 1992.

Gottschalk, Alfred. "Ordination Address." HUC-JIR, Los Angeles, May 16, 2004.

Grass, C. Nichole. "The Wind Chamber Works of Ernst Toch: A History and Comparative Analysis." D.M. diss., University of South Carolina, 2013.

Green, Arthur. "Renewal and Havurah: American Movements, European Roots." In *Jewish Renaissance and Revival in America: Essays in Memory of Leah Levitz Fishbane,* edited by Eitan Fishbane and Jonathan D. Sarna, 145–64. Waltham, MA: Brandeis University Press, 2011.

Grinstein, Hyman B. *The Rise of the Jewish Community of New York, 1654–1860.* Philadelphia: Jewish Publication Society, 1947.

Guttman, Adolph. "The Life of Salomon Sulzer." *Year Book of the Central Conference of American Rabbis* 13 (1903): 227–36.

Haas, Michael. "Eric(h) Zeisl: The One Who Nearly Got Away." *Forbidden Music,* March 24, 2014. https://www.forbiddenmusic.org/2014/03/24/erich-zeisl-1905-1959-the-one-who-nearly-got-away/

———. "The False Myths and True Genius of Erich Wolfgang Korngold." *Forbidden Music,* July 18,

2015. https://forbiddenmusic.org/2015/07/18/
the-false-myths-and-true-genius-of-erich-wolfgang-korngold/

———. *Forbidden Music: The Jewish Composers Banned by the Nazis*. New Haven, CT: Yale University Press, 2013.

———. "The 'Geographical' Journey of Dr. Ernst Toch." *Forbidden Music*, June 11, 2014. https://forbiddenmusic. org/2014/06/11/the-geographical-journey-of-dr-ernst-toch/

———. "Hitler's Musical 'Tabula Rasa'—Restitution— Restoration." PhD diss., Middlesex University, London, 2017.

Hammer, Reuven. *Entering the High Holy Days: A Complete Guide to the History, Prayers and Themes*. Philadelphia: Jewish Publication Society, 2005.

Heller, Charles. "Traditional Jewish Material in Schoenberg's *A Survivor from Warsaw*, op. 46." *Journal of the Arnold Schoenberg Institute* 3, no. 1 (1979): 69–74.

———. "The Traditional Jewish Sources of Schoenberg's *Kol Nidre*, op. 39." *Journal of Synagogue Music* 24, no. 1 (1995): 39–48.

———. *What to Listen for in Jewish Music*. Toronto: Ecanthus, 2006.

Henderson, Clayton. "Review of *PARADISI GLORIA: Psalms*," *Opera Today*, October 13, 2005. http://www.operatoday.com/ content/2005/10/

Heskes, Irene. *Passport to Jewish Music: Its History, Traditions, and Culture*. New York: Tara, 1994.

Hewitt, Ivan. "Swept Away, Kings Place, review." *The Telegraph*, June 21, 2015. https://www.telegraph.co.uk/culture/music/ classicalconcertreviews/11685727/Swept-Away-Kings-Place- review-astonishingly-ambitious.html

Hirsch, Lily E. *Anneliese Landau's Life in Music: Nazi Germany to Émigré California*. Rochester, NY: University of Rochester Press, 2019.

"Historical Resident Population City & County of Los Angeles, 1850 to 2010." Los Angeles Almanac. http://www.laalmanac. com/population/po02.htm

"History." Temple Beth El of Manhattan Beach. http://templebe-thelmb.org/history

"History of Agudas Achim." Agudas Achim. https://www.agu-dasachimnsc.org/history/index.html

Hoffman, Lawrence A. "*Kol Nidre* from *Union Prayer Book* to *Gates of Repentance.*" In *All These Vows: Kol Nidre*, edited by Lawrence A. Hoffman, 99–108. Woodstock, VT: Jewish Lights, 2011.

Hoffman, Lawrence A., and David Arnow, eds. *My People's Passover Haggadah: Traditional Texts, Modern Commentaries, Volume 2.* Woodstock, VT: Jewish Lights, 2008.

Horvitz, Eleanor F. "Temple Beth-Israel 1921–1981." *Rhode Island Jewish Historical Notes* 9 (1983): 30–67, 34–36.

Humphries, Reynold. *Hollywood's Blacklists: A Political and Cultural History.* Edinburgh: Edinburgh University Press, 2008.

Huneker, James. "Schoenberg: Musical Anarchist Who Has Upset Europe." *New York Times*, January 19, 1913.

"Itzhak Perlman celebrates Passover with a 'Musical Feast.'" Classical MPR, March 28, 2018. https://www.classi-calmpr.org/story/2018/03/27/a-musical-feast-forpasso-ver-with-itzhak-perlman

Jezik, Diane Peacock. *The Musical Migration of Ernst Toch.* Ames: Iowa State University Press, 1989.

Kaplan, Mordecai. *The Future of the American Jew.* New York: Macmillan, 1948.

Kaplan, Mordecai M. *Judaism as a Civilization.* New York: Macmillan, 1934.

Katter, Daniel. "Los Angeles, West Side and San Fernando

Valley Jewish Enclaves (California)." In *America's Changing Neighborhoods: An Exploration of Diversity through Places*, vol. 2, edited by Reed Ueda, 807–11. Santa Barbara, CA: Greenwood, 2017.

Katz, Mark. "Hindemith, Toch, and *Grammophonmusik*." *Journal of Musicological Research* 20, no. 2 (2001): 161–80.

Klontz, Mary Hannah. "The Heart and Mind of Arnold Schoenberg's '*De Profundis*,' Op.50B." PhD diss., George Mason University, 2015.

Korngold, Erich Wolfgang. *Prayer*. Mainz: B. Schott's Söhne, 1994.

Korngold, Julius. *Child Prodigy: Erich Wolfgang's Years of Childhood*. New York: Willard, 1945.

Kramer, William M. "The Founding of the Organized Jewish Community of Greater Los Angeles." In *The Jews of Los Angeles: Urban Pioneers*, edited by Norton B. Stern, 9–20. Los Angeles: Southern California Jewish Historical Society, 1981.

Kronzek, Lynn. "Fairfax: A Home, A Community, A Way of Life." *Legacy: Journal of the Jewish Historical Society of Southern California* 1, no. 4 (1990): 21–27.

Kun, Josh, ed. *Songs in the Key of Los Angeles: Sheet Music from the Collection of the Los Angeles Public Library*. Santa Monica, CA: Angel City, 2013.

Lace, Ian. "Review of *Erich Wolfgang Korngold* (ASV CD 1131, 2002, compact disc)." Music Web International. http://www.musicweb-international.com/classrev/2002/Dec02/KORNGOLD_Concert.htm

Landman, Isaac, ed. *The Universal Jewish Encyclopedia in Ten Volumes*, vol. 7. New York: Universal Jewish Encyclopedia, 1947.

Langer, Ruth. "The Censorship of Aleinu in Ashkenaz and its Aftermath." In *The Experience of Jewish Liturgy: Studies*

Dedicated to Menahem Schmelzer, edited by Debra Reed
Blank, 147–66. Boston: Brill, 2011.

Leader, Leonard. "The *B'nai B'rith Messenger*: Reviewing the
First 74 Years of the Newspaper's Community Service, 1897–
1971." *Western States Jewish History* 47, no. 1 (2014): 5–56.

Lek, Adrianus Jacobus. *Diegetic Music in Opera and Film: A
Similarity Between Two Genres of Drama Analysed in Works
by Erich Wolfgang Korngold (1897–1957)*. Amsterdam:
Rodopi, 1991.

Lessem, Alan. "The Refugee Composer in America: A Topic for
Twentieth-Century Music History." *Canadian University
Music Review* 6 (1985): 222–38.

Levin, Neil W. "Ernst Toch." Milken Archive of Jewish Music.
https://www.milkenarchive.org/artists/view/ernst-toch

———. "Joseph Achron." Milken Archive of Jewish Music.
https://www.milkenarchive.org/artists/view/joseph-achron

———. "Lazare Saminsky." Milken Archive of Jewish Music.
http://www.milkenarchive.org/artists/view/lazare-saminsky/

———. Liner notes to *Ernst Toch: Cantata of the Bitter Herbs* and
Jephta, Rhapsodic Poem. Naxos American Classics 8.559417,
2004, compact disc.

———. Liner notes to *Genesis Suite, Volume 17: Odes and Epics*.
Milken Archive of Jewish Music. https://www.milkenarchive.
org/music/volumes/view/odes-and-epics/work/genesis-suite/

———. Liner notes to *Vol. 7: Masterworks of Prayer*. Milken
Archive of Jewish Music (2011), digital album.

———. "Nathaniel Shilkret." Milken Archive of Jewish
Music. https://www.milkenarchive.org/artists/view/
nathaniel-shilkret/

Liszt, Franz. *The Gipsy in Music, Vol. 1*. Translated by Edwin
Evans. London: W. Reeves, 1926.

Litvak, Joseph. *The Un-Americans: Jews, the Blacklist, and*

Stoolpigeon Culture. Durham, NC: Duke University Press, 2009.

Loeffler, James. *The Most Musical Nation: Jews and Culture in the Late Russian Empire*. New Haven, CT: Yale University Press, 2010.

———. "Society for Jewish Folk Music." In *The YIVO Encyclopedia of Jews in Eastern Europe*, vol. 2, edited by Gershon David Hundert, 1170–71. New Haven, CT: Yale University Press, 2008.

MacDonald, Malcolm. *Schoenberg*, 2nd ed. Oxford: Oxford University Press, 2008.

Maegaard, Jan. "Schoenberg: The Texts He Used." *Danish Yearbook of Musicology* 25 (1997): 15–42.

Maleachi, Ruben. "Die Synagogen in Hamburg." *Mitteilungen des Verbandes ehemaliger Breslauer und Schleiser in Israel* 45 (April–May 1979).

Marcus, Kenneth H. *Musical Metropolis: Los Angeles and the Creation of a Music Culture, 1880–1940*. New York: Palgrave MacMillan, 2004.

———. *Schoenberg and Hollywood Modernism*. Cambridge: Cambridge University Press, 2016.

Marks, Nadine M., Heyjung Jun, and Jieun Song. "Death of Parents and Adult Psychological and Physical Well-Being: A Prospective U.S. National Study." *Journal of Family Issues* 28, no. 12 (2009): 1611–38.

Mayorek, Yoram. "Herzl and the Dreyfus Affair." *The Journal of Israeli History* 15, no. 1 (1994): 83–89.

Mehta, Zubin. *The Score of My Life*. New York: Hal Leonard, 2009.

Meltz, Jacob J., ed. *Mount Sinai Yearbook of 1946*. Los Angeles: Associated Organizations of Los Angeles, 1946.

Mendelsohn, Ezra. "On the Jewish Presence in Nineteenth-

Century European Musical Life." In *Modern Jews and Their Musical Agendas: Studies in Contemporary Jewry*, vol. IX, edited by Ezra Mendelsohn, 3–16. New York: Oxford, 1993.

Mendes-Flohr, Paul R., and Jehuda Reinharz, eds. *The Jew in the Modern World: A Documentary History*. New York: Oxford University Press, 1980.

"The Message of Music in Religion." Los Angeles Museum of the Holocaust. http://www.lamoth.info/index.php?p=digitallibrary/digitalcontent&id=3135/

Meyer, Michael A. *Response to Modernity: A History of the Reform Movement in Judaism*. Detroit: Wayne State University Press, 1995.

Millin, Aubin-Louis. "Le Sublime." In *Music and Aesthetics in the Eighteenth and Early Nineteenth Centuries*, edited by Peter le Huray and James Day, 206. Cambridge: Cambridge University Press, 1988.

Moddel, Philip. *Max Helfman: A Biographical Sketch*. Berkeley, CA: Judah L. Magnes Memorial Museum, 1974.

Moore, Deborah Dash. *To the Golden Cities: Pursuing the American Jewish Dream in Miami and L.A.* Cambridge, MA: Harvard University Press, 1994.

Morros, Boris. *My Ten Years as a Counterspy: As Told to Charles Samuels*. New York: Viking, 1959.

Nathan, Hans. *Israeli Folk Music: Songs of the Early Pioneers*. Madison, WI: A-R Editions, 1994.

Nathan, Isaac, and Lord Byron. *A Selection of Hebrew Melodies, Ancient and Modern*. Edited by Frederick Burwick and Paul Douglas. Tuscaloosa: University of Alabama Press, 1988.

Ne'eman, Joshua Leib. "Henle, Moritz." In *Encyclopedia Judaica*, vol. 8, edited by Fred Skolnik and Michael Berenbaum, 808. New York: Macmillan, 2007.

Norwood Stephen H., and Eunice G. Pollack, eds. *Encyclopedia of American Jewish History*, vol. 1. Santa Barbara: ABC-CLIO, 2008.

Nussbaum, Max. "Jacob Sonderling." *Proceedings of the Central Conference of American Rabbis* 75 (1965): 158.

"Orchestra Tickets from Society for Jewish Culture, 1944 and 1946." Los Angeles

Museum of the Holocaust. http://www.lamoth. info/?p=digitallibrary/digitalcontent&id=3138

"The Oriental and Occidental Beliefs, Expressed through the Arts." Hollywood Inter-Faith Forum. Newspaper advertisement, April 1946.

Patterson, Thomas. *Instruments for New Music: Sound, Technology and Modernism*. Berkeley: University of California Press, 2016.

Pauley, Bruce F. *The Habsburg Legacy: 1867–1939*. New York: Holt, Rinehart and Winston, 1972.

Peixotto, Benjamin Franklin. "Solomon Sulzer: Reminiscences of Vienna." *Menorah Journal* 8 (1890): 260–64.

Perry, Marvin, and Frederick M. Schweitzer. *Antisemitism: Myth and Hate from Antiquity to the Present*. New York: Palgrave Macmillan, 2002.

Phillips, Bruce A. "Los Angeles Jewry: A Demographic Portrait." *American Jewish Yearbook* 86 (1986): 126–95.

Powell, Bruce J. "Shlomo Bardin's 'Eretz' Brandeis." In *California Jews*, edited by Ava F. Kahn and Marc Dollinger, 171–84. Hanover, MA: Brandeis University Press, 2003.

Putterman, David. "The Academy's Place in Jewish Life." *The Jewish Music Forum Bulletin* 5, no. 1 (1944): 23–24.

Putterman, David, comp. *Mizmor L'David: An Anthology of Synagogue Music*. New York: Cantors Assembly, 1979.

"Rabbi Jacob Sonderling, Herzl Co-worker, Dead on Coast at 85." Jewish Telegraphic Agency, October 2, 1964.

"Rabbi Sonderling in Town Hall Services." Jewish Telegraphic Agency, September 10, 1933.

"Rabbi Sonderling, Zionist Aided Herzl." *New York Times*, October 1, 1964.

"Raise $65,000 at Los Angeles Jewish Appeal." Jewish Telegraphic Agency, July 18, 1934.

Raphael, Marc Lee. "Beyond New York: The Challenge to Local History." In *Jews of the American West*, edited by Moses Rischin and John Livingston, 52–65. Detroit: Wayne State University Press, 1991.

Raz, Carmel. "From Trinidad to Cyberspace: Reconsidering Ernst Toch's 'Geographical Fugue.'" *Zeitschrift der Gesellschaft für Musiktheorie* 9, no. 2 (2012): 227–73.

———. "The Lost Movements of Ernst Toch's *Gesprochene Musik*." *Current Musicology* 97 (2014): 37–59.

Rifkind, Donna. *The Sun and Her Stars: Salka Viertel and Hitler's Exiles in the Golden Age of Hollywood*. New York: Other, 2020.

Ringer, Alexander L. *Arnold Schoenberg: The Composer as Jew*. Oxford: Clarendon, 1990.

———. "Arnold Schoenberg and the Politics of Jewish Survival." *Journal of the Arnold Schoenberg Institute* 3, no. 1 (1979): 11–47.

Romo, Richardo. *East Los Angeles: History of a Barrio*. Austin: University of Texas Press, 2010.

Rosenbaum, Fred. *Cosmopolitans: A Social and Cultural History of the Jews of the San Francisco Bay Area*. Berkeley: University of California Press, 2009.

Rozenblit, Marsha L. *Jews of Vienna, 1867–1914: Assimilation and Identity*. Albany: SUNY Press, 1984.

Rubin, Barry. *Assimilation and Its Discontents*. New York: Random House, 1995.

Sacks, Jonathan, trans. and comm. *The Koren Yom Kippur Mahzor: The Rohr Family Edition*. Jerusalem: Koren, 2012.

Saleski, Gdal. *Famous Musicians of Jewish Origin*. New York: Bloch, 1949.

Saminsky, Lazare. *Music of the Ghetto and the Bible*. New York: Bloch, 1934.

Sanchez, George. "'What's Good for Boyle Heights Is Good for Jews': Creating Multiculturalism on the Eastside During the 1950s." *American Quarterly* 56, no. 3 (2004): 633–61.

Saperstein, Marc. "Sermons and History: The 'Marrano' Connection to *Kol Nidre*." In *All These Vows: Kol Nidre*, edited by Lawrence A. Hoffman, 31–38. Woodstock, VT: Jewish Lights, 2011.

Saunders, Richard Drake, ed. *Music and Dance in California and the West*. Hollywood, CA: Bureau of Musical Research, 1948.

Schallert, Edwin. "Philharmonic Makes Debut; New Orchestra Raises Tone of Local Music." *Los Angeles Times*, October 25, 1919.

Schiller, Benjie-Ellen. "The Hymnal as an Index of Musical Change in the Reform Synagogue." In *Sacred Sound and Social Change: Liturgical Music in Jewish and Christian Experience*, edited by Lawrence A. Hoffman and Janet R. Walton, 187–212. Notre Dame, IN: Notre Dame University Press, 1992.

Schiller, David Michael. *Bloch, Schoenberg and Bernstein: Assimilating Jewish Music*. New York: Oxford University Press, 2003.

Schleifer, Eliyahu. *Samuel Naumbourg: The Cantor of French Jewish Emancipation*. Berlin: Hentrich and Hentrich, 2012.

Schoenberg, Arnold. "A Four-Point Program for Jewry" (October 1938). *Journal of the Arnold Schoenberg Institute* 3, no. 1 (1979): 48–67.

———. *Kol Nidre*. Los Angeles: Belmont Music Publishers, catalogue no. 1027, 1976.

———. *Structural Functions of Harmony*, edited by Leonard Stein. New York: W. W. Norton, 1954.

Schoenberg, Barbara Zeisl. "Biographical Essay." Eric Zeisl: Austrian-American Composer. http://www.zeisl.com/essays-and-articles/biographical-essay-barbara-zeisl.htm

———. "The Reception of Austrian Composers in Los Angeles." Eric Zeisl: Austrian-American Composer. http://www.zeisl.com/essays-and-articles/the-reception-of-austrian-composers-in-los-angeles.htm

Schoenberg, Randol. Program notes to "Music of Arnold Schoenberg and Eric Zeisl." Los Angeles Zimriyah Chorale, Sinai Temple, Los Angeles, August 22, 2013.

Schreckenberger, Helga. "Salka Viertal's Transnational Hollywood Network." In *Networks of Refugees from Nazi Germany: Continuities, Reorientations, and Collaborations in Exile*, edited by Helga Schreckenberger, 161–78. Boston: Brill, 2016.

Schreiber, Emmanuel. *Reformed Judaism and Its Pioneers: A Contribution to Its History*. Spokane, WA: Spokane Printing, 1893.

Schwarz, Gerard. *Cantata of the Bitter Herbs*. Naxos American Classics 8.559417, 2004, compact disc.

Scult, Max, ed. *Communings of the Spirit: The Journals of Mordecai M. Kaplan, Vol. 1: 1913–1934*. Detroit: Wayne State University press, 2001.

Sendrey, Alfred, comp. *Bibliography of Jewish Music*. New York: Columbia University Press, 1951.

———. *Music in Ancient Israel*. New York: Philosophical Library, 1969.

———. *Music in the Social and Religious Life of Antiquity.* Rutherford, NJ: Farleigh Dickinson University Press, 1974.

———. *The Music of the Jews in the Diaspora (up to 1800): A Contribution to the Social and Cultural History of the Jews.* New York: T. Yoseloff, 1971.

Sendrey, Alfred, and Mildred Norton. *David's Harp: The Story of Music in Biblical Times.* New York: New American Library, 1964.

Singer, Isadore, and S. Funk. "Placzek, Baruch Jacob." In *The Jewish Encyclopedia,* vol. 10, edited by Cyrus Adler, 69. New York: Funk and Wagnalls, 1906.

Slide, Anthony. *The Encyclopedia of Vaudeville.* Jackson: University of Mississippi Press, 2012.

Slifkin, Natan. "The Most Fascinating Rabbi You've Never Heard Of." *Rationalist Judaism,* July 20, 2011. http://www.ratiuonalistjudaism.com/2011/07/most-fascinating-rabbi-youve-never.html

Slonimsky, Nicolas, ed. *Lexicon of Musical Invective: Critical Assaults on Composers Since Beethoven's Time.* Seattle: University of Washington Press, 1965.

Sonderling, Jacob. "A Rabbi Tells of God," *New Outlook* (September 1954): 15–19.

———. "Five Gates: Casual Notes for an Autobiography." *American Jewish Archives Journal* 16, no. 2 (1964): 107–23.

———. "The Jews Are Changing Their Music." *Los Angeles Times Sunday Magazine,* October 2, 1938.

———. Letter to Jacob R. Marcus, June 4, 1961. Sonderling Papers, Jacob Rader Marcus Center of the American Jewish Archives, HUC-JIR, Cincinnati, OH.

———. "Shalvi." Unpublished manuscript. Sonderling Papers, Jacob Rader Marcus Center of the American Jewish Archives, HUC-JIR, Cincinnati, OH.

———. "This Is My Life." Sonderling Papers, Jacob Rader Marcus Center of the American Jewish Archives, HUC-JIR, Cincinnati, OH.

———. "Unpublished Notes." March 16, 1961. Sonderling Papers, Jacob Rader Marcus Center of the American Jewish Archives, HUC-JIR, Cincinnati, OH.

Stein, Erwin, ed. *Arnold Schoenberg Letters*. Berkeley: University of California Press, 1987.

Stein, Leonard, ed. *Style and Idea: Selected Writings of Arnold Schoenberg*. Translated by Leo Black. New York: St. Martin's, 1975.

Steiner, Ena. "Schoenberg the Jew: On the 110th Anniversary of his Birth." *American Jewish Refugee Information*, October 10, 1984.

Steinhard, Erich. "Donaueschingen: Mechanisches Musikfest." *Der Auftakt* 6, no. 8 (1926): 183–86.

Stern, Lee. *Who is Who in Music: A Complete Presentation of the Contemporary Musical Scene, with a Master Record Catalogue*. New York: Lee Stern, 1941.

Stern, Norton B. "Jews in the 1870 Census of Los Angeles." In *The Jews of Los Angeles: Urban Pioneers*, edited by Norton B. Stern, 129–44. Los Angeles: Southern California Jewish Historical Society, 1981.

———. "The Location of Los Angeles Jewry at the Beginning of 1851." *Western States Jewish Historical Quarterly* 5, no. 1 (1972): 25–32.

Streeter, Kurt. "At 93, Rabbi Leonard Beerman still stirs passions with pacifist views." *Los Angeles Times*, November 26, 2014.

Stuckenschmidt, Hans H. "Arnold Schoenberg's 'Kol Nidre' and the Jewish Elements in His Music." *Journal of Synagogue Music* 11, no. 1 (1981): 51–57.

Sulzer, Salomon. *Schir Zion*, Wien: Artaria and Co., c. 1840.

Szasz, Ferenc Morton. *Religion in the Modern American West*. Tucson: University of Arizona Press, 2000.

Tabory, Joseph. *JPS Commentary on the Haggadah*. Philadelphia: Jewish Publication Society, 2008.

Tarsi, Boaz. "*Moses and Aaron* as a Reflection of Arnold Schoenberg's Spiritual Quest." *Musica Judaica* 12 (1991–92): 52–64.

"Temple Israel of Washington Heights." New York City Organ Project. https://www.nycago.org/Organs/NYC/html/TempleIsraelWHts.html

Thomas, William I., and Florian Znaniecki. *The Polish Peasant in Europe and America*. New York: Alfred A. Knopf, 1927.

"To Hold New Religious Service in Full Dress." Jewish Telegraphic Agency, August 30, 1932.

Toch, Ernst. "The Credo of a Composer." *Deutsche Blätter*, April 1945.

———. "How *Cantata of the Bitter Herbs* Was Created." *The Amor Artis Bulletin* 2, no. 1 (December 1962).

———. "Musik für mechanische Instrumente." *Musikblätter des Anbruch* 8, nos. 8–9 (1926): 346–49.

———. *The Shaping Forces in Music: An Inquiry into the Nature of Harmony, Melody, Counterpoint, Form*. New York: Criterion, 1948.

Trollope, Frances Milton. *Vienna and the Austrians: With Some Account of a Journey through Swabia, Bavaria, the Tyrol, and the Salzbourg*. London: R. Bentley, 1838.

Union Hymnal: Songs and Prayers for Jewish Worship. New York: CCAR, 1932.

Union Prayerbook for Jewish Worship, Part II. New York: CCAR, 1945.

"Unsigned and Undated Notes." Sonderling Papers, Jacob Rader Marcus Center of the American Jewish Archives, HUC-JIR,

Cincinnati, OH.

"Unsigned Biographical Summary." Sonderling Papers, Jacob
Rader Marcus Center of the American Jewish Archives,
HUC-JIR, Cincinnati, OH.

"Untermyer Scores Hitler's New Move; Tells Los Angeles
Audience the German Step is Challenge to Civilized World."
New York Times, March 13, 1935.

Ussher, Bruno David. "Los Angeles Philharmonic Makes Its
Debut." *Pacific Coast Musical Review*, October 25, 1919.

———. "Philharmonic Orchestra of Los Angeles Plays to Packed
Houses." *Pacific Coast Musical Review*, November 8, 1919.

Vinaver, Chemjo, ed. *Anthology of Jewish Music*. New York:
Edward B. Marks, 1953.

Vorspan, Max, and Lloyd P. Gartner. *History of the Jews of Los
Angeles*. San Marino, CA: Huntington Library, 1970.

Vorspan, Max, and Sheldon Teitelbaum. "Los Angeles." In
Encyclopedia Judaica, vol. 13, edited by Fred Skolnik and
Michael Berenbaum, 195–211. New York: Macmillan, 2007.

Wagner, Guy. *Korngold: Musik ist Musik*. Berlin: Matthes and
Seitz, 2008.

Wallace, David. *Exiles in Hollywood*. Pompton Plains, NJ:
Limelight, 2006.

Wegele, Peter. *Max Steiner: Composing,* Casablanca*, and the
Golden Age of Film Music*. Lanham, MD: Rowman and
Littlefield, 2014.

Weisgall, Hugo D. "Jewish Music in America." *Judaism: A
Quarterly Journal of Jewish Life and Thought* 3, no. 4 (1954):
427–36.

Weiss, Sam. "The *Cantus Firmus* of Arnold Schoenberg's 'Kol
Nidre.'" *Journal of Synagogue Music* 9, no. 2 (1979): 3–9.

Weisser, Albert. *The Modern Renaissance of Jewish Music: Events
and Figures, Eastern Europe and America*. New York: Bloch,

1954.

Werner, Eric. *From Generation to Generation: Studies on Jewish Musical Tradition*. New York: American Conference of Cantors, 1967.

———. "The Tunes of the Haggadah." *Studies in Bibliography and Booklore* 7 (1965): 57–83.

White, Pamela Cynthia. *Schoenberg and the God-Idea: The Opera Moses und Aron*. Ann Arbor, MI: YMI Research, 1985.

Williams, T. F. "A Form-Critical Classification of the Psalms According to Hermann Gunkel." *Resources for Biblical, Theological, and Religious Studies* (October 2006): 1–4.

Wilson, Karen S., ed. *Jews in the Los Angeles Mosaic*. Los Angeles: Autry National Center of the American West, 2013.

Winters, Ben. *Erich Wolfgang Korngold's* The Adventures of Robin Hood. Lanham, MD: Scarecrow, 2007.

Yasser, Joseph. *A Theory of Evolving Tonality*. New York: American Library of Musicology, 1932.

Zach, Miriam Susan. "The Opera Works of Ernst Toch." M.M. thesis, University of Florida, 1990.

Zeisl, Eric. *Requiem Ebraico*. New York: Transcontinental, catalogue no. 266, 1946.

Zeisl, Gertrud. "Biographical Essay." Eric Zeisl: Austrian-American Composer. http://www.zeisl.com/essays-and-articles/biographical-essay-gertrud-zeisl.htm

Index

ABOUT THE AUTHORS

JONATHAN L. FRIEDMANN is Professor of Jewish Music History and Associate Dean of the Master of Jewish Studies Program at the Academy for Jewish Religion California, President of the Western States Jewish History Association, Director of the Jewish Museum of the American West, and the author or editor of twenty-five books on Judaism, music, and religion.

After almost thirty years as a labor lawyer, **JOHN F. GUEST** returned to his first love, music, and was ordained a cantor. He now works as a substitute cantor and tutors b'nei mitzvah students in the Los Angeles area, and he serves as Vice President of the Western States Jewish History Association. (Photo courtesy of Allison Weiss Bluestein.)

www.ingramcontent.com/pod-product-compliance
Lightning Source LLC
Chambersburg PA
CBHW021355090426
42742CB00009B/865